Baseball Research Journal

Volume 49, Number 1
Spring 2020

Published by the Society for American Baseball Research

BASEBALL RESEARCH JOURNAL, Volume 49, Number 1

Editor: Cecilia M. Tan
Design and Production: Lisa Hochstein
Cover Design: Lisa Hochstein
Copyediting assistance: Keith DeCandido
Proofreader: Norman L. Macht
Fact Checker: Clifford Blau

Front cover photo: Courtesy of the Boston Red Sox

Published by:
Society for American Baseball Research, Inc.
Cronkite School at ASU
555 N. Central Ave. #416
Phoenix, AZ 85004

Phone: (602) 496–1460
Web: www.sabr.org
Twitter: @sabr
Facebook: Society for American Baseball Research

Paper: 978-1-970159-29-5
E-book: 978-1-970159-28-8

Contents

Note from the Editor

One thing I have learned through my long association with SABR is that sometimes "it all depends on how you count it." If you consider that our goal is typically to get the spring issue of the *BRJ* to press before Opening Day, this issue is not yet late! But if one uses the other calendar methods, well, we are now about two months into Quarantine Time as I write this. And Quarantine Time is measured not in days or weeks, but by flattened curves.

I was on my way to Florida when the announcement came that Major League Baseball was suspending spring training. The night before my flight, the news broke that Utah Jazz basketball player Rudy Gobert had tested positive for coronoavirus. (Who could have predicted that the guy who cavalierly made light of the encroaching crisis by touching all the microphones of reporters after a press conference would be the one to catch it? Funny that.) Gobert's diagnosis was a huge wake-up call not only to him—he would later apologize profusely for not taking things seriously enough—but to the entire USA. This young paragon of health, a major star athlete, in the middle of the country (the Jazz were in Oklahoma City at the time), caught it and didn't even have any idea where he got it from.

The virus was already inside the borders. And it seemed like overnight, people suddenly believed it. Individual case counts and dire stories from Seattle and epidemiological facts didn't make people see. But a single major sports figure getting the virus: that made the threat real.

Though some in government didn't want to recognize the seriousness or urgency of the situation right away, every sport shut down operations within the 48 hours after the Gobert announcement. The NCAA basketball tournament, which had already been scheduled to go forward without fans in the seats, was called off entirely (as were all NCAA championships in every sport). The NBA and NHL "suspended" their seasons. MLB called off spring training. Even the PGA Tour, which flirted with the idea of holding a golf tournament without fans, in the end decided to cancel it.

I believe the cancellations themselves drove home the severity of the situation to many who were still hoping the pandemic might "blow over." This isn't solely about sports, of course. The news about Tom Hanks's diagnosis broke at the same time as Gobert's. Broadway went dark, and a few days after the sports-pocalypse, Walt Disney World closed its doors. The tangible effect of the pandemic on these cultural touchstones and the mass media that connect us is what made it all real for the first time. Historians, take notes. The effect of this global "pause" will be studied and written about for generations to come.

Now, of course, we live the "new normal." I only leave the house for groceries, where I stand in a line six feet apart from other shoppers, wearing my facemask and disposable gloves, and I pine for baseball, which would be the perfect distraction from the dire mortality statistics I can do nothing about. As I write this, MLB and the players are discussing outlandish plans for how to conduct a half-season (starting in July) safely and equitably. But there is no guarantee that any kind of a season will happen. The future is uncertain, and the present is on pause, so looking backward at the past is all we have for the moment. Classic games on television and in our SABR Games Project archives, the #SABRatHome initiative, and, of course, the *BRJ* right here in your hands.

May you all live to see baseball return.

— Cecilia M. Tan, May 2020

Before We Forget

The Birth, Life, and Death of The Sporting News Research Center

Steve Gietschier

More than a decade has passed since American City Business Journals (ACBJ), a subsidiary of Advance Media, the company that bought the Sporting News in 2006, moved the publication's editorial office from St. Louis to Charlotte, North Carolina, and closed The Sporting News *Research Center. This essay is an attempt to tell the story of how the research center came to be, what it accomplished over twenty-two years, and how it met its demise. My recollections have been aided by those of Jim Meier, who worked for TSN for nearly twelve years and without whose expertise we would have achieved much less.*

HOW IT BEGAN

Sometime before the Sporting News Publishing Company marked its centennial on March 17, 1986, president and chief executive officer Richard Waters recognized that his domain included a variety of historical artifacts and research materials that needed and deserved better care than the company had provided to that point. Waters contacted his friend, Charles P. Korr, professor of history at the University of Missouri–St. Louis (UMSL) and later the author of *The End of Baseball as We Knew It: The Players Union, 1960–81*, and asked for advice. Korr suggested Waters consult with Anne Kenney, the director of special collections at UMSL and a professional skilled in caring for historical materials. Kenney recommended that Waters hire an archivist, preferably one familiar with sports and sports history. She helped craft the job description and the advertisement published in the November/December 1985 newsletter of the Society of American Archivists.

I read that advertisement and mailed my letter of application on New Year's Eve, 1985. At the time I was both a historian, with a doctorate from Ohio State, and an archivist, having worked for three years at the Ohio Historical Society and more than seven years at the South Carolina Department of Archives and History. I was neither a sports historian nor a sports archivist. I didn't even know if those two fields existed. I was, however, a very committed sports fan. To prepare for the interview I hoped would come, I began buying *The Sporting News* at a local drugstore. I had read the publication on and off as a youngster but, in truth, had focused most of my sports reading on books and *Sports Illustrated*. Fortunately, on the very date on which *TSN* became a hundred years old, *SI* published

a long, celebratory essay by the inimitable Roy Blount Jr. Through it, I learned a lot about *TSN*'s past and especially about a man named Paul Mac Farlane, a former copy editor turned company historian.

Shortly thereafter, TSN's human resources director, Char Strahinic, invited me to St. Louis for an interview. This full-day experience took place on April Fool's Day, 1986. In the morning, I met with Waters, chief financial officer Jim Booth, and editor Tom Barnidge. I spent time in the afternoon with Mac Farlane and Lowell Reidenbaugh, who had just written *The Sporting News: The First Hundred Years, 1886–1986*, a hardcover, coffee table book that would become my concordance to the "Bible of Baseball." Lowell and I talked mostly about the Civil War, his other passion besides baseball. As for Mac Farlane, we talked mostly about his other passion, the Boston Red Sox.

I returned to South Carolina enthusiastic, believing I had a good shot at the job. How many other people could there be, I wondered, who were historians, archivists, and sports fans? Very few, apparently, because within a few days, Char called with a job offer that I accepted. I entered the company's offices for the first time as an employee on the Tuesday after Labor Day, 1986.

WHERE IT BEGAN

The building the company owned at 1212 N. Lindbergh Boulevard in suburban St. Louis was a big place, 41,000 square feet, the company's first home since leaving downtown in 1969. Offices located around the perimeter were huge and had ceiling-to-floor windows. The editorial staff worked in two open spaces bereft of walls or cubicles with a telephone and a computer terminal on every desk. The wallpaper was custom-made, reproducing pages from TSN's inaugural issue, and the carpeting was a very vibrant burnt orange. Along the walls were rows of book shelves and file cabinets, each with drawers painted alternately the same burnt orange and beige. Adjacent to the editorial areas was the lunch room—or "corporate dining area," as some insisted it be called. Its wallpaper was also custom-made, featuring baseballs on a sky-blue background. In the past, I learned, when major league players had visited the building, they were sometimes persuaded to autograph a wallpaper baseball. Fastened to these walls were wooden racks that held sets of the commemorative bats produced by Hillerich & Bradsby to mark each All-Star Game and World Series. We had complete runs of these bats plus dozens of extras stored in a back room: a warehouse from which we mailed books, guides, and registers and retained boxes of back issues of *TSN* itself dating back more than fifty years.

Mac Farlane—or Mac, as everyone called him—had an interior office that measured about fifteen feet by twelve feet with no windows. That was where I was supposed to work, but it was too cluttered. Blount called this space a "historical storehouse." True. Mac's desk was overwhelmed with books, letters, envelopes, scraps of paper, coffee mugs, pens, pencils, and a standard typewriter. The adjacent shelves groaned under a century of tradition. In front of his desk, partially blocking the doorway, was a table-top model of Fenway Park, maybe three feet by four feet, around which everyone who wanted to enter had to maneuver. Under his desk and known to almost no one, sat a hidden case of Laiphroaig scotch whisky, delivered once a year by a mysterious stranger.

I found work space in the room adjacent to Mac's, the vault. It really was a vault. Its entrance was through a bank vault door, the combination to which was one of the sacred baseball numbers to which Mac paid homage, 4–0–6. In the vault, the company kept precious things: Beadle guides, Spalding and Reach guides, a copy of *The Base Ball Player's Pocket Companion*, published in 1859, and two file cabinets—called fireproof because they were made of steel and concrete. This is where I went to work each day, opening the combination lock and sitting at a small desk wedged into impossibly crammed space.

WHAT TO DO?

The job description called for someone to be responsible "for preserving and maintaining a sports collection, documents and reports, designing and implementing retrieval and storage systems, and assisting sales and marketing staffs with historical presentations," but how to do these things was up to me. Technically, the position was situated within the editorial department, and Barnidge was my boss, but he was content to let me fashion the job as I saw fit. I spent my first weeks getting to know everyone else and understanding that the company included several departments besides human resources and editorial: circulation, advertising, production, books, accounting, public relations, and customer service. My goal was to make sure that everyone knew who I was and that I was available as a resource to assist them however appropriately. The closest relationships were with public relations and advertising, particularly when the ad sales staff tried to use the company's history as a tool to sell advertising pages. In one instance I recall, we helped the Chicago sales office put together some trivia questions on Chicago sports history.

I learned that the editorial staff was divided into two groups: a bunch of mostly senior people responsible for "putting out the paper," as the saying went, and a group of younger people who worked on the books—guides, registers, record books, hardcover books, and season preview magazines called "yearbooks." Both concentrated on the sports we called the Big Six: baseball, college and pro football, college and pro basketball, and hockey. Most of both groups were men, and most had no idea who I was or what I was supposed to do. Many were fixed in their ways.

OUR HOLDINGS

Mac's office and the vault contained only some of the company's historical materials. He controlled complete runs of staples like the *Spalding Guide*, the *Reach Guide*, the *Baseball Blue Book*, the *American League Red Book*, the *National League Green Book*, the *Little Red Book of Baseball*, and others. Outside his office were open shelves on which were stored several thousand trade books in complete disarray. Scattered about were periodicals, media guides, and our own guides, registers, and record books. File cabinets adjacent to the newsroom held our photographs, probably more than 600,000 prints, mostly black-and-white, plus a smattering of negatives. File cabinets near the book editors held a resource of incalculable value: our clipping files.

In 1986, *TSN* subscribed to over a hundred daily newspapers. There were stacks of newspapers all over the newsroom. Editors, in their spare time, read these papers and clipped relevant articles. An editorial assistant placed each clipping in the proper brown envelope within a massive filing system for untold thousands of clippings, some dating from the first years of the twentieth century or even earlier. Some clips were filed biographically, but there was also an elaborate—and yet unindexed—subject file. These clips covered not just baseball, but other sports as well. The file cabinets that housed the clips stood six drawers high, and there were, memory suggests, more than fifty cabinets.

The same editorial assistant also updated our file of player contract cards: 3 x 5 index cards on which we recorded the contract history of every professional baseball player. Our staff used these cards, but so did I, learning how to document minor league careers for customers who wrote inquiring about family members. SABR founder Ray Nemec maintained his own set of cards, and we frequently worked together to fill in gaps. With a player's contract history in hand, it was a simple task to check the relevant guides and develop a player's statistical record. Mac Farlane had told Blount that "the FBI uses this," referring to the card file. I could not say.

Buried within the clipping files was an extraordinary collection of player questionnaires. From the early days of the *Baseball Register*, first published in 1940, our correspondents would ask players in spring training to fill out biographical questionnaires. They did so, year after year, creating a trove of data in the players' own hands that were filed in each player's folder.

Also sitting on the shelves were two boxes of correspondence between the Spinks, Taylor and his son, C.C. Johnson Spink, and Ty Cobb. Nearly a hundred letters passed back and forth, most dating from the 1950s until 1961, the year of Cobb's death.

THE FIRST ARCHIVES

Waters soon said that our goal was to construct an addition to the existing building that would become the new, professionalized archives. We began meeting with an architect, a man whose practice had included designing Burger King restaurants and an addition to the Waters residence. We developed a floor plan that met some of our needs: office space, storage space maximized by a system of compact shelving, and work tables for staff members and—I hoped—outside researchers. Waters also said this addition would be my work space, but not Mac's. As construction proceeded, Mac would walk back to inspect it, and he began to wonder if it was going to be big enough for the two of us. My job was to deflect such questions. No one else told him his days were numbered. When construction was completed, the treasures moved from the vault and Mac's office into the new space. It was awkward, to say the least. The new space opened on April 8, 1988, complete with its own air conditioning system. Mac's last day came a week later.

Opening the new archives gave us a chance to begin treating some of our research materials with the respect they deserved. Two examples will suffice. To prepare the coffee table books the company was publishing regularly, the book editors had been using what we called "bound volumes," all the issues of a full year of *TSN* bound between hard covers. Obviously, newsprint does not age well, and repeated use of the bound volumes from our early years was causing substantial and irreversible deterioration. Night after night, the cleaning crew had to vacuum myriad bits of paper from the floor. We had *TSN* on microfilm, but no way to use it. Once we had archival space, we bought a microfilm reader-printer, trained the editors in how it worked, and retired the bound volumes from use. We were also able to gather together the sports books littering shelves here and there and re-shelve them on our compact shelving. We no longer had a random collection of books. We had a library.

On the other hand, the budget that built the new archives had a limit, and so, too, did the space we created. The clipping files remained where they were, and so did the photo files. Frankly, I could not imagine a budget large enough to create a space that could house everything we held. The key toward securing these materials was to assert control. Emptying the vault and Mac's office helped. So, too, did the requirement that we lock the archives upon leaving each night. Editors soon learned that I was the resource person for finding what they needed. To give one more example, I removed the player questionnaires from the clipping files and brought them together in the new archives: fifty questionnaires in an acid-free folder, thirteen folders in an acid-free archival box, forty-seven boxes in all. Still, I was pretty much operating on my own without making any real contribution to our editorial products. Not until John Rawlings succeeded Barnidge and refashioned the editorial staff did I become part of the editorial team that planned each issue and begin to do research that helped writers and editors prepare stories for publication.

TSN AND SABR

I attended my first SABR convention when the organization met in St. Louis for the second time in 1992. Frankly, I was leery about going, guessing, incorrectly as it turned out, that once people knew I worked for *TSN*, I would be overwhelmed with requests for research assistance. Such was not the case. We also arranged for convention attendees to tour our office, sort of a trip to a baseball mecca. We thought we had planned for one bus with thirty people whom we would divide into three tour groups of ten. To our great surprise, three buses showed up, each with thirty people. It was time to scramble, which we did, making a lot of SABR friends in the process.

THE CONLONS

Early on, Mac had told me about those two fireproof file cabinets. Inside were his pride and joy, glass-plate negatives, some 5 x 7 and some 4 x 5, all of them photographs taken by Charles Martin Conlon. This was a name I did not know, but I soon began to appreciate Conlon's skill as a photographer and his place in baseball's visual history. Moreover, I learned that while these file cabinets contained glass-plate negatives, our regular photo files contained many other Conlon photographs, some vintage prints made by Conlon himself, some more recent prints made by others, and thousands of negatives shot on acetate film after Conlon switched from glass plates. We pulled all the Conlons together in one place and counted more than seven thousand images, truly one of baseball's grandest treasures.

Some Conlon prints had already been on public display. The National Portrait Gallery, part of the Smithsonian Institution, had mounted a Conlon exhibit called "Baseball Immortals" that opened in 1984. Perhaps the Smithsonian had been aware that a small St. Louis company, World Wide Sports, had used Conlon's images to produce a set of one hundred oversized baseball cards in 1981 and a set of sixty cards to commemorate the fiftieth anniversary of the All-Star Game in 1983. The Smithsonian made exhibit prints directly from the glass plates and developed a new set of sixty cards. Marketed under the logo "Baseball Americana," these cards plus posters and other ancillary products were produced by another St. Louis company, Marketcom, whose principal business was oversize posters of *SI* covers. After the Washington show closed, the exhibit joined the Smithsonian's SITES program and traveled around the country for two years. After that, all the "Baseball Americana" materials became Marketcom's property.

How did *TSN* come to own the Conlons? No one around in 1986 knew for sure. We did know that Conlon began taking pictures in 1904, stopped in 1942, and died in 1945. All we could surmise, absent any paperwork, was that some time after Conlon stopped taking pictures, he sold his collection to *TSN*. How

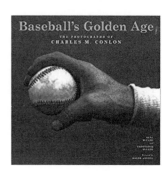

In 1993, the publication of Baseball's Golden Age: The Photographs of Charles Martin Conlon, *by Neal McCabe and Constance McCabe, brought the work of baseball's best photographer to a new public.*

everything moved from suburban New York, where Conlon lived, to St. Louis remained a mystery. After spending a little time with his life's work, I became convinced of two things. First, the negatives needed help from professional photo conservators. And second, his best images deserved to be published in a book. Conlon was frugal. To store his negatives, he used ordinary cardboard boxes. He placed each negative in an envelope cut in half and wrote on it the player's last name, an abbreviation for his team, and two digits for the year, say, "23," for 1923. Frequently, he reused these envelopes, scribbling out the data on one side and writing new information on the other, indicating, so it seemed, that he must have destroyed hundreds, if not thousands, of negatives.

What survived needed work. We bought archival-quality sleeves and boxes and, without a computer, wrote a thorough database, but that was only the beginning. One of the nation's foremost paper conservators, Mary Lynn Ritzenthaler, suggested an art conservator, Connie McCabe. She worked at the National Gallery of Art and co-owned, with Stephen Small, a business called PPS, Photo Preservation Services. Speaking to me on the telephone, Connie was far from convinced that these photos were worth her expertise, but PPS needed the work, and she agreed to take on the project. The trip from St. Louis to Alexandria, Virginia, in a Ford Taurus station wagon was fraught with the fear of a rear-end collision, but we made it unscratched.

PPS cleaned the negatives, re-shot them to archival standards, produced a second generation called interpositives and a third generation called reproduction duplicates. Every use to which we put the Conlons after that used this iteration. We retired the originals, regarding them as precious artifacts. Just as significantly, McCabe, once she saw the negatives, fell in love with them as works of art. She was not a baseball fan, but her brother Neal, a postal employee in Los Angeles with a degree in music composition, was. When Connie told Neal that she was working on an extraordinary collection of baseball images, his skepticism duplicated hers from a few months previous. But he visited her and changed his mind. Thus began the saga that led to the publication of *Baseball's Golden Age: The Photographs of Charles M. Conlon*, perhaps the most stunning book of baseball photography ever published.

A book proposal went to *TSN*'s own book department, experienced in the production of low-cost, hardcover books that did not sell especially well. The best-selling title had been *Take Me Out to the Ball Park*, reproducing illustrations by Gene Mack and Amadee Wohlschlaeger. The proposal suggested that a book of Conlon photographs should be produced to a higher standard and printed on glossy paper. The head of the book department, as skeptical as Connie and Neal had been, rejected the proposal, but she agreed to forward the idea to a New York-based publisher called Harry N. Abrams. *TSN* had been a Times Mirror company since 1977, and so was Abrams, and their specialty was high-end art books. Somehow, Abrams said yes, but the editor they assigned to the project was less than enthusiastic. Conlon got his book. Neal selected the pictures and wrote the captions, Connie did the technical work, but the editor insisted that the McCabes' suggested title, *The Baseball Photographer*, the title of an essay Conlon himself wrote, should be abandoned for the more prosaic *Baseball's Golden Age*. Abrams published the book and even hosted a launch party in New York but did not see fit to invite the authors to celebrate their own work. Instead, *TSN* assigned me to represent the book. I got to talk about it on live television with sportscaster Len Berman, and I got the party's special guests, former players Tommie Agee and Ed Kranepool, to autograph a copy. The book got excellent reviews. It sold very well and even appeared in a paperback edition, highly unusual for an art book. And it led eventually to a sequel, *The Big Show: Charles M. Conlon's Golden Age Baseball Photographs*, that had an ever longer tumultuous and serpentine genesis.

THE COBB SLIDE PHOTO

Conlon's most famous photo shows Ty Cobb sliding into third baseman Jimmy Austin. Well before the McCabes' book was published, this image had been reproduced many times, never credited to Conlon or *TSN*. What no one knew until one auspicious day was that the photo as published was a cropped version of the original. On that day, a woman from our accounting department walked into the archives and said, "We are clearing out a safe. Do you want this?" She handed me a brown, padded mailing envelope on which was written in pencil "Cobb slide—original." We knew we had this image on a 4 x 5 glass negative, but when I gingerly removed the contents of the envelope, I saw another glass plate, this one 5 x 7. The glass was cracked, but incredibly, the emulsion was still intact. We had, I knew, uncovered one of baseball's most precious artifacts, the Cobb slide, not as it had been cropped, but as Conlon had photographed it. Connie McCabe repaired the glass, and Neal, working from the photo's internal evidence, was able to date it precisely to July 23, 1910. Another treasure rescued.

BASEBALL CARDS

Baseball's Golden Age put Conlon on the map, but so, too, did "The Conlon Collection," baseball cards produced by a company called MegaCards. Before the book's publication, TSN received an inquiry: would we be interested in a multi-year set of baseball cards using Conlon photos? Yes, subject to obtaining the proper licenses. So began a project that was supposed to last five years, 330 cards per year, numbered consecutively. MegaCards issued full sets in 1991, 1992, 1993, and 1994, but in 1995, with baseball embroiled in a labor dispute, the company hedged its bets and released only 110 cards, withholding the other 220, subject to unfolding events. No more ever appeared.

OPEN FOR RESEARCH

Both the Ohio Historical Society and the South Carolina Department of Archives and History made their holdings available to the researching public. I expected to do the same in St. Louis, to allow researchers to use our resources, even though we were a private company. Little did I know that *TSN* had long held a proprietary attitude toward the information we held even to the point of restricting sales of a locally-produced microfilm edition. To my knowledge, the only researchers *TSN* had ever allowed inside had been Dorothy and Harold Seymour. One can only imagine the conversations that transpired between two titans of their trades, J.G. Taylor Spink and Dr. Harold Seymour.

Only some private companies have archives, and only a few of these are open to the public. Waters was amused that I wanted to open our facility to researchers, especially those working on books, and even more amused that I wanted to do so without charging visitors a fee. When I explained that most researchers' books would not earn them much money, he was befuddled. "Why," he asked, "would anyone write a book that won't make any money?" Still, he placated me, "so long as you don't neglect your other duties," and we were able to announce that *The Sporting News*

Archives, as we first called it, was open to researchers. They arrived slowly but rather steadily.

We were also able to extend the company's internship program, which each summer took on college journalism students, to the archives. One of our interns later earned a doctorate in sport history. Another got a job in collegiate sports management. A third stayed with us for quite some time and worked quite nearly as a full-time employee. Later, two students in archival studies did internships with us.

KEN BURNS AND *BASEBALL*

When documentarian Ken Burns announced that Florentine Films' next large project after *The Civil War* would cover the history of baseball, *TSN* got involved. We thought that our collection of photographs, Conlons included, would prove essential. Producer Lynn Novick and cinematographer Buddy Squires came to St. Louis for an extended visit. They took video of many photos, and *TSN* got a nice on-screen credit at the end of each episode. We also thought that we might be offered a chance to comment on the script and maybe even become one of Burns's famous "talking heads," but after critiquing a very early version of the script—maybe the first—no more came of that. Burns, *TSN*, and General Motors worked out a tri-partite agreement. We gave Burns access to our photos at no charge. General Motors paid for an advertising supplement to our regular issue just before the film premiered in 1994. Burns agreed to make some personal appearances at *TSN* functions although no such occasions ever occurred. In similar fashion, we helped filmmaker Aviva Kempner as she worked on *The Life and Times of Hank Greenberg*, which made its debut in 1998.

HIRING JIM MEIER

One revenue stream we were able to explore was licensing the use of our photos for a fee. We began to sell prints to individuals for personal use, and we hired a person, who stayed with us for a while, to develop a more robust market among authors, publishers, and commercial users. Expanding the breadth of the archives and turning it into a research center followed the company's decision to hire another professional, Jim Meier, in 1995. Jim arrived with impeccable credentials. He was an athlete and a sports fan. He had a bachelor's degree in economics and three master's degrees in business, sports management, and library science, plus experience in a library. He complemented what we already had and enabled us to move forward.

In 1996, the company sold its headquarters and moved into leased space less than a quarter-mile away. Jim organized the move, working with a company skilled in moving library resources, so that the contents of each shelf at 1212 N. Lindbergh got to the right shelf at 10176 Corporate Square Drive. After we worked consecutive fifteen-hour days, the new research center was ready to go when the editorial staff returned to work on the next issue without any significant downtime.

Before Jim arrived, we had in place contracts to supply our content to the Nexis database and the LATimes syndicate. Jim assumed responsibility for fulfilling these contracts, and he wrote procedural manuals and trained others to do this work. He also expanded our photo licensing business, adding to it the sale of "Keepsake Covers" reproduced from the weekly, and increased annual revenues in this area to six figures.

Jim's other contributions were substantial. He created a networked online catalog to our book collection, grown to more than ten thousand volumes, available to all editorial staff members. He developed a section of the *TSN* website called "The Vault" where he posted all sorts of historical data. He and I both sat on small committees, editorial content teams, that planned coverage of our various sports.

Jim also helped expand our effort to do public research, that is, answer queries that arrived by letter, by telephone call, and later, via email. We helped athletes, broadcasters, students, scholars, genealogists, and incarcerated people. We handled questions from around the world, and we let people do their research in person. I particularly remember one man who visited from Australia several Januarys in a row to do research on the National Football League.

The results of this policy are dozens of baseball books on shelves everywhere. Authors like to see their names on title pages. Archivists and librarians like to see their names on acknowledgments pages. Our names are in lots of books. For this honor, gratitude goes to the editors under whom we worked, Barnidge and Rawlings, and the presidents who followed Waters and allowed us to continue: Tom Osenton, Nick Niles, Jim Nuckols, and Rick Allen.

PAPER OF RECORD

Jim and I were regularly able to attend the annual conference of the Special Library Association where we were members of the News Division along with researchers and archivists from many other newspapers, magazines, and broadcast media. In San Antonio in 2001, we listened to a presentation from a Canadian firm called Cold North Wind. Their goal was to take newspapers that had been microfilmed but not digitized and convert the microfilm into digital files that would be full-text searchable and available online. Jim and I agreed, "This is for us." We had *TSN* on microfilm, of course, but there was no index, making searching tedious. Besides, Cold North Wind said that their product, Paper of Record, would bring our company revenue. We set in motion a process that eventually added *TSN* to the Paper of Record database. Researchers gained easy access to it for a reasonable fee, and the search capability worked surprisingly well, given the uneven quality of the microfilm images. One of SABR's most valuable membership perks is access to Paper of Record, largely because of the archives of *TSN*. (Google later acquired Cold North Wind, and SABR's access to Paper of Record was suspended, but SABR worked with Google to reopen it as a member benefit.)

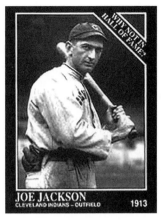

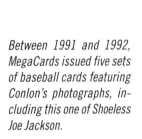

Between 1991 and 1992, MegaCards issued five sets of baseball cards featuring Conlon's photographs, including this one of Shoeless Joe Jackson.

AND OTHER DUTIES AS ASSIGNED

The editorial content of *The Sporting News* changed significantly as the company confronted competition from cable television and the Internet. From April 1990 until October 1997, I wrote a biweekly book review column, showcasing the work of SABR members and other sports authors. For an additional year, the column continued online and as an occasional part of a print column called "My Turn."

TSN redesigned the *Baseball Guide* in 1992, and I took over writing the "Year in Review" essay from the beloved Cliff Kachline. I wrote this essay until the *Guide*'s final edition in 2006. Bittersweet though the demise of the Guide was, it was pleasant to know that the idea of an annual guide and an annual year-in-review essay had originated with Henry Chadwick, the "Father of Baseball," who published the first edition of *Beadle's Dime Base Ball Player* in 1860.

Similarly, late in 2003, the company asked me to assume editorship of *The Complete Baseball Record Book*. Knowing nothing about how to do this, I said yes. Fortunately, SABR friends came to the rescue, especially Pete Palmer, who had been helping with the *Record Book* for years, and Lyle Spatz, then the chair of SABR's Records Committee. A sensible decision was recruiting a roster of SABR volunteers, each of whom agreed to follow one team for the season in a plethora of records categories. Thanks to this help, the book improved every year. *TSN* published the final print edition in 2006 and produced two more after that as PDF files, made available on our website for no charge.

HOW IT ENDED

Perhaps the beginning of the end came in the late 1990s when the company ordered the sale of all our artifacts. We had previously sold an array of commemorative and souvenir items, most of them gifts to the Spinks, that had graced display cases in the lobby of 1212 N. Lindbergh, including autographed baseballs and photos, letters from presidents, and pieces of memorabilia once belonging to the American League's founding president, Ban Johnson, such as his diploma from Marietta College. In this second sale, anything that did not bear directly upon the company's history or have research value had to go. There was no room for sentiment. We contracted with a sports auction house and devised a plan we hoped would maximize revenue. On the auction block went all the souvenir Louisville Sluggers and thousands of original illustrations that the country's most prominent sports artists had submitted for publication.

The company's ownership history is instructive as a guide to the further demise of the research center. The Spink family owned the company from its founding in 1886 until 1977 when the Times Mirror Company became the new owner. In 2000, Times Mirror sold to Vulcan Media, owned by Microsoft co-founder Paul G. Allen, and in 2006, Vulcan sold to Advance Media and ACBJ. Part of this last transaction was leaving leased space at Corporate Square Drive in May 2006 and moving to smaller leased space that had no room for a research center. We packed everything we had in bankers' boxes, put a barcode label on every box, and sent them to an off-site storage facility from which we could retrieve materials as needed. The research center was closed.

The father-and-son executive duo that ran ACBJ said they would keep *The Sporting News* in St. Louis. Yet, within a year, they moved all phases of the operation except the editorial staff to Charlotte, and in July 2008, they transferred the editorial staff as well and adjusted the publication schedule from weekly to bi-weekly and later to monthly. In 2012, print publication ceased, and only digital publication remained.

In 2013, ACBJ entered into a joint venture with Perform Group, an international sports data company that bought 65 percent of the company at first and purchased ACBJ's remaining stake in 2015.

THE LEGACY

Once ACBJ announced the move to Charlotte and said that I need not come along, we developed a proposal to keep the history of *The Sporting News* in St. Louis. We retrieved the bankers' boxes from off-site and lined them up like coffins in a spare room. We approached three local universities, asking them if they would be willing to acquire the archives and create what might have been called the *Sporting News* Center for the Study of Sports in America. All three were receptive. ACBJ executives were less enthusiastic. One hundred days after receiving the proposal, the CEO walked into the room where the materials were lying. He opened one box and said, "Oh, books about Ty Cobb. Ship them all to Charlotte." Except for the bound volumes—whose safe transfer to the Missouri Historical Society, a St. Louis institution, ACBJ did approve—none of the research materials stayed in St. Louis. Everything went south.

The *St. Louis Post-Dispatch* quoted another ACBJ executive on the future of the research center. "It is sad to see it leaving St. Louis, but it's a happy time as well, to know that we're able to keep it in the company," he said. "From the company's standpoint, this is a valuable resource—one that doesn't exist anywhere else—and is a real benefit to what we do."

Unfortunately, that "valuable resource" remains in Charlotte but unavailable to researchers. Tom Hufford, one of SABR's founding members, was able to convince ACBJ to donate the player contract cards to SABR in 2013, and in November 2019 the Sporting News Player Contract Card Collection went live online, making available biographic details about the lives of over 180,000 major and minor league players and over 10,000 umpires and team executives.

Much more tragic was the fate of the photo collection, including the Conlons. In 2010, ACBJ sold the entire photo archives to Rogers Photo Archive for a reported $1 million. John Rogers faced numerous legal difficulties, and in August 2016, the Conlon negatives sold at auction to an anonymous buyer for $1,792,500. After the sale, I tried to offer my services to the buyer, but Heritage Auctions, the company that handled the sale, said it was unable to forward my offer.

One final, sad note. When the company was preparing to leave 1212 N. Lindbergh for 10176 Corporate Square Drive, we located roughly twenty boxes of correspondence and records dating from before 1977. These were, so to speak, the corporate archives of the Spink years, boxes that contained priceless material documenting the relationship between both Taylor Spink and Johnson Spink and executives throughout Organized Baseball. Without involving me, the company sent these boxes to an off-site storage facility and never retrieved them. Where exactly they went and what became of them is unknown.

With sustained corporate support, *The Sporting News* Research Center, developed from scratch, became one of the outstanding sports research facilities in North America. Our message to baseball researchers was this: "If you live in the East, by all means try to get to the National Baseball Library in Cooperstown. If you live in the West, consider the Amateur Athletic Foundation of Los Angeles [now LA84]. But if you live in the Midwest and can't travel far, come to St. Louis." Many did, and baseball scholarship is the richer for it. ∎

24 Years Before Jackie, There Was Charlie Culver

Christian Trudeau

In 1946, all eyes were on the Montreal Royals and Jackie Robinson as he was readying to break baseball's color line. But 24 years earlier, without any publicity, an African American ballplayer had already played six games for the Montreal team in the Class B Eastern Canada League. Charlie Culver's presence didn't ruffle many feathers—except on the semi-pro team that had previously signed him.

BACKGROUND AND HIRING

Montreal had lost the International League Royals after the 1917 season, leaving the city without a professional team. To fill the absence, several semi-pro leagues had popped up, with many teams vying for the city championship, as well as other towns and cities across Quebec competing for the provincial title. In 1921 Joe Page—a Canadian Pacific Railway employee, baseball promoter, and Chicago White Sox scout—unsuccessfully tried to start a new league with teams in Montreal, Sherbrooke, Granby, Trois-Rivières, and Ottawa.[1] The following year, a scaled-down version of the Page project came to life with the creation of the Eastern Canada League in late March 1922. The league would be centered in Montreal with a local team there and rivals to the southwest in Valleyfield, to the west in Ottawa, and to the east in Trois-Rivières. At an early April meeting, it was announced that the league had received a Class B accreditation from the National Association of Professional Baseball Leagues.[2]

With Opening Day set for May 11, teams scrambled frantically to fill their rosters. Naturally, the best players in the local semi-pro leagues were prime candidates, and the first to sign up. One of these was a multi-talented, all-around player, named Charlie Culver.[3] Culver had excelled both at the plate and on the mound over his previous two seasons in Montreal, playing mostly at shortstop when not pitching. His success was not surprising given his background: before arriving in Montreal, Culver had played high-level baseball between 1916 and 1920 with two top independent Negro teams—the New York Lincoln Giants and the Pennsylvania Red Caps. His teammates had

included Joe Williams and Fats Jenkins, among others.[4] In September 1919, he landed in Montreal along with Pop Watkins and his Havana Red Sox.[5] The following spring the team returned, and Culver was offered a contract to also play with St. Henri, a Montreal team vying for the city championship. During the weekend of May 22–23, Culver not only pitched a complete game for the Havana Red Sox, he then went the distance the next day in a marathon game for St. Henri, eventually losing it, 6–5, in 20 innings.[6]

In the United States, Culver had no choice but to play on Negro League teams because black players had been effectively banned from the major and minor leagues. Throughout the twentieth century, there had been attempts to disguise black players as Native American (Jimmy Claxton with the 1916 Oakland Oaks) or hispanic (many light-skinned Cubans signed by Cincinnati and Washington).[7]

Somehow, the "gentleman's agreement" excluding black players does not seem to have reached the Eastern Canada League. When the Montreal management, led by president Fred Gadbois and manager Larry Carmel, started assembling its lineup, Culver was a natural fit. He signed with the team on April 25. The daily newspaper *La Presse* ran the story the next day, along with a photo, but made no mention of his race or the color line. The article congratulated the team on a solid hiring.[8] Other newspapers in Montreal, as well as those outside of the city, did not carry the story.

Nevertheless, over the next few days, two negative reactions were published in the local newspapers. The first had nothing to do with the color line. On April 27, *La Presse* ran a letter expressing the concerns of a baseball team in St. Hyacinthe, some 70 kilometers (45 miles) east of Montreal. The team, seeking Quebec baseball supremacy, had signed Culver to a contract a month earlier, and had no intention of giving him up. St. Hyacinthe was certainly capable of attracting top talent, both from the province and neighboring regions, with presumably good pay. But the Eastern Canada League played six games a week, while St. Hyacinthe only played on weekends. The letter carefully attacked the Montreal team and the new league, but not Culver himself.[9]

Then on May 2, the other French-language Montreal daily newspaper, *La Patrie*, published parts of a long letter it had received which further complained about Culver's hiring. These concerns were also directed at the new league, but this time made a point of addressing the matter of the color line by pointing out how unusual it would be for a team in Organised Baseball to hire any black player. As such, the letter wonders about the legitimacy of the alleged Class B status for the league:

> How can the new organization pretend to be in Organized Baseball, that prohibits hiring colored players on its teams? Aren't we trying to fool the public in this story?[10]

While the letter is signed by "a group of baseball fans," it was evident that this "group" also managed the rival (semi-pro) City league, which stood to lose serious revenue because of the arrival of the professional league.

> Those that were the first to ostracize Calvert a few years ago when he arrived in the City league are the same characters who today are offering a king's ransom to hire him in an organization supposedly in Organized Baseball. Don't we just want to hurt the City league and baseball in general?[11]

None of this prevented Culver from getting ready for the Eastern Canada League season. League President Joe Page, keen to properly launch the league, had used his baseball contacts to arrange high profile visits throughout the season, and the Boston Braves

LA PRESSE, MARCH 26, 1921

Culver signing his 1921 contract with the St. Henri semi-pro team.

were the first in town on April 30. Arriving with most of their regular lineup, they beat Culver's Montreal team by a score of 7–2. Culver played shortstop, and was penciled in the third spot of the lineup. He amassed two of the four hits against Braves pitcher Jigger Lansing, including a double that was described as the best shot of the day.[12] The *Boston Globe* ran a short article on the game, with no mention of Culver.[13]

If there was any attempt to hide or disguise Culver, it seems to have been a poor one. While touting an exhibition game against Trois-Rivières before the official start of the season, *La Presse* mentioned that "Cuban pitcher" Charlie Culver was to be on the mound.[14] It is not clear if this was a reference to his arrival with the Havana Red Sox—who had no link to Cuba, and used the name as a marketing gimmick—or to his mysterious origins (more on that later). In general, local newspapers didn't shy away from describing him as black or colored. As for the exhibition game, it was rained out.

PLAYING IN THE EASTERN CANADA LEAGUE

In the late afternoon of Thursday May 11, 1922, in front of about 3,000 fans at Atwater Park in Montreal, Culver took the mound against the visiting Ottawa team. He gave up single runs in each of the first two innings, but a two-run home run by teammate Edward Singher evened the score at 2–2. Culver switched into second gear in the third: slotted in the fifth spot in the lineup, he hit a three-run homer, and blanked Ottawa the rest of the way. Montreal won, 7–2, with Culver giving up the two runs on seven hits and a single walk, striking out 10. He added a double to his long ball to finish 2 for 4.[15]

La Presse ran a short story on the game, not mentioning Culver's background or race. If there were reactions from the crowd or the teams, they did not make it into print. The article was accompanied by pictures of the two teams as well as the umpires.

The following afternoon, Culver was moved to right field, and while he was limited to one hit in four at-bats, it was a big one. His second home run in two days tied the score at 2–2 in the eighth inning. Montreal sealed the deal in the ninth to beat Ottawa, 3–2.[16]

On May 13, Montreal completed the sweep against Ottawa with a 6-4 win, as Calvert finished with one hit in two at-bats and a run scored. He sat out the next day, a 3–2 loss at home against Valleyfield.[17]

On May 15, he was back on the mound, and his teammates gave him an early five-run lead. It was 9–2 in the eighth inning when Culver let his guard down and let in three runs. In total, he surrendered

Newly signed Charlie Culver and Franklyn Wallace visit St. Hyacinthe in the spring of 1922.

LA PRESSE, APRIL 26, 1922

five runs on 11 hits and a walk, striking out three batters. However, for the first time, he was held hitless at the plate in two at-bats, scoring one run and committing an error.[18]

The next day, he returned to right field, producing a double in three at-bats, scoring three runs in an 8–4 win.[19] The final game of the series against Valleyfield occurred on May 17, with Culver managing to go 1–4 in an 11–2 loss.[20]

Trois-Rivières then came in town for a series starting on May 18, but Culver was not in the lineup. Newspapers of the day ran brief stories focusing mostly on the previous day's game. No reason was given for Culver's absence, but he would not return. A few days later, on May 22, *Le Nouvelliste de Trois-Rivières* reported that "Culver, formerly of Montreal, will be obliged to play for St. Hyacinthe, with whom he had signed a contract at the beginning of the season."[21]

Although his name would continue to appear sporadically in the media for his play in semi-pro ball, Charlie Culver's career in organized baseball was over after six games. Culver appears, absent a first name, in the official statistics of the league. At the plate, he went 6 for 19 with two doubles and two home runs, scoring seven times. On the mound, he was 2–0 with 18 hits and seven runs allowed in 18 innings. He struck out 13 batters and gave two free passes.

Despite their good start, the Montreal team finished last in the league with a 55–69 record. Midseason, Valleyfield moved to Cap-de-la-Madeleine, just across the Saint-Maurice River from Trois-Rivières, which won the pennant with a 69–53 record. The Cap-de-la-Madeleine team then moved to Quebec City for the 1923 season. In 1924, the league added two teams in Vermont, in Rutland and Montpelier, while Trois-Rivières was replaced by a second team based on the island of Montreal. The league rebranded itself as the Quebec-Ontario-Vermont league. The Vermont teams

disbanded at mid-season, and the league itself ceased its operations after the season.

Semi-pro leagues in Quebec continued to attract black players in the following years. Chick Bowden, a catcher who had come to Montreal with the Manhattan Giants, eventually settled in Quebec and had a long baseball career across the province. By the late 1920s, Chappie Johnson was sponsoring an all-black team in Montreal leagues, an experience that continued sporadically until 1937, when a team called the Black Panthers was part of the Provincial League. Culver and Bowden alternated playing with these teams and with local teams.[22]

ON CHARLIE CULVER

Quebec newspapers are not especially generous about Charlie Culver's origins.[23] By drawing information from the Seamheads Negro League Encyclopedia and making contact with one of his great-grand-daughters we can produce a rough sketch of his life. He was born on November 17, 1892, in Buffalo, New York, presumably the out-of-wedlock son of Joseph Edwin Culver and an unidentified mother.[24] He was thus approaching 30 years of age when he played in the Eastern Canada League in 1922. According to his WWI registration card, by 1917 Charlie was living in New Jersey and working as a porter at Pennsylvania Station in New York City (and, as previously mentioned, playing for the Red Caps, a Negro independent team made up mostly of his coworkers). He was married, although the name of his wife is not reported.[25]

By 1920 he had made it to Montreal, and shortly after he married Paula Saint-Arnaud, a widow with a young son. Her husband had succumbed to the Spanish flu while serving in the Canadian Army. He adopted her son Gérard, who took the last name of Calvert, and the couple had a son (Joseph, 1924) and a daughter (Dolores, 1927) together. Paula was shunned by her family for marrying a black man. Tragedy struck when Paula passed away in 1930, a victim of a typhoid epidemic.[26] Left alone with three children, Culver eventually gave his two youngest, Joseph and Dolores, up for adoption, while Gérard was left to fend for himself.[27]

Culver seems to have stayed in Quebec for the rest of his life, devoting most of it to baseball. He continued to play semi-pro ball across southern Quebec until the mid-1940s, often as player-manager.[28] By the 1950s, he had transitioned to coaching junior baseball in Montreal. According to various voters lists, he seems to have complemented his income with factory work, being listed as a Canadian Vickers employee, then later as a foreman.[29] Along the way he remarried to Marie-Jeanne Martel.[30]

He passed away on January 4, 1970, in Montreal. He was still known well enough for a few newspapers to run stories reflecting back on his career. Denis Brodeur, the father of NHL Hall of Famer Martin Brodeur, who himself had a sound athletic career in baseball and hockey before becoming the official photographer of the Montreal Canadiens, remembered playing for Culver:

> Mr. Culver was one of my first managers, and together we won the Montreal junior championship. He was respected by all his players. In 1949, he was managing an all-star junior team that was to play a Brooklyn all-star team. I remember the game. Around the 7th inning, we were leading by a run, and a ball was hit between Marcel Durand and I. We let it drop, and the opposing team took advantage to score the tying run. Culver immediately came to see us and said: "Don't worry, you'll have other opportunities." In the 13th inning, Durand hit a double, and I was hitting next. Culver said: "Here's your chance. Take your time." I followed with a double and we won 4–3.

"Culver dedicated his whole life to baseball," concluded Brodeur.[31]

POSTSCRIPT

Many questions remain unanswered. While it looks like the contractual dispute with St. Hyacinthe was the main reason for Culver's departure from the league, one must wonder if there was some pressure from the National Association to get rid of him. The truth might lie between these extremes, with the Montreal management advising Culver to fulfill his contractual

LE SAMEDI, FEBRUARY 25, 1950

Culver, right, being honored as manager of the 1950 Montreal junior champions.

obligations with St. Hyacinthe when faced with the prospect of not only an uncertain legal battle with St. Hyacinthe but also the potential difficulties with the National Association.

The other open question is what exactly were the managements of the Montreal team and of the league thinking when they signed Culver? Given the experience of league president Joe Page and the recent presence of the Montreal Royals, they were unlikely to be ignorant of the color line. One possibility is that they believed, maybe with the support of the National Association, that the color line did not extend to an all-Canadian league. But given that Culver was not re-invited for 1923 or 1924, nor were any other black players there nor in other all-Canadian leagues (including the 1940 Provincial League in Quebec) that seems improbable. One can imagine that it would have quickly become untenable for the National Association to allow blacks players in some regions but not others.

In the end, it seems to have taken close to 100 years for the historic significance of Culver's exploits to be noticed. Even in Quebec where he was a known figure, his pioneering experience in organized baseball was never mentioned. Some of the journalists who covered Jackie Robinson with the 1946 Montreal Royals were surely around 24 years earlier when Culver broke the color line, but nobody seemed to remember. It is not even clear if Culver knew the significance of his presence. It is possible that in its infancy, the Eastern Canada League was not much different from the City league against which it was competing, with the National Association accreditation looking like a marketing gimmick. In fact, the presence of Culver might have been a proof to some that this could not be true, giving an incentive for the league management to let him go to St. Hyacinthe.

In the end, while Culver's week in Organized Baseball went unnoticed, his long career as a trailblazer helped set the stage for Jackie Robinson's arrival. But one is left wondering what would have happened if he had not signed that contract with St. Hyacinthe, or if he had been able to get out of it. ■

Acknowledgments
I'd like to thank Jodie Calvert and Tina Marie for helping me with the details of Charlie's life. I'm also grateful to Patrick Carpentier and Alexandre Pratt for assistance on the Montreal baseball scene of the 1920s. Gary Fink and Bill Young also provided helpful comments on early drafts.

Notes
1. "Sherbrooke likely to have pro team," *Sherbrooke Daily Record*, April 27, 1921, 10.
2. "L'inauguration le 11 mai," *Le Devoir*, April 10, 1922, 7.
3. Charlie Culver was also known as Charlie Calvert. The name, more frequent in the French media, was also taken by his sons. Official documents like voters lists and his obituary used Culver. A 1938 article confirms that Calvert/Culver are one and the same, with Culver being the real name (Le Samedi, 2 juillet 1938, Dans le monde sportif). No reason is provided for the switch, but one reason might be that Culver translates to "butt worm" or "green butt" in French. Victor Power switched to his mother's maiden name, from Pellot, for similar reasons after playing in the 1949–50 Provincial League.
4. *The Seamheads Negro League Encyclopedia.*
5. "Les Red Sox Havanais gagnent et perdent ici," *Le Canada*, September 29, 1919, 2.
6. "Le Saint-Arsène gagne la plus longue partie de baseball jouée à Montréal," *La Presse*, May 24, 1920, 7.
7. Joel Zoss and John Bowman, *Diamonds in the Rough: The Untold History of Baseball*. Lincoln: University of Nebraska Press, 2004, 146–49.
8. "Boston viendra ici dimanche," *La Presse*, April 26, 1922, 8.
9. "Le Saint-Hyacinthe et Charlie Calvert," *La Presse*, April 27, 1922, 8.
10. "On critique l'engagement de Calvert," *La Patrie*, May 3, 1922, 6.
11. "On critique l'engagement de Calvert," *La Patrie*, May 3, 1922, 6.
12. "Boston défait le club local au Shamrock," *La Presse*, May 1, 1922, 14.
13. "Braves victors, 7–2," *Boston Globe*, May 1, 1922, 7.
14. "Eugène Grenier contre Calvert," *La Presse*, May 4, 1922, 8.
15. "Home runs par Charlie Calvert et Ed. Singher," *La Presse*, May 12, 1922, 10, and "Le Montréal défait l'OUawa," *La Patrie*, May 12, 1922, 6. *La Presse* and *La Patrie* disagree, with *La Patrie* crediting Culver with 11 strikeouts.
16. "Valleyfield jouera demain au Shamrock," *La Presse*, May 13, 1922, 14.
17. "Premier échec de Montréal après trois succès," *La Patrie*, May 15, 1922, 6.
18. "Montreal bat le Valleyfield à Westmount," *La Presse*, May 16, 1922, 8.
19. "Home runs par Jos Delisle et Ed. Singher," *La Presse*, May 17, 1922, 8.
20. "Belle besogne des frappeurs de Valleyfield," *La Presse*, May 18, 1922, 8.
21. "Le Trois-Rivières prend la tête de la ligue de l'est," *Le Nouvelliste*, May 22, 1922, 3.
22. See John Virtue, *South of the Color Barrier*, McFarland & Co Inc, 2007, 48, and Christian Trudeau, *Le baseball à Montréal en 1927*, SABR-Québec website archives.
23. An exception is when he signs his 1921 contract. Media coverage mentioned his Negro teams background, and the fact that he only considered playing in Montreal, New York, Philadelphia or Buffalo. See "Le Saint-Henri aura un fameux club cet été," *La Presse*, March 26, 1921, 18.
24. Joseph Edwin Cutler appears in the 1900 and 1910 U.S. censuses, with a Charlie born in November 1892 as part of his household. Charlie is listed as son in 1900 but step-son in 1910. Although his color is listed as "white" on both occasions, this is most likely an attempt to hide a potentially scandalous situation. Other evidence that this is the same Charlie Culver is that the WWI registration card lists a Jersey City address, a city where the Joseph Edwin Culver's family had lived for generations.
25. "United States World War I Draft Registration Cards, 1917–1918," database with images, FamilySearch, New Jersey > Jersey City no 5; A-H > image 1816 of 4082; citing NARA microfilm publication M1509 (Washington, DC: National Archives and Records Administration, n.d.).
26. Ancestry.com. Quebec, Canada, Vital and Church Records (Drouin Collection), 1621–1968 [database online]. Provo, UT, USA: Ancestry.com Operations, Inc., 2008. Original data: Gabriel Drouin, comp. Drouin Collection. Montreal, Quebec, Canada: Institut Généalogique Drouin.
27. The stories in this paragraph were obtained through an email conversation with Jodie Calvert, granddaughter of Gérard.
28. For instance, Culver threw at shutout in 1944, at age 52. "Le Saint-Jean gagne à la 11ème manche," *Le Devoir*, 12 juin 1944, 9.
29. Voters Lists, Federal Elections, 1935–1980. R1003-6-3-E (RG113-B). Library and Archives Canada, Ottawa, Ontario, Canada.
30. "Naissances, décès, remerciements, in memoriam," *La Presse*, January 5, 1970, 39.
31. "Le Miroir des Sports," *La Presse*, January 6, 1970, 24.

A Global Fiasco

Walter Dilbeck tried to create a third major league. He wound up in prison.

Warren Corbett

Shifty. That's a good word for Walter Dilbeck, the huckster who launched the Global Baseball League in 1966. And launched it again in 1968. And crashed it in 1969. The barely believable saga of Dilbeck and his self-styled third major league involves 11 Hall of Famers, a former vice president of the United States, a crooked preacher, and an international incident, with cameo appearances by Frank Sinatra and Howard Hughes.

The world was not exactly clamoring for another baseball league in 1966. The American and National leagues had recently expanded to 10 teams each, with a promise of more. The minors had shrunk from 59 circuits to 18 in a decade and a half, and some of the survivors were teetering. Professional football was ascendant. It was fashionable—again—to proclaim baseball dying or dead.

Undaunted, Dilbeck hatched his scheme on October 21, 1966, when he announced that representatives from 14 cities had met in Evansville, Indiana, to adopt a charter for the new league. He said the Global would begin play in 1968 in contiguous US cities and later extend its reach to the Philippines, Japan, and Puerto Rico.[1] "We can find better players than there are in the major leagues," he declared. "I'd say there are only 20 or so in each league who would be good enough to play in our league."[2] That laughable exaggeration set the tone for all that came later.

Walter J. Dilbeck Jr. was a 48-year-old Evansville real estate developer who claimed to have played briefly in the minors and was part-owner of the Class-A Rock Hill, South Carolina, club. He was a decorated World War II hero; the Associated Press reported that he had been awarded two Distinguished Service Crosses for valor, the Army's second-highest medal, as well as four Bronze Stars and four Purple Hearts (though not all of these awards could be verified). "He's not inclined to let you forget it," Bill Fleischman wrote in *The Sporting News*.[3]

His postwar record was less distinguished. He had run twice for mayor of Evansville unsuccessfully, once garnering only 586 votes. *Sports Illustrated* reported

that he had lost his Indiana real estate license in 1955.[4] Now he was promoting land deals in Kentucky. A stout man with a neat Clark Gable mustache, he described his wardrobe as "flashy clothes, lively clothes."[5] Dilbeck projected a salesman's glib confidence, but he was a moderate-sized fish in a small pond, a trout aspiring to be a whale.

After additional meetings in November and January, he declaimed, "When some old boys who have held the reins since 1900 tell us this nation of 200,000,000 people is not capable of fielding three major leagues, I challenge this." He identified five cities that had anted up $50,000 deposits toward a franchise: Milwaukee, Phoenix, Jersey City, Indianapolis, and San Diego.[6] As subsequent events showed, this was almost certainly false.

A month later Dilbeck shifted to a new roster of cities including Louisville, Charlotte, and Omaha. But he was vague about stadium leases and declined to discuss the league's financing. If he had a plan, it depended on securing a network television contract. He said he was in negotiations toward that end.[7]

The baseball establishment weighed in through the game's bible, *The Sporting News*, with a warning to prospective investors. Editor C.C. Johnson Spink wrote that the Global League "got off on the wrong foot" by failing to seek an audience with Commissioner William Eckert and pledge allegiance to Organized Baseball. If it dared to proceed as an "outlaw," Spink predicted, failure would be swift and sure.[8]

The Global League was fully capable of failing without Spink's advice. By mid-1967 the circuit had vanished. Dilbeck shifted his focus in a new direction. In October he paid a reported $65,000 for the bankrupt Toronto Triple-A franchise and persuaded the International League to move it to Louisville.

Louisville had been without professional baseball since 1962, when the American Association folded. Kansas City A's owner Charlie Finley had teased the city with a proposal to bring his team there, but nothing came of it. Now Dilbeck bragged, "I'm going to make a major league town out of Louisville in two years or so." Pumping up his bona fides to the local paper, he touted his real estate projects in Kentucky and dropped the names of Governor Ned Breathitt and the late Senator Alben Barkley. He confided that Hollywood was making a movie of his wartime exploits.[9]

The Louisville Colonels scored a working agreement with the Boston Red Sox, who named former big leaguer Eddie Kasko as manager. Dilbeck promised him a $15,000 bonus for winning the pennant.[10] The club finished fifth in 1968, but led the league in attendance with more than 225,000.

When the major leagues announced a new round of expansion for 1969, Dilbeck entered his horse in the race. "Money and financing are not our problems," he wired National League President Warren Giles. "We have the desire, therefore it will come.[11]" The NL chose San Diego and Montreal for its new franchises. With both majors now comprising 12 teams, no further expansion was likely any time soon.

Seeing the setback as an opportunity, Dilbeck pulled the Global League off the trash heap in June 1968. He had one of his allies write a letter to Commissioner Eckert seeking Organized Baseball's blessing for a third major league, but Eckert's reply was noncommittal boilerplate.[12] Dilbeck charged full speed ahead.

This time around, he said four Japanese teams would join franchises in Louisville, Jersey City, Dallas, and Mexico City. Players? No problem: "I'm sure out of 200 million people in this country you'll find some good baseball players."[13] They would play a 100-game schedule beginning in 1969 with tickets priced at $5.[14]

In an interview with *The Sporting News*, he said, "We wouldn't be competing with the majors. We would be somewhere between Double-A and Triple-A." But not just another minor league. The games would pause during the fifth inning for a halftime show featuring "Geisha girls" among other entertainment[16]

Jack Corbett, a longtime minor-league owner with connections in Japanese baseball, came aboard as executive vice president (no relation to the author). He said the league would not raid the majors or minors for players. The Globals advertised for investors to establish farm clubs for the new circuit.

To skeptics, Dilbeck said he had arranged a multi-million-dollar line of credit with an unnamed Indianapolis bank. The league planned to begin its 1969 season in June and cap it off with a true World Series in September. Dilbeck offered the job of managing the Louisville entry to Eddie Stanky, former Cardinals and White Sox manager. Stanky said he was considering it.[17]

In October Dilbeck rolled out another big name. Former baseball commissioner Happy Chandler agreed to serve as commissioner of the Global League. The 70-year-old Chandler, a former Kentucky senator and governor, had been forced out of the major league commissioner's office back in 1951. He and Dilbeck presided over the signing of the Global's first player, Arnold Edward Davis, a 21-year-old pitcher from Evansville.[18]

Continuing his media blitz in the fall, Dilbeck raised his sights: "We plan for this to be the third major league in not too many years. We're here to compete with Organized Baseball." He had shifted again and was now talking of a six-team circuit with three in the United States and three in Japan. Dilbeck said Louisville and Jersey City were set and he planned to award the remaining franchise to Tampa investor Bunny Mick. But Mick said, "I think he's getting a little ahead of himself." He had not applied for a franchise.[19]

Dilbeck claimed he had an agreement with the National Association, the governing body of the minors, to play in minor league parks when the home teams were on the road. But National Association President Phil Piton said there was no such agreement. He did point out that any "barnstorming team" could rent a ballpark.[20]

Retired slugger Johnny Mize signed to manage one Global team; he didn't know which one. Former American League umpire Bill McKinley was appointed supervisor of umpires. Stanky was offered the position of vice president of player development at $75,000 a year, but he was not interested.

In February 1969 the league scheduled tryout camps in four cities with former major leaguers Mize, Enos Slaughter, Gordon Jones, and Stu Miller in charge. Another shift: Dilbeck now said the circuit would include San Juan, Puerto Rico, and Caracas, Venezuela.

One big red flag: except for Dilbeck in Louisville, none of the other team owners had revealed themselves. The unknown Dilbeck was the only public face of the league. Commissioner Chandler had retreated to his old Kentucky home.

Just a decade earlier the Continental League had declared itself the third major. The Continental had many advantages over the Global. It attracted deep-pocketed owners in eight large cities and enlisted the visionary executive Branch Rickey as its president and spokesman. While the majors had resisted expansion beyond the Northeast and Midwest for more than half a century, new cities had grown up with a thirst for big-league status. There was pent-up demand for baseball.

But despite its bona fides, the Continental League disbanded before it played a game—when the two major leagues agreed to expand. "It was ridiculed as a sham," one of the organizers, Houston's Craig Cullinan Jr., said, "but on the contrary it was an enormous success because it ran what became the biggest bluff in the history of professional sports."[21]

Walter Dilbeck didn't have the cards to run such a bluff. He had to play the hand he had dealt himself.

He made a high-stakes bet to strengthen his hand, according to several bizarre stories that broke in the spring of 1969. Bob Addie of the *Washington Post* wrote that the Global League had offered "fabulous contracts" of $500,000 over four years to a glittering lineup of 10 major league stars: Don Drysdale, Ron Santo, Juan Marichal, Brooks Robinson, Roberto Clemente, Jim Bunning, Jim Fregosi, Joel Horlen, Jim Maloney, and Bill Mazeroski. Addie said Drysdale was recruiting more players.[22]

Robinson and Fregosi confirmed the offers, and Hank Aaron said he had been approached with the same deal. Robinson said Dilbeck had met with the players and told them he was negotiating with the Hughes Television Network to provide the money and broadcast the league's games.[23] Sandy Grady of the *Philadelphia Bulletin* also reported that Hughes TV money was the bait[24]

The billionaire hermit Howard Hughes had bought Sports Network Inc., a syndicator of sports programs, put his name on it, and was looking to expand. But Hughes Network President Dick Bailey called the stories "ridiculous." He said he had never discussed a proposal from the Global League.[25] The network was preparing to bid for Major League Baseball and NFL broadcast rights. Flirting with a competing league could kill its chances.

While Dilbeck was silent, the league's vice commissioner, Hillman Lyons, denied any attempt to raid the majors for players. Still, the story had a ring of plausibility. During the offseason the Major League Baseball Players Association had orchestrated a mass holdout, with the vast majority of players refusing to sign their 1969 contracts in a standoff over the pension plan. As spring training approached, uncertainty hung over the game.

Several of the named stars were nearing the end of their careers and might be tempted by a big payday. Fregosi was being threatened with a salary cut after a bad year. Drysdale was struggling to recover from a shoulder injury that would force him to retire a few

months later. And Dilbeck had a history of making extravagant promises.

Without a TV contract, Addie reported, the Global League was "on the verge of extinction."[26] The league spokesman called that speculation "a big joke."[27]

The Global League reached its high tide on April 2, 1969, when about 150 players reported for spring training in Daytona Beach, Florida, under the direction of Mize and Slaughter. The league now had actual players on an actual ball field coached by actual major leaguers. Former all-star shortstop Chico Carrasquel led a contingent from his native Venezuela, and a retired Japanese star, Toru Mori, brought the sharpest-looking team to camp. Former Giants pitcher Ruben Gomez was prepping the Puerto Rican entry. A Dominican team was said to be on the way. The U.S. clubs represented Jersey City and Mobile, Alabama, at least on paper. Their hopefuls included a former big-league pitcher, Ed Rakow, and a future one, Oscar Zamora (who soon left), but few had professional experience.[28]

Mize disclosed that the league would play a revolutionary brand of baseball: unlimited pinch-hitters and pinch-runners, and free substitution, with players allowed to exit the game and return. "It could be a whole new concept of baseball—offensive and defensive teams like in college football," he said.[29]

One of the players, third baseman Bobby Bragan Jr., said Dilbeck "was kind of an odd character. He had all these rules. You can't smoke. You can't drink. You can't cuss. You can't go anywhere after 11PM. Of course, nobody paid any attention to 'em." After a couple of weeks of practice games, Dilbeck took the players out for steaks and booze and gave each one a $100 bill. That was just about the last money Bragan ever saw from the Global League.[30]

Soon the league announced it was ready to begin its season—in Latin America. Opening Day was set for April 24 with games in San Juan, Puerto Rico; Santo Domingo, Dominican Republic; and Caracas, Venezuela. "The major leagues lose money the first month of the season," Dilbeck explained, "and I can't see playing baseball in the States in April and May."[31]

It was a strategic error born of desperation. After scrambling to cover the heavy expenses of spring training, Dilbeck was counting on big crowds south of the border to replenish his bank account. His advance men in Venezuela assured him that enthusiasm was high. But playing in the Caribbean and South America meant no coverage in U.S. newspapers.

Dilbeck told his hometown *Evansville Press* that 20,000 people had turned out for the opener in Caracas, with just one hitch. When the American flag was raised, anti-American demonstrators stormed the field. Dilbeck said he had restored order by threatening to "kill the first s.o.b. who touched the flag."[32] Unfortunately, no U.S. reporter was present on the scene to verify this dramatic tale.

The games in Puerto Rico and the Dominican Republic were a bust; Dilbeck acknowledged that they had drawn only about 1,500 spectators. He said all six teams would play in Caracas before coming to the United States.

The league effectively disappeared for a month. When news stories resumed, they were worse than no stories. On May 23 the Associated Press reported that one Caracas hotel had refused to serve meals to Global players because of unpaid bills. "We've only been playing three weeks, we don't even have nicknames and already we're in trouble," said James Purcell, manager of the New York club. "My boys have to eat."[33] (Dilbeck had rebranded the U.S. teams as New York and Los Angeles, which sounded more "major league" than Jersey City and Mobile.)

A United Press International reporter found 87 ballplayers stranded in Caracas with hotels threatening to throw them out in the street unless the league paid $90,000 that it owed. Paul May, a Global representative in Venezuela, said the funds were "held up by formalities at local banks." A spokesman for the U.S. Embassy commented, "We haven't seen any money yet." Several players had filed a complaint with police charging breach of contract, and May had been briefly detained.[34]

"It is hard to describe the confusion that existed when we arrived in the Caribbean," said Johnny Mize, who had already come home along with Slaughter. He revealed that the teams had played before mostly empty seats. "The men Dilbeck sent to Central and South America must have been on vacations. They didn't do much, if anything, for the league. They painted a great picture for Dilbeck and kept wiring him for more money. I think he deserved better than that because he really put his heart into this thing."[35]

Jack Corbett and Stu Miller had also jumped ship with the league owing them back pay. "The Global League was the most mixed-up affair I've ever seen," the veteran executive Corbett remarked. "Dilbeck is quite a guy and I really like him, but he had no setup and talked a good game." Miller, who had coached for only a few weeks before opening his eyes, said, "I was conned." When a reporter called the normally loquacious Dilbeck, he hung up.[36]

Another reporter sought a comment from Happy Chandler. The figurehead commissioner didn't know that the league had started its season. "I have heard very little from them in the last six months," he said, adding that he had not been paid his reported $4,000-a-month salary.[37]

Within a week, league spokesman Jack White said almost all the players had been brought out of Venezuela. He said the league would continue its season in U.S. minor league parks and accused the majors of sabotage because they refused to allow Global League games in their parks. "They're fighting us in every conceivable way," White complained. "They don't want competition."[38]

Not everyone had been rescued. Some U.S. players asked the embassy for emergency loans to get home.[39] The Japanese were also left behind. When the league sent them plane tickets, Venezuelan authorities blocked them from leaving until their hotel bills were paid. At one point they made it as far as the airport but were ordered off the plane. The Japanese Embassy was said to be arranging their ransom.[40]

Dilbeck surfaced in June to announce that he had sold the Global League to the Los Angeles-based Baptist Foundation of America for $3 million. Foundation President T. Sherron Jackson said the league fit with the group's philosophy of "clean bodies and clean minds." Dilbeck's no-smoking, no-drinking, no-cussing rules were apparently worth $3 million. He continued as president.[41]

While some Global League employees, such as Mize and Corbett, remained sold on the salesman, Dilbeck's creditors were not so understanding. Hotels in Venezuela and the Dominican Republic filed lawsuits in U.S. courts demanding payment of past-due bills. So did a supplier of uniforms and equipment. The Japanese players showed up in Evansville in August, free at last and looking for their back pay. Several were suffering from vitamin deficiencies brought on by malnutrition.[42]

An Evansville semipro team announced that it would play an exhibition against the Japanese "Tokyo Dragons" on August 27.[43] If the game was played, it was evidently the only Global League contest ever staged in the United States.

Dilbeck had also lost his International League team. The league seized the Louisville Colonels and sold the franchise to a local businessman, William A. Gardner, a nephew of Red Sox owner Tom Yawkey. The club was reportedly $160,000 in debt.[44]

The Baptist Foundation of America turned out to be a scam, not affiliated with the Baptist church. It later shut down after the U.S. attorney in Sacramento charged that it had run "a highly sophisticated and intricate international conspiracy to defraud the public of many millions of dollars." The Rev. Dr. Jackson was sentenced to prison for conspiracy and mail fraud. Dilbeck said he was stuck with worthless stock in a company controlled by the foundation.[45]

After the Global League passed into history, Walter Dilbeck continued to seek the spotlight. He raised funds for the legal defense of American soldiers accused of massacring Vietnamese women and children at My Lai and spearheaded a Reagan for President drive in 1972, when Ronald Reagan was not a candidate.

Three years later he announced that the disgraced former Vice President Spiro T. Agnew had joined his company as a rainmaker to bring in Arab investors for real estate projects. Dilbeck said the two had met at Frank Sinatra's house. He boasted that he was paying Agnew $100,000 a year plus profit participation that would make the crooked politician a multimillionaire. After the publicity stirred a backlash, Agnew canceled the contract, saying with a straight face that Dilbeck had exploited him "at the expense of my integrity."[46]

Dilbeck's past reared up to bite him in 1976. A federal grand jury in Indianapolis indicted him on five counts of income tax evasion in the years 1968 through 1972. He blamed his dispute with the IRS on losses from the Global League, but investigators charged that he had done worse than stiff a few hotels and ballplayers. They accused him of "using other people's credit and securing loans in other people's names" while dodging taxes on at least $2.3 million in unreported income. In a plea bargain with prosecutors, he admitted guilt to a single count.[47]

Since prosecutors made no sentencing recommendation, the huckster faced up to three years in prison. U.S. District Judge William Steckler said Dilbeck's wife, Dorothy, had written to him describing her husband as "a flamboyant person, high living, money coming in very easy and going out very easy." The judge said Dilbeck's victims included his own sister, who was out $125,000, and two people who had died of heart attacks after learning of their losses. Then Judge Steckler shocked courtroom spectators by sentencing Dilbeck to just 60 days confinement. He justified leniency because of the defendant's war record and poor health; doctors said he had diabetes and high blood pressure.[48]

The caress on the wrist smelled so bad that *Indianapolis News* reporter David Rohn began investigating. He discovered that the wife of Indiana Senator Vance Hartke had visited the judge privately in chambers to urge him to go easy on Dilbeck, who had been a big contributor to the senator's failed presidential campaign. Rohn said the prosecutors cut a deal because their case relied largely on evidence that was "unsubstantiated or hearsay," and a conviction was no sure thing if it had gone before a jury. Courthouse sources believed Judge Steckler was regretting the light sentence.[49]

After serving his time, Dilbeck found God. He and Dorothy knocked on doors to spread the gospel on behalf of the Baptist church. When he was no longer able to pound the pavement, he preached to passersby outside a supermarket.[50] He filed for bankruptcy in 1984, listing debts of $1.3 million and assets of $8,300. He told the court he had lost $3.5 million on his baseball venture.[51] That was the epitaph of the Global League.

Walter Dilbeck died of heart and kidney disease at 72 on May 30, 1991. He was a man of grand ambition and little scruple. The movie of his life has not yet been made. ∎

Source

McKenna, Brian. "The Global League." SABR BioProject, https://sabr.org/bioproj/topic/global-league.

Notes

1. Associated Press, "World Wide Baseball: That's Global League," *Pittsburgh Post-Gazette*, October 22, 1966: 7.
2. "The Third What?" *Sports Illustrated*, November 26, 1966, https://www.si.com/vault/1966/11/21/609976/scorecard, accessed July 21, 2019.
3. Bill Fleischman, "Capt. Dilbeck Sees Good Ship Global Sink in Red Ink," *The Sporting News* (hereafter *TSN*), June 28, 1969: 25.
4. "The Third What?"
5. Lloyd Shearer, "Spiro Agnew—He's Becoming a Multimillionaire in Real Estate," *Parade*, January 19, 1975: 5.
6. Associated Press, "Global League Seeks College Players," *Baltimore Evening Sun*, January 17, 1967: B9.
7. "Global, As In a Long Way from Anywhere," *Dallas Morning News*, February 24, 1967: 2.
8. C.C. Johnson Spink, "We Believe," *The Sporting News*, March 25, 1967: 14.
9. Earl Ruby, "'Private Dilbeck' to send Colonels to the majors?" *Louisville Courier-Journal*, October 19, 1967: B9.
10. Ron Coons, "High Finish Means Cash for Kasko," *Louisville Courier-Journal*, December 13, 1967: B10.
11. "Big Time?" *Louisville Courier-Journal*, April 21, 1968: C12.
12. Al Dunning, "All in the Game," *Evansville* (Indiana) *Press*, July 3, 1967: 17.
13. Coons, "Louisville Starts Move for Third Major League," *Louisville Courier-Journal*, July 14, 1968: C8.
14. Coons, "Louisville To Have 2 Baseball Teams?" *Louisville Courier-Journal*, July 30, 1968: B7.
15. Fleischman, "Dilbeck Enthuses Over Global Loop; Is He Just Dreamer or Big Dealer?" *TSN*, September 8, 1968: 15.
16. Dave Kindred, "Global League Set…and Stanky Isn't Scoffing," *Louisville Courier-Journal*, September 26, 1968: B5.
17. Kindred, "Global League Set."
18. David Reed, "Chandler 'Happy' To Be Commissioner of New Global Baseball League," *Lexington* (Kentucky) *Herald*, October 29, 1968: 10.
19. Fred Girard, "Global Loop Stirring World of Unrest in Minors," *TSN*, November 23, 1968: 41.
20. Girard, "Global Loop."

21. Robert Reed, *Colt .45s, a Six-Gun Salute* (Houston: Lone Star Books, 1999), 34.

22. Bob Addie, *Washington Post* News Service, "Stars Sought; Lack of TV Threatens Plan," *Arizona Republic* (Phoenix), March 5, 1969: 27.

23. Associated Press, "Robinson Reveals Global Offer," *Columbia* (South Carolina) *Gazette*, April 28, 1969: 4-D; "Fregosi Says He Nixed $500,000 Global Offer," *TSN*, March 29, 1969: 30; Associated Press, "Aaron Says Global Offer $500,000," *Richmond* (Virginia) *Times Dispatch*, June 15, 1969: E-6.

24. Sandy Grady, "When Howard Hughes Tried to Raid Majors," *TSN*, May 10, 1969: 10

25. "Story Linking Hughes Video Net to Global League Called 'Ridiculous,'" *TSN*, May 17, 1969: 22.

26. Addie, "Stars Sought."

27. "Global Loop Condition Is Claimed OK," *Muncie* (Indiana) *Star Press*, March 7, 1969: 22.

28. United Press International, "Five Global League Teams Begin Workouts in Florida," *Evansville Press*, April 4, 1969: 15; Jimmy Mann, "The Global League Story" *St. Petersburg* (Florida) *Times*, April 22–23, 1969.

29. UPI, "Five Global League Teams."

30. Frank Luksa, "Bragan Between Jobs in Global League," *Fort Worth* (Texas) *Star-Telegram*, June 15, 1969: 27.

31. United Press International, "Global League Opens Play Next Thursday," *Jasper* (Indiana) *Herald*, April 18, 1969: 10.

32. Dunning, "Global League games a riot in Venezuela," *Evansville Press*, May 1, 1969: 26.

33. Associated Press, "Global Players Hungry," *Evansville Courier and Press*, May 23, 1969: 23.

34. United Press International, "Global League Farce Still Running Rampant," *Lexington Herald*, May 27, 1969: 10.

35. Fleischman, "Capt. Dilbeck."

36. Fleischman, "Capt. Dilbeck."

37. David Reed, "Who's on First?" *Lexington Herald*, June 4, 1969: 10.

38. David Reed, "Who's on First?"

39. "Ball players Dilbeck hired asking loans," *Evansville Press*, June 12, 1969: 1.

40. Associated Press, "Japan Set to Bail Out Club," *Evansville Courier and Press*, August 1, 1969: 18.

41. "Dilbeck Sells Global League for $3 Million," *Evansville Press*, June 18, 1969: 29; Associated Press, "Baptist Faith Gets Test in Global League," *Lexington Herald*, June 19, 1969: 26.

42. Associated Press, "Where's Dilbeck?" *Louisville Courier-Journal*, August 13, 1969: B8.

43. "Mattingly Benefit Game Set Tonight," *Evansville Press*, August 27, 1969: 30.

44. Mike Kallay, "Louisville Businessman Buys Colonels Franchise," *Louisville Courier-Journal*, April 21, 1969: 1.

45. Associated Press, "Phony Religious Group Indicted for Big Frauds," *Tacoma* (Washington) *News Tribune*, April 18, 1973: B-5; "Ex-LaVerne minister receives prison sentence," *Pomona* (California) *Progress-Bulletin*, April 19, 1976: 1.

46. Shearer, "Spiro Agnew"; Associated Press, "'Victim' Spiro drops partner," *Chicago Tribune*, February 8, 1975: 3.

47. "Dilbeck's Dealings Revealed," *Indianapolis News*, December 2, 1976: 28.

48. "Dilbeck Gets 60 Days for Tax Fraud," *Indianapolis News*, February 7, 1977: 3.

49. David Rohn, "Steckler Dismayed at Dilbeck Term?" *Indianapolis News*, February 17, 1977: 21.

50. Dave DeWitt, "Flamboyant local businessman Walter Dilbeck dies at age 72," *Evansville Courier and Press*, May 31, 1991: 5.

51. Associated Press, "Walter J. Dilbeck Jr., 72, World War II Hero," *Lafayette* (Indiana) *Journal and Courier*, May 31, 1991: 18.

Tom Loftus

The American League's Forgotten Founding Father

John T. Pregler

In 1877, an auburn-haired 20-year-old from St. Louis, Missouri, took the field for George McManus's St. Louis Brown Stockings. The career of baseballist Thomas Joseph "Tom" Loftus parallels the story of the first 35 years of pro ball. Born on November 15, 1856, Loftus was a minor and major league baseball player, team captain, scout, manager, league organizer, club owner, and magnate.[1]

Over his career, Loftus helped develop numerous players in the minors whom he would go on to coach, manage, or play against in the majors: Hall of Famers Charles Radbourn, Charles Comiskey, and Rube Waddell, and other players like Tom "Sleeper" Sullivan, Joe Quinn and Billy Sullivan, to name but a few.[2]

Toward the end of Loftus's career, he stood shoulder to shoulder with Ban Johnson and Charles Comiskey during the rise of the American League and was at the center of some of the most pivotal events during that first critical year in 1899. He is the American League's forgotten founding father.

Loftus's name has been lost in time and history because he quit major league baseball in 1904 and died in 1910, four years before Babe Ruth's major league debut. Johnson and Comiskey would live two decades longer than Loftus, and their eventual falling out and larger-than-life egos ended up bumping Loftus's name from the front-page box score of history. It did not help Loftus's legacy that he lived in Dubuque, Iowa, a small Midwestern city without a major-league team or a large media spotlight. A review of newspapers of the era shows that Loftus's life in baseball was significant and warrants the same recognition now that was afforded him by his peers and contemporary sportswriters.

Loftus's major league career included two years as a player for the National League's St. Louis Brown Stockings late in the 1877 season and the American Association's St. Louis Browns at the beginning of the 1883 season. Loftus appeared in nine games over his MLB career, going 6-for-33 for a batting average of .182. In and around those two cups of coffee, Loftus would play in the semi-pro and minor leagues for about a decade.[3]

Loftus started his major league managing career in 1884 with the Milwaukee Brewers of the Union Association, which was only in existence for that one year. In 1885, Loftus and Ted Sullivan founded the Western Base Ball League.[4] Loftus would guide the Cleveland Blues of the American Association in 1888, then migrate the Cleveland club into the National League for the 1889 season. In 1890 and 1891, Loftus managed the Cincinnati Reds. During a stint as owner-manager of the Western League's Columbus Senators 1896–99, Loftus aided in the creation of the American League. Loftus sold his AL Cleveland club and became manager of the Chicago Orphans of the NL for the 1900–01 seasons. And finally, Loftus, part owner of the Washington Senators, managed his AL team in the 1902–03 seasons. In all, Loftus managed 1,055 games in MLB going 454–580 for a .439 won-loss average.[5]

Loftus had stepped away from the big leagues after the 1891 season because of the rising mean-spiritedness in all aspects of major league baseball that would come to undermine baseball in the 1890s. In November 1895, Loftus rejoined Johnson and Comiskey when he became owner of the Columbus Senators in the Western League. From 1896 through 1899, the Western League continued to grow in popularity, profits, and power in the baseball world. But not all was well with our national pastime.

By 1898 baseball was at a crossroads that could either lead to its further decline and a baseball war or turn the pastime around and send it into a new era of prosperity, ensuring the game's survival for future generations. MLB no longer consisted of multiple leagues, and the struggling NL grew to a 12-city circuit with the collapse of the American Association in 1891. Club owners had become complacent with their monopoly over their industry and their players, and the quality of play on the field was more rowdy and vulgar than it had been in the prior 30 years. Fan attendance was down in NL cities, while attendance was rising in Western League cities. By mid-1899 men in baseball circles, initially lead by Al Spink, founder of the *St. Louis Sporting News*, were quietly suggesting the time was right to form a successful rival league to the NL. Their efforts would lead to the second attempt in five years to revive the American Association, which had operated as a major league from 1882–91.[6] At the same time the threat of a revived American Association was rising against the NL, the powers in the Western League started to see their long-awaited chance to migrate their minor league into major league status in direct competition with the NL. They knew the process would be difficult, fraught with risk, and take more than one or two seasons to accomplish.[7]

Before the Western League could transform into the American League in 1900 and declare itself a major league in 1901, it had to overcome several critical issues that existed within and between the National and Western Leagues.

First, there was the 1899 sale of the St. Louis Browns and a related move of the NL Cleveland club players to St. Louis, which would free up Cleveland for the American League in 1900.[8] Second, an attempt to revive the American Association and the desire of both the Association and the Western League to place a team in Chicago in 1900 posed a threat to the NL.[9] And finally, the abandonment of the existing National Agreement between professional baseball leagues, including the arbitrary National and its junior league partner, the Western League, would ensure a costly baseball war for owners and clubs between the two leagues.

The Western League triumvirate central to resolving these critical issues were league president Ban Johnson, St. Paul, Minnesota club owner Charles Comiskey, and Columbus, Ohio club owner Tom Loftus. These three were not alone in working through the multitude of issues associated with founding and sustaining the AL. Other giants of the era who played pivotal roles included Henry and Matthew Killilea of Milwaukee and John Bruce of St. Louis, who provided the AL executive leadership with legal advice critical to the progression of the league. Their opinions weighed heavily in decisions made regarding the sale of the NL St. Louis club in 1899 and the sale of the AL Detroit club in 1900.[10]

In addition, Jim Manning of Kansas City (1894–1900) and Washington (1901) and Charles Somers, who owned the Cleveland AL club, were also critical to the success of the AL. Somers would be the AL's financier and have investments in several ballclubs in the league besides his Cleveland Indians.[11]

Loftus, Johnson, and Comiskey started charting the course that resulted in the AL when they took full control of the Western League executive leadership in the fall of 1896, with Loftus and Comiskey elected to the league's Board of Directors.[12] A week after being elected to the board, the three met in the Hotel Julien in Dubuque, Iowa, to discuss their plans to develop a reputable league to rival the NL.[13] They wanted a league that played clean ball for the love of the game, a league in which a mother and her children could attend a game without offense, a reputation the NL lacked.

Loftus and Comiskey had history in the legendary baseball town of Dubuque. Both men had played professional ball there in the late 1870s and early 1880s, before going on to play for Chris Von Der Ahe and the St. Louis Browns of the American Association.[14] Both men married Dubuque women,[15] and both lived and had children in Dubuque.[16] Loftus lived there his entire adult life, while Comiskey would frequently visit Dubuque family and friends after moving back home to Chicago in 1891.[17]

When Comiskey left the Browns in 1890 to play for the Chicago Pirates of the newly formed Players League, Loftus went from managing the 1889 Cleveland Spiders of the NL to managing the 1890 Cincinnati Reds. During Loftus's time in Cincinnati, he got to know Johnson, the *Cincinnati Commercial Gazette*'s sports editor, quite well. Johnson admired the older business-minded Loftus and would accompany Loftus and his Reds on road trips, referring to him respectfully in the *Gazette* as "Sir Thomas" or warmly as "Tommie" Loftus.[18]

After the 1891 season, Cincinnati's new owner John T. Brush replaced Loftus as the Reds manager with Comiskey. It was while managing the Reds that both Loftus and Comiskey got to know Johnson. It was at Comiskey's urging, and with Brush's reluctant support, that a reconstituted Western League hired Johnson as their league president in 1894. Comiskey would enter the Western League in 1895 as owner of the St. Paul club, and Loftus would do likewise in 1896 as the Columbus club's owner. Johnson would come to personally know and respect Loftus and Comiskey—both men Johnson's senior and early mentor—for their sage advice.

The problems facing professional baseball as it neared the 20th century were complex and not always public. With back-room deals and different factions vying for power and monopolistic control of major league baseball, the stakes for the magnates who owned the clubs and controlled the leagues had never been higher.

In December 1898, the NL let Johnson and the Western League in on their plans for 1899, which included Frank and Stanley Robison of the Cleveland NL club buying out Chris Von Der Ahe of the St. Louis

NL club and moving their Cleveland players to St. Louis, essentially abandoning Cleveland and freeing it for Loftus's Columbus club to move in.[19] Loftus had worked for the Robisons as manager of Cleveland in 1888 and 1889, when the brothers moved their club from the American Association into the NL. The brothers, however, did not wish to vacate Cleveland to the Western League free and clear...emphasis on free![20] The Robisons had built a ballpark in Cleveland and felt they were treated poorly by the fans' low attendance the last few years, making Cleveland a poor financial performer. The Robisons, therefore, wanted Loftus and the Western League to compensate them for the Cleveland club, even though the Cleveland players would be moved to St. Louis if the Robison brothers purchased Von Der Ahe's club at public auction.

Von Der Ahe had gotten into financial trouble over the prior four years and his Browns suffered for it. His refusal to sell his St. Louis interests to the Robisons to resolve his personal financial problems, while strengthening the league and the Browns' financial position, delayed the NL's and the Robisons' plan. Von Der Ahe chose to fight off his financial creditors in court in an effort to save his ball club, which ultimately led to Judge Spencer issuing a court-ordered public sale of the Browns.[21] Because it was not a private sale, it opened the door to outside interests with the result being the NL owners could not dictate who ultimately bid on or bought the club.

In late February 1899, John T. Brush, powerful owner of the Cincinnati Reds, released a statement pronouncing on behalf of the NL magnates that no undesirable person or persons could be forced upon the league through the mere purchase of the St. Louis Browns organization at the sheriff's auction on March 14, 1899. Brush's public statement was directed at Loftus, his former employee, who had shocked the baseball world earlier by announcing his intention to bid at the public auction.[22]

Loftus, Johnson, and Comiskey had been meeting on a frequent basis in January, February, and March leading up to the sale of the Browns, trying to figure out how to leverage the opportunity the forced public sale of the St. Louis club presented them.

On February 3, 1899, the *Dubuque Daily Times* proclaimed, "President Ban Johnson is Here for Conference with Tom Loftus." The article stated, "Men in a position to know the ins and outs of base ball [sic] politics declare that Johnson, Loftus, Manning, Comiskey and other Western league magnates will meet in Dubuque today and indulge in the luxury of a secret conference."[23] The primary topics of discussion were the sale of the Browns and the completion of the Western League circuit for 1899. The public announcement coming out of this meeting of magnates was that "President Johnson and Manager Loftus will not announce the eighth city of the Western League until the National League has placed its teams."[24]

On Thursday, February 16, Johnson and Comiskey met in Chicago with president Jim Hart of the Chicago NL team. That Saturday, the two men boarded a westbound train for Dubuque to meet in conference with Loftus for another week of Western League strategic planning. The primary topics were the sale of the St. Louis Browns and the league's desire to move Loftus's Columbus club into Cleveland and Comiskey's club into Chicago, part of the Western League's effort to become a rival league by having teams in major league cities.[25] The magnates also needed to decide how they wished to address the group of baseball men, many of them personal friends, who wished to revive the American Association.

While the Western League executives held their second February conference in Dubuque, John T. Brush released his statement on behalf of the NL in response to Loftus's announced intentions to bid on St. Louis.

The Western League's response was to publicly clarify the legal reasons why the NL could not prevent the purchaser of the St. Louis club from entering the league. This response was drawn up by the elder Killilea brother of the Milwaukee Western League club, who was a brilliant legal mind and practicing lawyer:

> The National League must recognize the purchase of the St. Louis franchise, as it is a corporation, and a corporation is simply an artificial being created by the supreme authority of the State, is invisible, intangible and endowed with perpetual existence. The corporate rights of the St. Louis Club being sold at a public sale make the obligation binding on the National League to accept the purchaser, who while unable to secure by purchase the players held by the St. Louis Club, can acquire the reserve to the players now held by the corporation of which Chris Von Der Ahe was President.[26]

Johnson, Comiskey, and the Killilea brothers were not helping Loftus so he could become an NL magnate, although on the surface they all denied there was any ulterior motive in Loftus bidding on the Browns. Loftus, Johnson, and Comiskey knew they would need to start moving some of their smaller ball clubs into major league cities. Going into the 1899 season, the

Western League had clubs in Milwaukee, Detroit, Kansas City, Minneapolis, Buffalo, Indianapolis, St. Paul, and Columbus. Only Buffalo was in the top 10 in U.S. population.[27] The three most desirable cities for the Western League to migrate into first were Cleveland, St. Louis, and Chicago.

St. Louis, the fourth largest city in the U.S., was desirable for a variety of reasons.[28] First, St. Louis was a great baseball city that could financially support a well-run major league team. Second, Loftus was born in St. Louis and started his major league career playing for the Brown Stockings of the NL in 1877, and again for the Browns of the American Association in 1883.[29] Third, Comiskey had been player-manager of those same Browns for most of their existence, and had won four league pennants and a World Series against Cap Anson's Chicago White Stockings.[30] And finally, St. Louis presented a potential pathway into Cleveland, free and clear.

If Loftus lost St. Louis to the Robison brothers, the Western League could still move Columbus into Cleveland once the latter was vacated by the Robisons.[31] During numerous private conferences in Dubuque among Loftus, Johnson, and Comiskey, the three league field marshals carefully laid out their plans to move Loftus's Columbus team to Cleveland and Comiskey's St. Paul team to Chicago. Chicago would present a bigger problem, so they first decided to focus on Loftus, Cleveland, and the sale of the St. Louis Browns.

The Robison brothers did not want to just give up Cleveland, and yet they planned on securing St. Louis and transferring their Cleveland players there. So it became the strategy of the Western League magnates to have Loftus make it known that he was going to St. Louis to bid on the Browns, having the effect of driving up the cost for the Robison brothers. Loftus ultimately worked out a deal with the Robisons, if it had not been the plan all along (as some had suggested), that he would not bid on St. Louis if the Robisons would clear the way for Loftus and the Western League to move a combined Columbus-Grand Rapids club into Cleveland.[32]

Frank Robison, with assistance from John T. Brush, ended up purchasing the St. Louis Browns organization through a local partner, Edward C. Becker. Loftus and Robison worked out a deal to allow Loftus to move his team to Cleveland after the 1899 season.[33]

As the dust settled from the St. Louis sale, the respective leagues prepared for their 1899 championship seasons. Because of the short time between the sale of the St. Louis team and the start of the season, the NL did not vacate Cleveland until after their record-setting 20–134 season. Loftus's club then moved to Cleveland for the 1900 season.

In the summer of 1899, word came out of Chicago and Dubuque that the Western League was planning a new rival league. The announcement made such a stir in the baseball world that Johnson, Loftus, Comiskey, and the other league magnates immediately started walking back the announcement.

The storm arose when newspapers ran a story from a statement released by Johnson on July 15 from the league's Chicago office. The *Indianapolis News* headline read, "Rival Baseball League—President Ban Johnson Makes the First Authoritative Announcement." The statement said, in part, "There will be another baseball organisation [sic] next year, a rival of the National League, and the Western League will be affiliated with It. In fact, it will practically be a Western League merged into a national organization. The conditions of baseball are such at present that a rival organisation is bound to spring up, and for business reasons the Western League must go in with It."[34]

Johnson went on to suggest the new league would include St. Louis, Chicago, Milwaukee, and Detroit in the West, and New York, Boston, Pittsburgh, and Philadelphia in the East. At the time, the Western League only had clubs in Milwaukee and Detroit. Clearly the league needed to move into more top-10 cities in the United States if they wished to declare themselves a major league.

The article went on to say that Loftus, Comiskey, Jim Manning of Kansas City, and Matt Killilea of Milwaukee would be the leading magnates identified with the new league, with Johnson as the probable league president. It was also stated for the first time, but not for the last, that Loftus would move his Columbus club into the South Side of Chicago, while Comiskey would take his St. Paul team down the Mississippi River in a return home of sorts to St. Louis. Killilea would keep his team in Milwaukee and Jim Manning would take his Kansas City team to Boston.[35]

The following day a sports page story showed up in the *Cincinnati Commercial Tribune* and newspapers across the nation that read, "Dubuque, IA, July 15 – It is stated here that Ban Johnson, Jimmy Manning, Charles Comiskey and Tom Loftus are planning for a new baseball league for next season. In distribution it is said Loftus is to be given Chicago, and he will have the park on the South Side. In an interview tonight Loftus admitted there was something in the scheme, and arraigns the National League, pronouncing its policy narrow and arbitrary."[36]

The *Cincinnati Commercial Tribune* and *Chicago Daily Tribune* ran another syndicated article with more detail that came from the same Loftus interview referenced in the story with the Dubuque dateline. Here again, it was suggested that Loftus "Will Head (an) Opposition Baseball League Team In Chicago." It was again suggested Comiskey would be back in St. Louis, where the man and the city had great memories and great chemistry with one another. Consideration had long been given to finding a place in the league for team ownership for Connie Mack, who had been a loyal league man and manager of Killilea's Milwaukee Brewers. Mack would have to wait until the 1901 season before he would get his own team, the Philadelphia Athletics.[37]

The *Dubuque Daily Times* printed a different story that was also being published around the nation at the same time: "Chicago, July 15 – Ban R. Johnson, president of the Western League, made the following announcement in part today: 'The Western league as a body has no idea of fostering a proposition to organize a rival to the National league and institute a fight against the present major organization. It would be suicidal for the western league to attempt to foster an organization on the lines of the old brotherhood for the simple reason it could not possibly hope for success.'" The article went on to state that Cap Anson was certain a new league would be created, and Johnson and Anson agreed a new league could be successful against the NL.[38]

The same day that Johnson released his initial statement, Matt Killilea suggested Johnson was misquoted. "I honestly believe that Mr. Johnson was either misquoted or that he did not talk for publication," Killilea told a Milwaukee reporter. Killilea, like many others, believed a new league would result in a baseball war of financial attrition that would ultimately be won by the NL due to superior financing. Johnson was likely speaking off the record and not for publication, for everything he stated would come to pass. It could also have been his way of testing the temperature of the NL to gauge how big a fight they would have on their hands as they proceeded with their plans laid out in January and February.[39]

Within two days of Johnson's initial statement and the conflicting newspaper reports published on July 16–17 around the country, Johnson, Loftus, Comiskey, and all the Western League magnates were proactively adamant in their denials a new league was being planned. Johnson clarified his statement, saying that if a new league were to be formed, alluding to the rumors of a revival of the American Association by Al Spink and friends, some of the individual club owners in his league may be inclined to join that new association, but the Western League was not interested in being part of any new organization. The *Indianapolis News* concluded, "It is thought from the qualifying statements which Johnson has made since Saturday that someone has advised him to go slow."[40] Johnson and the league pulled back on their public talk of forming a new league for a couple of months.

The NL magnates met in Chicago for an unscheduled meeting on July 27–28 to undoubtedly discuss their strategy to address the formation of a potential rival league. John T. Brush, Jim Hart, and Frank Robison had been meeting in Indianapolis to discuss the matter prior to the league meeting in Chicago. Comiskey and Johnson were in conference in Chicago on July 26–27 also discussing the matter. Comiskey spent part of the day on July 27 in conference with Brush.[41]

The *Cincinnati Commercial Tribune* zeroed in on what appears to be nearer the truth than any of the other stories regarding a new league published that July, apart from Johnson's original statement that started the storm. The *Tribune*'s July 28 story on the NL meeting in Chicago summed up the reality of the situation in a single paragraph:

The magnates declare they are not meeting to discuss the league situation, yet from all over the country come stories of the forming of a rival league. It is said the National League magnates have decided to form the rival league themselves, splitting the twelve-club circuit and, with the assistance of Western League magnates, forming two eight-club leagues. Comiskey and Loftus, of the Western League, are close to the National League promoters. Both are anxious to get into a bigger circuit, and Comiskey has been with the magnates all week.[42]

A month later, Ban Johnson wrote Spink that he still needed to speak with Loftus and that he had recently spoken with Ted Sullivan, another promoter for a new league. Spink was still trying to get the Western League to join his group of Association revivalists, which included Sullivan, Von Der Ahe, John McGraw, and Cap Anson. Spink was trying to persuade Johnson and the Western League to attend the American Association's first official meeting in hopes of them joining the Association in taking on the NL.[43]

On September 17, 1899, the American Association had its first meeting as a new organization in Chicago to elect officers. The Western League magnates were invited to attend. Loftus and Johnson had been elected to represent their league at the meeting.[44]

It just so happened that during these two league meetings in Chicago, Frank Robison was in town and held a long meeting with Loftus.[45] On September 16, the day before the Association's official organizing meeting, the Western League announced its circuit for 1900: Minneapolis, Milwaukee, Kansas City, Indianapolis, Detroit, and Buffalo, all teams that were in the 1899 circuit, along with relocated teams in Chicago and Cleveland. It was again suggested Loftus was to move into Chicago and this time Comiskey would take Cleveland, and not St. Louis.[46]

Loftus was the only representative of the Western League to attend the September 17 meeting of the American Association. He sat quietly and listened, and before the end of the first day's meeting, he informed the Association the Western League would not be joining their new organization and left it at that. This effectively killed the chances of a revived American Association for the 1900 season.[47]

The suggestion the *Cincinnati Commercial Tribune* made on July 28 that the NL would address the rise of the rival Association by working with the Western League to create a new rival league was true. In 1900 both the American League and the National League would have eight teams, the National League being down from 12 the year before. And key was Hart of the Chicago National League permitting a team in Chicago and Robison of the Cleveland–St. Louis clubs officially abandoning Cleveland as NL territory, opening those major league cities to the soon-to-be renamed American League.

The Western League formally changed its name at an October 11, 1899, meeting in Chicago.[48] The AL would still be a minor league in 1900, but it was accomplishing a lot of what it set out to do when they started planning their move in January and February of 1899. Loftus was able to skillfully deal with Robison and the St. Louis Browns sale, ultimately forcing the NL's hand and freeing up Cleveland for the AL in 1900. Loftus was also instrumental in getting Comiskey and the AL into Chicago.

Hart had been courting Loftus for the prior two years to become manager of the Orphans, since Anson's departure after the 1897 season.[49] The two men had known each other just a little over a decade, going back to 1888 and the forming of the reconstituted Western Association, when Loftus managed the St. Louis Whites and Hart the Milwaukee Brewers. The following year the two men managed against each other in the NL, Loftus with Cleveland and Hart with Boston.[50] Hart said, "Loftus I consider the best manager in the league, barring none." Chicago sportswriters agreed, saying Loftus was "the shrewdest man in the game."[51] Hart saw his opportunity to finally sign Loftus in November 1899.

Hart feared the American Association moving into Chicago more than he did the Western League. The Western League was still governed by the baseball laws established in the National Agreement. The American Association was not. And Anson was still wildly popular in Chicago and was said to be backed by millionaires who already had land for a new ballpark.[52]

Both the Western League and American Association had announced their intention to move into Chicago for the 1900 season. Hart preferred Comiskey and the Western League in his territory competing against his Orphans for fan and fare over Anson and the Association. Hart and Comiskey were friends and Comiskey would presumably be less ruthless toward him than Anson, who did not see eye to eye with Hart. Comiskey told Hart, Brush, and the other NL magnates, "Let us start this American League of ours and we'll put the American association [sic] beneath the daisies before spring comes around."[53]

Hart agreed to allow Comiskey and the AL into Chicago if Loftus would manage the Orphans. Hart had wanted Loftus and preferred the Western League over the Association in Chicago, and Comiskey and Loftus relished competing against each other with different teams in the same city, as they had done in 1888 when they both managed teams for Von Der Ahe in St. Louis.

Hart met with Loftus, Comiskey, and Johnson at a Western League meeting in Chicago on November 18, 1899. Loftus told Hart he would manage his Orphans if he had full control of the team and players *and* his friend "Commy" be allowed to move his St. Paul team to Chicago. Hart told the triumvirate it was alright to place a ball club in Chicago and to go ahead and make the announcement, pre-empting the Association.[54]

The November 29, 1899, *Chicago Daily Tribune* announced to the baseball world, "Loftus Succeeds Burns." "Loftus has been one of the most successful baseball managers in the business since the game started. His success has been uniform wherever he had a club."[55]

The *Tribune* also made mention in the middle of the article, "Another interesting announcement was made when President Ban B. Johnson [sic] of the American league confirmed the report that Comiskey would manage a Chicago American league club, a rival of the National league organization."[56]

The AL and Comiskey finally had Chicago, Hart finally had Tom Loftus, and Loftus and Comiskey got to manage in arguably the best baseball city in the world. Now all the two leagues needed to do was play well together and sign a new national agreement without getting into a war.

By late winter of 1899–1900 things were coming together for the AL. Tom Loftus and Ban Johnson were able to get the Columbus team, which merged with the failing Grand Rapids team and moved into Cleveland for the 1900 season under new local ownership. Comiskey was able to move into Chicago as promised, despite Hart's efforts to renege on his word in early 1900.

In January 1900, some NL magnates were expressing their dislike for the idea of allowing the AL into major league cities, criticizing the Chicago deal. Feeling the pressure, Hart joined in, saying he never consented to allow the AL into Chicago. Comiskey fought back in early March. "If we were good enough to get permission to run here when the Anson crowd and the American Association threatened President Hart's territory," he said, "we are good enough now." Comiskey went on to say, "Certainly, we got it [Hart's permission]. Didn't he come to our meeting at the Great Northern and assure Johnson it was all right for us to place a club here and to go ahead and make the announcement? It would be absurd for us to invent any such a story."[57]

Loftus stepped in, bringing all parties together to mediate a resolution. The *Indianapolis News* reported, "A Meeting Held and a League War May be Averted. A telegram received this morning Indicated that an agreement had been reached between President Johnson and Charley Comiskey, of the American League, and James A. Hart, of the Chicago club of the National League, by which the American League can place a club in Chicago this season. … It is a fact that, through the friendly offices of Tom Loftus, the three men were brought together Tuesday, and were in conference for over two hours. The report is that both sides made concessions."[58]

Once the question of Chicago was finally put to rest on March 14, the AL had two of its four major hurdles cleared. Besides placing teams in Cleveland and Chicago, they were able to change their name and brand from the regionalized Western League to the nationwide American League.

The last two hurdles would have to be addressed after the first season as the AL in 1900 was over. First, they had to be declared a major league, which required some additional reorganization. That happened on January 28, 1901, with expansion occurring in 1901 and 1902, during the "baseball wars" that led to the final hurdles to peaceful coexistence, the combining of rules, agreement on schedules and the creation of a new national agreement. Loftus managed the Chicago NL club for the 1900 and 1901 seasons. It became immediately clear Hart was not going to give Loftus the control of the club as he had promised. It also became clear that Loftus was still connected to the AL when Loftus failed to extend his contract with Hart and bought into the ownership of the Washington Senators of the AL in the fall of 1901. Kansas City owner Jim Manning, a stalwart of the Western League, moved his club to Washington as part of the expansion into additional major league cities for the 1901 season. Manning, with Johnson's support, decided to sell his interest in the Washington club after its inaugural season to Loftus and Fred Postal of Detroit. Loftus was immediately announced as the new Washington manager for the 1902 season.[59]

In December 1902, the news out of the AL related to placing a team in New York City. And the man chosen by the league magnates to take on the job of managing the New York Highlanders was Tom Loftus. The AL was planning on moving the Baltimore Orioles club, which joined the League in 1901, to New York for the 1903 season.[60] The move would satisfy two needs. First, it brought a ready-made team, a familiar Eastern team, into the largest baseball market in the world. Second, it removed any potential negative effects on the Washington club of having a nearby franchise competing for fans and fare.

Loftus relished the chance to manage a club in New York City. His co-owner in the Washington Senators was not as thrilled. When Loftus insisted he was taking the New York job, Postal threatened to sell or move his club out of Washington if he lost Loftus as manager.[61]

Loftus had built a solid reputation as a player's coach and manager over his twenty-five-year professional baseball career. Although his managerial won-loss record in the Major Leagues is not impressive at 454–580,[62] Loftus's genius in the early days of building up the national game was in providing organizational structure and discipline on and off the field that led to financial success.[63] As a manager, Loftus was a team coach first, a field manager second, and—not uncommon in the day—the general manager of the club responsible for overall operations. Loftus was a successful businessman outside of baseball and his skill was in financially stabilizing clubs and selecting quality players who in turn bring fans into the ballpark, which provides financial capital to make the whole operation economically viable. Baseball, while a game, was a business at the major league level, and Loftus was recognized as a shrewd baseball businessman. And Loftus wanted New York.

Postal dug in. Loftus and Johnson desired to keep the peace and recognized it would not be hard to find a manager for New York. So, they gave in to Postal's demand and Loftus stayed in Washington for the 1903 season.[64] New York would go on to be managed over its first six seasons in the American League by one of Loftus's former players on the Chicago Orphans, Hall of Famer Clark Griffith.[65]

By the end of the AL's second MLB season in 1902, it became clear to both leagues that the baseball war needed to end so all could prosper, or most would fail financially. A peace agreement came at a joint American-National League conference in Cincinnati on January 10, 1903.[66]

The terms called for both leagues to agree to clauses related to player contractual issues, such as honoring the player reserve rule, and a prohibition on two clubs in the same city consolidating players. The agreement also called for the creation of a Rules Committee and a Schedule Committee to work out the particulars for peaceful coexistence. The clauses of the peace agreement and the resulting work of the Rules and Schedule Committees would be used to formulate a new national agreement, paving the way toward long-term peace within major league baseball.[67]

On January 30, 1903, President Ban Johnson appointed Loftus, Benjamin Shibe of Philadelphia, and John Bruce of St. Louis to the joint American-National League Rules and Schedule Committees. President Harry Pulliam of the National League appointed Hart, Barney Dreyfuss of Pittsburgh, and Charles Ebbets of Brooklyn to the Schedule Committee. Pulliam also appointed Hart, Julius Fleischmann of Cincinnati, and Ned Hanlon of Brooklyn to the Rules Committee. The meeting of the committees was the next step and direct result of the peace treaty negotiated by the two leagues in Cincinnati twenty days earlier.[68]

The day Johnson appointed Loftus to the Rules and Schedule Committees, Loftus was in conference with Charles Comiskey in Dubuque.[69] Loftus was still vying for the New York club. And there were rules up for debate as the leagues standardized the game with a uniform baseball code.

Baseball's rules had varied between leagues through the years since the establishment of the Knickerbocker Rules in 1845. Rules were different among the NL, the AL, and the different minor league organizations that wished to participate in a new national agreement in 1903. Rules up for consideration included a designated hitter rule, establishing a standard height for the pitcher's mound, requiring the first and third base foul lines to be level, determining whether to make foul balls strikes, and whether to ban baseball mitts with pockets or webbing used to scoop the ball "as one would scoop a butterfly."[70] Over time, the pitcher's mound continued to get higher, and no two fields had it at the same height. Some groundskeepers were also building up the foul lines along first and third base so bunts rolling foul would be pushed fair.

The joint Rules Committee did not adopt a designated hitter rule in 1903. It would be another 70 years before the AL would adopt the DH. Loftus was able to get a new section added to Rule No. 1 to address his two biggest issues going into the meeting.[71] Section 2 states: "The pitcher's box shall be no more than fifteen inches higher than the base lines and home plate. The base lines and home plate shall be perfectly level, and the slope from the pitcher's box toward the base lines and home plate shall be gradual."[72]

The Rules Committee voted unanimously to adopt the foul strike rule used by the NL. This instituted the rule throughout baseball that a foul ball is called a strike if it is your first or second strike. In the AL, you could foul off any number of pitches and not have a strike against you. The American League went into the Rules meeting against the foul strike rule, but Loftus acquiesced when it was agreed to amend the balk rule to include the following definition, "A balk shall constitute any delivery of the ball to the batsman by the pitcher while either foot of the pitcher is back of the pitcher's plate."[73] The joint Rules Committee was able to agree to a uniform code of baseball rules. The following day, the Schedule Committee met and developed a schedule that met Hart's one requirement, namely that all leagues must share the same opening day of the season.[74]

The only thing left to do after the Rules and Schedule Committees met was to finalize the draft of the new National Agreement of 1903 and have the NL, AL, and the National Association of Professional Baseball Leagues (NAPBL) Boards of Directors adopt and sign the new agreement. The two major leagues acted quickly. The NAPBL took the bulk of the 1903 season to agree to adopt the new agreement, finally signing it on September 11, 1903, in Cincinnati.[75]

Loftus had started 1903 as Johnson's pick to lead the new AL club in New York, but Loftus agreed to stay in Washington to stop Postal from selling or moving the club. Then Postal sold his 52% interest in the club on August 4, 1903, to the minor shareholders.

Vice President Charles Jacobsen became the new president of Washington, while Loftus retained his 25% interest in the club and position as manager.[76]

Both Postal and Loftus were tiring of the rapid changes occurring in baseball that continued to give team owners and managers less control over their assets and the league office more. Loftus tried to make a go of it with the new Washington executive leadership, but when the club was sold to locals Thomas Noyes and William J. Dwyer in March 1904, Loftus decided to sell his interest in the club and retire from major league baseball before the start of the season.[77]

Loftus would contemplate a return that fall. During one of Loftus and Comiskey's famous hunting-fishing trips into Northern Wisconsin with Johnson, sportswriter Jack Tanner, and others in October, it was stated that a place in the league in the 1905 season had been identified for Loftus, and all he needed to do was decide if he wished to come out of retirement.[78]

However, he decided to stay engaged only in local baseball, as he re-engaged in his Dubuque businesses. In 1908, Loftus was elected the president of the Illinois–Indiana–Iowa (Three-I) League in a successful effort to prevent that minor league from going under.[79]

In March 1910, Comiskey and his Chicago White Sox were at spring training in California preparing for the 1910 season when Comiskey received word from Loftus's doctor in Dubuque that Loftus, who had been battling throat cancer, was on death's door. Comiskey immediately left his team for Dubuque and his best friend's bedside. Comiskey and his wife spent two days with Loftus and his wife before Comiskey had to return to California to rejoin his White Sox. Comiskey would return to Dubuque to visit Loftus again in early April, as did Ted Sullivan, the man who first brought Loftus and Comiskey together in Dubuque in 1879. Former *Chicago Inter Ocean* sports editor Lou Housemann also came to Dubuque to see Loftus one last time.[80]

On April 17, headlines around the nation announced the passing of "one of the great builders-up of our National Game." The *Chicago Daily Tribune* announced to a mournful baseball world, "Tom Loftus Dies in Dubuque." The "Great Friend of Comiskey" was 54 years old.[81]

Funeral services for Loftus were held in Dubuque on April 19, 1910, at St. Raphael's Cathedral. Honorary pallbearers included Comiskey, Johnson, Sullivan, James "Tip" O'Neil, and Chicago baseball writer Hugh E. Keough. Future United States Senator and local newspaper editor Richard Louis Murphy served as one of three ushers at the Cathedral. The Reverend

M. H. Carey officiated the funeral and the graveside absolution. Thomas Joseph Loftus was laid to rest in Mt. Olivet Catholic Cemetery in Key West, Iowa.[82]

Loftus left behind a legacy of deep personal friendships and mutual respect for the men who built major league baseball in its first 27 years. Highlighting his role in the baseball wars between 1899 and 1903 and the rise of the American League sheds long overdue light on the American League's forgotten founding father. ∎

Additional Sources

Baseball-Reference.com. Accessed November 2019. https://www.baseball-reference.com.

"Manager Hart – Something about the Man who runs the Boston Team," *Boston Daily Globe*, June 7, 1889, 11. https://newspaperarchive.com/boston-daily-globe-jun-07-1889-p-11.

Chicago Daily Tribune. 1903. "Johnson Names Dual Committee." January 30: 7.

2019. Clark Griffith. Accessed December 26, 2019. https://www.baseball-reference.com/players/g/griffcl01.shtml.

Dubuque Daily Times. 1900. "SPORTING CIRCLES – Tom Loftus' Arrival in Chicago is Eagerly Awaited." February 11: 2. https://newspaperarchive.com/dubuque-daily-times-feb-11-1900-p-2.

Dubuque Telegraph-Herald. 1910. "Loftus Crosses Great Divide." April 17: 6. https://newspaperarchive.com/dubuque-telegraph-herald-apr-17-1910-p-6.

Dubuque Telegraph-Herald. 1903. "Will Not Head League." November 19: 3. https://newspaperarchive.com/dubuque-telegraph-herald-nov-19-1903-p-3.

Indianapolis News. 1900. "President Killelea Gives Legal Advice on the Detroit Case." January 13: 24. https://newspaperarchive.com/indianapolis-news-jan-13-1900-p-24.

2019. SABR. Accessed November 2019. sabr.org.

St. Louis Sporting News. 1918. "A Birthday for the American League." January 10: 5. https://newspaperarchive.com/st-louis-sporting-news-jan-10-1918-p-5.

St. Louis Sporting News. 1886. "The New Association." August 30: 1. https://newspaperarchive.com/st-louis-sporting-news-aug-30-1886-p-1.

2019. Tom Loftus. November 2. https://www.baseball-reference.com/bullpen/Tom_Loftus.

2020. Tom Loftus. Accessed March 15, 2020. https://www.baseball-reference.com/register/player.fcgi?id=loftus002tom.

Notes

1. Tom Loftus player page, Baseball-Reference.com. Accessed March 15, 2020. https://www.baseball-reference.com/register/player.fcgi?id=loftus002tom.

2. SABR Bioproject, SABR.org. Accessed November 2019; Baseball-Reference.com, November. Accessed November 2019.

3. Tom Loftus player page, Baseball-Reference.com. Accessed March 15, 2020. https://www.baseball-reference.com/register/player.fcgi?id=loftus002tom.

4. "BASE BALL: Western League Successfully Organized at Indianapolis," *Cincinnati Commercial Gazette*, February 13, 1885: 1. https://newspaper-archive.com/cincinnati-commercial-gazette-feb-13-1885-p-1/.

5. Tom Loftus player page, Baseball-Reference.com. Accessed March 15, 2020. https://www.baseball-reference.com/register/player.fcgi?id=loftus002tom.

6. Bill Lamb, "Thrice Stillborn: Turn-of-the-Century Attempts to Resurrect the Once-Major League American Association," *Base Ball 11 – New Research on the Early Game*, edited by Don Jensen, 140-166.

7. Alfred H. Spink, *The National Game*, (St. Louis, MO: National Game Publishing Co., 1910).

8. "VON DER AHE LOST – Franchise of St. Louis Club No Longer His," *Washington Post*, January 24, 1889: 8.
9. John B, Foster, "25 Years of Ban Johnson." *Oakland Tribune*, January 17, 1928: 36. https://newspaperarchive.com/oakland-tribune-jan-17-1928-p-36/.
10. "IS TOM LOFTUS BLUFFING? The Announcement That He will Bid for Browns a Bombshell," *Cincinnati Commercial Tribune*, February 21, 1899: 3. https://newspaperarchive.com/cincinnati-commercial-tribune-feb-21-1899-p-3/.
11. "Cleveland Bought," *Philadelphia Inquirer*, March 4, 1900: 14. https://newspaperarchive.com/philadelphia-inquirer-mar-04-1900-p-14/.
12. "The Base Ball Meetings," *Indianapolis News*, November 13, 1896: 1.
13. "NOTED BALL MEN," *Dubuque Daily Times*, November 25, 1896: 5. https://newspaperarchive.com/daily-times-nov-25-1896-p-5/.
14. "TOM LOFTUS DIES IN DUBUQUE – Great Friend of Comiskey," *Chicago Daily Tribune*, April 17, 1910: C1.
15. "United in Marriage," *Dubuque Daily Times*, September 1882: F1; "Mrs. Tom Loftus Claimed by Death," *Dubuque Telegraph-Herald and Times-Journal*, June 11, 1930: 18. https://newspaperarchive.com/dubuque-telegraph-herald-and-times-journal-jun-11-1930-p-18/.
16. J. Louis Comiskey. Accessed December 29, 2019. https://www.baseball-reference.com/bullpen/J._Louis_Comiskey; "Mrs. Tom Loftus Claimed by Death."
17. "What Makes a City Known," *Dubuque Daily Herald*, June 26, 1887: 1. https://newspaperarchive.com/dubuque-daily-herald-jun-26-1887-p-1/; "Our Base Ball Boodlers," *Dubuque Daily Times*, December 3, 1890: 5. https://newspaperarchive.com/dubuque-times-dec-03-1890-p-5/.
18. "Base Ball," *Cincinnati Commercial Gazette*, February 22, 1891: 7. https://newspaperarchive.com/cincinnati-commercial-gazette-feb-22-1891-p-7/; "Base Ball Gossip," *Cincinnati Commercial Gazette*, April 20, 1891: 6. https://newspaperarchive.com/cincinnati-commercial-gazette-apr-20-1891-p-6/.
19. "Baseball Gossip," *Cincinnati Commercial Tribune*, January 20, 199: 3. https://newspaperarchive.com/cincinnati-commercial-tribune-jan-20-1899-p-3/.
20. "CLEVELAND OUT OF LEAGUE," *Washington Post*, January 24, 1899: 8.
21. "VON DER AHE LOST – Franchise of St. Louis Club No Longer His," *Washington Post*, January 24, 1899: 8.
22. "IS TOM LOFTUS BLUFFING?"
23. "TALK BASE BALL – President Ban Johnson is here for Conference with Tom Loftus," *Dubuque Daily Times*, February 3, 1899: 5. https://newspaperarchive.com/dubuque-daily-times-feb-03-1899-p-5/.
24. "Waiting on National League," *Cincinnati Commercial Tribune*, February 4, 1899: 3. https://newspaperarchive.com/cincinnati-commercial-tribune-feb-04-1899-p-3/.
25. "THE EIGHTH CITY – Comiskey, Ban Johnson and Loftus have Conference about it," *Dubuque Daily Times*, February 17, 1899: 5. https://newspaperarchive.com/dubuque-daily-times-feb-17-1899-p-5/.
26. "IS TOM LOFTUS BLUFFING?"
27. Biggest US Cities by Population – Year 1900. Accessed December 22, 2019. https://www.biggestuscities.com/1900.
28. Biggest US Cities By Population.
29. Tom Loftus, November 2. https://www.baseball-reference.com/bullpen/Tom_Loftus.
30. Baseball-Reference.com.
31. "CLEVELAND OUT OF LEAGUE," *Washington Post*, January 24, 1899: 8.
32. "Browns Sold to Becker," *Chicago Daily Tribune*, March 18, 1899: 6.
33. "Browns Sold to Becker."
34. "RIVAL BASEBALL LEAGUE – President Ban Johnson Makes the First Authoritative Announcement," *Indianapolis News*, July 15, 1899: 16. https://newspaperarchive.com/indianapolis-news-jul-15-1899-p-16/.
35. "RIVAL BASEBALL LEAGUE."
36. "ANOTHER WAR STORY. Tom Loftus Quoted as Saying That There is Something in the Scheme," *Cincinnati Commercial Tribune*, July 16, 1899: 3. https://newspaperarchive.com/cincinnati-commercial-tribune-jul-16-1899-p-3/.
37. "TOM LOFTUS. Will Be at the Head of the New Baseball League," *Cincinnati Commercial Tribune*, July 16, 1899: 3. https://newspaperarchive.com/cincinnati-commercial-tribune-jul-16-1899-p-3/; "LOFTUS TO COME HERE – Will Head Opposition Baseball League Team in Chicago," *Chicago Daily Tribune*, July 16, 1899: 6.
38. "Talk of New Ball League," *Dubuque Daily Times*, July 16, 1899: 6. https://newspaperarchive.com/daily-times-jul-16-1899-p-6/.
39. "JOHNSON WAS MISQUOTED. President Killilea Says That a New League Is Out of the Question," *Cincinnati Commercial Tribune*, July 16, 1899: 3. https://newspaperarchive.com/cincinnati-commercial-tribune-jul-16-1899-p-3/.
40. "THE NEW BALL LEAGUE. President Johnson's Story Vigorously Denied on All Sides," *Indianapolis News*, July 17, 1899: 6. https://newspaperarchive.com/indianapolis-news-jul-17-1899-p-6/.
41. "VAUGH GOES TO ST. PAUL – Comiskey Announces the Deal – Brush Leaves Indianapolis Suddenly," *Cincinnati Commercial Tribune*, July 18, 1899: 3. https://newspaperarchive.com/cincinnati-commercial-tribune-jul-18-1899-p-3/; "MAGNATES AT CHICAGO," *Cincinnati Commercial Tribune*, July 28, 1899: 3. https://newspaperarchive.com/cincinnati-commercial-tribune-jul-28-1899-p-3/.
42. "MAGNATES AT CHICAGO."
43. Spink, *The National Game*.
44. "NEW LEAGUE LEADERS MEET TODAY – Johnson and Loftus to Represent Interests of the Western," *Chicago Daily Tribune*, September 17, 1899: 6.
45. "NEW LEAGUE LEADERS MEET TODAY."
46. "MAY LET THE WESTERN LEAGUE IN – Chicago Likely to Grant the Minor Body a Desired Concession," *Chicago Daily Tribune*, September 18, 1899: 6.
47. "NEW LEAGUE ORGANIZES – Johnson Does Not Attend," *Chicago Daily Tribune*, September 18, 1899: 10.
48. "AMERICAN BASEBALL LEAGUE," October 12, 1899: 6.
49. "Chicago After Loftus," *Dubuque Daily Herald*, November 18, 1899: 8.
50. Baseball-Reference.com. Accessed November 2019.
51. "Mr. Hart is Huffed," *Dubuque Daily Times*, January 19, 1900: 8.
52. "New Base Ball League," *Dubuque Sunday Herald*, November 19, 1899: 3.
53. John B. Foster, "25 Years of Ban Johnson," *Oakland Tribune*, January 17, 1928: 36. https://newspaperarchive.com/oakland-tribune-jan-17-1928-p-36.
54. "Chicago After Loftus;" "League Magnates to Meet," *Dubuque Sunday Herald*, November 19, 1899: 3.
55. "Loftus Succeeds Burns," *Chicago Daily Tribune*, November 29, 1899: 6.
56. "Loftus Succeeds Burns."
57. "Charles Comiskey was in a defiant mood," *Cincinnati Commercial Tribune*, March 4, 1900: 7. https://newspaperarchive.com/cincinnati-commercial-tribune-mar-04-1900-p-7/.
58. "Report of an Agreement," *Indianapolis News*, March 15, 1900: 2. https://newspaperarchive.com/indianapolis-news-mar-15-1900-p-2/.
59. "SAY LOFTUS WILL SUCCEED – Dubuque Man to Become Managing Owner of Washington Team," *Dubuque Daily Times*, October 30, 1901: 1. https://newspaperarchive.com/daily-times-oct-30-1901-p-1/.
60. "QUICK BASEBALL MEETING – Americans Give the Baltimore Franchise to New York," *Baltimore Sun*, December 23, 1902: 6. https://newspaperarchive.com/baltimore-sun-dec-23-1902-p-6/.
61. Anaconda Standard. 1903. "TO TRANSFER FRANCHISE – The Invasion of New York." January 2: 12. https://newspaperarchive.com/anaconda-standard-jan-02-1903-p-12/.
62. https://www.baseball-reference.com/bullpen/Tom_Loftus.
63. Ed J.Grillo, "New York Must Have Strong Team," *Cincinnati Commercial Tribune*, October 21, 1902: 14. https://newspaperarchive.com/cincinnati-commercial-tribune-oct-21-1900-p-14/; "HITCH IN PEACH TREATY – Loftus Causes Some Friction," *Chicago Daily Tribune*, December 23, 1902: 6.

64. "SELBACH A SENATOR — Tom Loftus to be at Helm," *Washington Post*, December 29, 1902: 8.

65. Clark Griffith player page, Baseball-Reference.com. Accessed December 26, 2019. https://www.baseball-reference.com/players/g/griffcl01.shtml.

66. "Base Ball Peace." *Dubuque Daily Times*, January 11, 1903: 9. https://newspaperarchive.com/daily-times-jan-10-1903-p-9/.

67. "Base Ball Peace."

68. "Baseball Committees Named," *The New York Times*, February 3: 6. https://newspaperarchive.com/new-york-times-feb-03-1903-p-6/.

69. "Chas. Comiskey in the City," *Dubuque Daily Times-Journal*, January 31, 1903: 6. https://newspaperarchive.com/daily-times-jan-31-1903-p-6/.

70. Tim Murnane, "Murnane's Baseball," *Boston Sunday Globe*, February 1, 1903: 40. https://newspaperarchive.com/boston-sunday-globe-feb-01-1903-p-40/.

71. "NEW BASEBALL RULES — Loftus Wants Pitcher's Box Lowerer. Why Bunts Roll Fair," *Baltimore Sun*, February 23, 1903: 9. https://newspaperarchive.com/baltimore-sun-feb-23-1903-p-9/.

72. "Peace Reigned at Committee Meet," *Cincinnati Commercial Tribune*, February 24, 1903: 7. https://newspaperarchive.com/cincinnati-commercial-tribune-feb-24-1903-p-7/.

73. "The Foul Strike Rule," *Atchison Daily Globe*, June 23, 1903: 6. https://newspaperarchive.com/atchison-daily-globe-jun-23-1903-p-6/; "Peace Reigned at Committee Meet," *Cincinnati Commercial Tribune*, February 24, 1903: 7. https://newspaperarchive.com/cincinnati-commercial-tribune-feb-24-1903-p-7/.

74. "Wants All Leagues to Open on Same Day," *Cincinnati Commercial Tribune*, January 30, 1903: 10. https://newspaperarchive.com/cincinnati-commercial-tribune-jan-30-1903-p-10/.

75. "All Sign It," *Boston Daily Globe*, September 12, 1903: 2. https://newspaperarchive.com/boston-daily-globe-sep-12-1903-p-2/.

76. "Pres Postal Sells Out," *Boston Daily Globe*, August 4, 1903: 16. https://newspaperarchive.com/boston-daily-globe-aug-04-1903-p-16/.

77. "Loftus is Coming Home," *Dubuque Daily Times*, March 25, 1904: 5. https://newspaperarchive.com/daily-times-mar-25-1904-p-5/.

78. "Tom Loftus Home from Hunting Trip," *Dubuque Telegraph-Herald*, October 27, 1904: 9. https://newspaperarchive.com/dubuque-telegraph-herald-oct-27-1904-p-9/.

79. "Call Loftus 'The Man of the Hour,'" *Dubuque Telegraph-Herald*, March 27, 1908: 9. https://newspaperarchive.com/dubuque-telegraph-herald-and-times-journal-mar-27-1908-p-9/.

80. "COMISKEY IS HERE — Tom Loftus' Lifelong Friend Arrived Sunday Morning," *Dubuque Daily Times-Journal*, April 19, 1910: 3. https://newspaperarchive.com/dubuque-times-journal-apr-19-1910-p-3/.

81. "TOM LOFTUS DIES IN DUBUQUE — Great Friend of Comiskey," *Chicago Daily Tribune*, April 17, 1910: C1.

82. "IN ETERNAL SLEEP — Thos. J. Loftus Laid to Rest in Mt. Olivet," *Dubuque Daily Times-Journal*, April 20, 1910: 2. https://newspaperarchive.com/dubuque-daily-times-apr-20-1910-p-2/.

The 1967 Dixie Series

Jeb Stewart

From 1920 to 1958, baseball fans across the Deep South and Southwest looked forward to the annual Dixie Series, a best-of-seven postseason matchup between the playoff champions of the Southern Association and the Texas League. In 1967, after an 8-year hiatus, owners in the Double-A Texas League and the newly created Southern League resurrected the Series, but it would prove to be one last hurrah.

The games between the Birmingham Athletics and the Albuquerque Dodgers proved exciting and included three one-run, extra-inning contests. Another was won on a grand slam in the ninth. With the final out in Game Six recorded on September 11, 1967, at Rickwood Field, the A's were crowned champions of the last Dixie Series ever played.

THE END OF THE ORIGINAL DIXIE SERIES: TWO LEAGUES HEADING IN OPPOSITE DIRECTIONS

To understand the reasons for reviving the Dixie Series in 1967, and why it failed to catch on as an annual event, it is instructive to review its demise from 1948 to 1958. In 1948, the Birmingham Barons drew a whopping 28,319 fans to its only two home games in the Dixie Series: 17,071 in the first game and 11,248 in the second. The latter crowd was smaller because of bad weather.[1] Big crowds meant healthy profits for both owners and players, as *The Sporting News* reported:

> The [1948] Dixie Series, which was won by Birmingham, four games to one over Fort Worth, drew a gate of 56,254 and receipts, less taxes, of $94,025.75, Secretary Milton Price announced, October 8.

> The players' pool of $38,706.35 was the largest pool since 1931, when the Barons and Houston Buffs cut up a $39,548.64 melon. Birmingham's players divided $23,222.81 from this year's pot, while the losing Cats received $15,482.54.

> Each league received $9,402.57 and each club $18,257.13.[2]

If the Series was near its high-water mark in 1948, over the next decade the financial incentive to play the Dixie Series waned. By 1958, the situation was such that before the season, Nashville's management announced that if the Vols won the league, they would skip the Series unless the Southern Association agreed to cover financial losses. The worry was justified: Ticket sales for the entire six-game Series in 1958 barely exceeded 18,000, less than one-third of the 1948 Series.[4]

Changes in baseball also exposed a stark difference in the two leagues, which threatened the continuation of the Series. The Texas League had desegregated in 1952,[5] while the Southern Association remained stubbornly all-white.[6] During the Texas League playoffs, Austin's owner announced the Senators would not play in the Dixie Series if its black players could not play in Birmingham, which was a decidedly segregated city.[7] However, when Corpus Christi won the Texas League playoffs, the Giants agreed to leave their black players in Texas when they traveled to Alabama to play the Barons.[8] The end of the original Dixie Series, which was more bitter than sweet, finally came in the winter of 1959 when the Southern Association voted to shorten its own Shaughnessy playoff format and the Texas League refused to follow.[9]

For the Texas League, the death of the Dixie Series opened the door, albeit briefly, to a Pan-American partnership with the Mexican League.[10] The Texas League has survived with limited interruptions since 1902. Losing the Dixie Series was a canary in a coal mine for the Southern Association, however. The league was already in financial trouble as total attendance fell from 854,941 in 1958 to only 639,386 in 1959.[11] The mortal wound came following the 1961 season, when the Southern Association collapsed and permanently ceased operations after 60 years of professional baseball.

"BACK TO THE FUTURE"

The Southern Association's demise was not the end of organized baseball in the Deep South, or its member cities. In 1964, the South Atlantic League, also known as the SALLY, changed its name to the Southern

League, and added the Birmingham Barons, the new Double-A affiliate of the Kansas City Athletics.[12] Franchises in other former Southern Association cities—Chattanooga, Knoxville, and Macon—were included in the newly minted and integrated league.[13]

Before a pitch was even thrown, Southern League owners immediately began considering renewing the Dixie Series.[14] Jim Burris, the president of the Texas League, signaled an interest in resuming the Series, but cautioned that "it will take a meeting of the minds to get the Dixie Series revived, but it can be done…"[15] By August of 1964, the leagues shelved bringing back the interleague series due to monetary considerations.[16] The idea lingered; and in November 1966, discussions began again:

> The Dixie Series, once one of the most famous playoffs in the minor leagues, may be revived next season by the Texas and Southern leagues. A joint announcement by Hugh Finnerty, Texas president, and Sam Smith, Jr., Southern president, said the series would be resumed if the directors of the two circuits approve. They will meet during the minor leagues' winter convention at Columbus, O.[17]

The following month, the leagues agreed to the return of the Series.[18] By January 1967, baseball fans received the news that the best-of-seven Series was finally back.[19] The Texas League champions would host the first three games and would finish the Series in the city of the Southern League's winner. Finnerty predicted the Series would boost attendance for his league and players would enjoy the competition.[20]

1967: "THE SUMMER OF GLOVE"[21]
The Birmingham A's

W. Albert Belcher had owned the Barons in the Southern Association when the league ceased operations. In the new Southern League, he again owned the Barons in 1964–65, but crowds were small at Rickwood Field. Before the 1966 season Belcher sold the franchise to colorful Birmingham-area native and insurance magnate, Charles O. Finley, who also owned the Kansas City Athletics.[22] Birmingham's reprieve as a professional baseball town was briefly interrupted, and the future of Rickwood Field was threatened, as Finley moved the Barons to Mobile and rebranded them as the A's.[23] The A's won the Southern League in 1966 under manager John McNamara.

However, Finley returned the club to Birmingham in 1967 and named Paul Bryant, Jr. as his general manager.[24] Birmingham's roster was stocked with a talented group of prospects including Reggie Jackson, Joe Rudi, Dave Duncan, and Rollie Fingers. Future Hall of Fame manager Tony La Russa appeared in 41 games but did not play in the Dixie Series. Birmingham featured the following typical starting lineup:

C	Dave Duncan
1B	Joe Rudi
2B	Michael Dobbins
3B	Weldon "Hoss" Bowlin
SS	Arturo Miranda
RF	Stan Wojcik (and LF)
CF	Wayne Norton
LF	Reggie Jackson (and RF)

Leading the pitching staff, which compiled a team-ERA of 2.63, were Rollie Fingers, George Lauzerique (13–4, 2.30), Mike Olivo (13–6, 2.66), Vern Handrahan (8–4, 1.50), Robert Guzek (7–9, 3.10), and Joe Grzenda (6–0, 1.20).[25] Both Lauzerique and Olivo could not complete no-hitters due to a 100-pitch limit, which Kansas City imposed for its minor league affiliates.[26] However, on July 6, in the first game of a twin-bill, Lauzerique needed only 85 pitches to complete a 7-inning perfect game.[27]

Fingers and Jackson, two future Hall of Famers, played big roles with the A's, although their introductions to Rickwood Field were starkly different. On opening day, a blistering line drive hit by Evansville's Fred Kovner struck Fingers in the face. The ball fractured his jaw and cheek bones. Fingers spent time on the DL but started 17 games and had a 2.21 ERA over 102 innings and a 6–5 record. Early in the spring, Jackson introduced the baseball world to his uncanny ability to create dramatic headlines at critical moments.

On April 22, Jackson stepped to the plate in the bottom of the ninth with two outs, the bases loaded, and the A's trailing the Knoxville Smokies, 6–3. With University of Alabama football coach (and the GM's father) Bear Bryant in the stands, and facing a 2–2 count, the future Mr. October crushed a grand slam over Rickwood's 390-foot right-center-field fence to win the game, 7–6.[28] "The A's hero leaped with joy the last two-thirds of his joyous trip around the bases and the crowd of 1,648 cheered him all the way to the dressing room."[29] On July 8, Jackson hit for the cycle and walked in a thrilling 9–7 win over the Macon Peaches. His homer was an opposite field moon shot, which sailed high over Rickwood's left-center-field scoreboard. However, only 758 fans saw the game.[30]

Wayne Martin was a young sportswriter for *The Birmingham News* in 1967. Although he was not the

The 1967 Birmingham Barons

Front Row (L–R): Reggie Jackson (34), Arturo Miranda (17), Bob Frati (23), George Lauzerique (25), John McNamara (1), Hoss Bowlin (2), Don O'Riley (29), Mickey Dobbins (5), Vern Handrahan (18)

Back Row (L–R): Santiago Rosario (21), Bob Guzek (27), Dave Duncan (11), Stan Wojcik (32), Joe Rudi (15), Joe Grzenda (41), Gil Blanco (30), Rollie Fingers (26), Mike Olivo (20), Wayne Norton (24), Nicky Curtis (12), Danny Garrett (Trainer).

beat writer for the A's, he spent most of his nights at Rickwood that summer and would often use his access to walk along the roof towards right field. Martin remembered one of Jackson's homers:

> The old stadium had its flaws as age and neglect took its toll, but from the roof in right you didn't see the blemishes. You saw the beauty of the green grass, the red dirt of the skinned portions of the infield, a batter taking a mighty swing, and from 300-plus feet away you heard the crack of the bat a moment later.

> One night in 1967, I had taken my nightly stroll to right field and Reggie Jackson came to bat. I think it was about the seventh inning, late enough that a few fans were getting an early start home. I saw Jackson swing, heard the crack of the bat and saw the ball sailing straight toward me. It would have been too high to catch (if I had a glove) and soared into a small parking lot beyond the right field fence. Its flight ended at the feet of a couple of startled fans on the way to their car. They didn't get hit, but they did pick up a Reggie Jackson home run ball.[31]

Jackson batted .293 and led the team with 17 home runs, 17 triples, 26 doubles, 17 stolen bases, 84 runs scored, and a .562 slugging average. Jackson's numbers would have been even more impressive had he not missed nearly 25 games after a June promotion to Kansas City. With Jackson, and A's RBI leader Joe Rudi (70), Birmingham finished near the top of the Southern League in most offensive categories.

Despite Jackson's heroics, the Evansville White Sox raced to a 22-6 record and led the second place A's by 6.5 games on June 3. The White Sox soon slumped, and the Montgomery Rebels surged into first place with a 41-26 record by the end of June, with the 35-26 A's in third place trailing by three games. After going 16-8 in late June and July, the A's finally moved into first place with a 51-34 record. On August 1, the three teams remained clustered at the top of the Southern League standings. The A's were 59-43 and had a razor thin half-game lead over the second place Rebels (58-43), with the White Sox only one game behind in third (57-43).

By September, the three-way pennant race, which seemed to be a marketing dream for its owners, forced the league to reveal that the Dixie Series' return might not happen. The six franchises struggled to turn a profit, and only 240,566 fans attended for the season, just over 288 per game.[32] The owners voted to allow the pennant-winner to opt out of the Series if its management determined participating would cause a monetary loss. Montgomery and Evansville were not eager to play in the Series fearing the travel costs—expected to total $2,500—would exceed gate receipts. Although the A's only sold 53,053 tickets for the whole season—just 758 per game—they were able to break even in the Series. The club possessed another key advantage over the Rebels and White Sox: Birmingham was the only franchise in the Southern League owned by a major league club.[33] Charlie Finley would underwrite the team's expenses.

The A's ended any concerns about canceling the Dixie Series by finishing 25-12 to capture the Southern League pennant with an 84-55 record. The Rebels finished 3.5 games behind in second (80-58); and the White Sox finished a distant third (76-63). The A's were great on the road, as they went 43-23 and also swept 10 doubleheaders away from Rickwood. After winning his second consecutive pennant, McNamara said, "It just shows what I have been saying all along as we got out front and stayed there. Every man on this team has done something in the clutch."[34] Outfielder Stan Wojcik, who led the A's with a .375 on-base average and batted .296 (good for second in the Southern League), and Joe Rudi were later named Topps Double-A All-Stars.[35]

After clinching the Southern League, the A's had some fun at the end of a long summer. McNamara honored Hoss Bowlin at Rickwood Field:

Hoss Bowlin, Birmingham's regular third baseman, displayed his versatility on a night in his honor as the Athletics wound up their regular-season appearance at home August 31. Bowlin played all seven of the infield and outfield positions before taking the mound in the eighth with a 3–1 lead over Montgomery. The Rebels greeted his arrival with a single by Jim Leyland. After a force out, Bob Christian tripled and scored the tying run on an error. Montgomery then beat reliever Marcel Lachemann in the ninth, 4–3. Bowlin was scheduled to catch in the final frame, but an eye irritation forced him to relinquish the job.[36]

THE ALBUQUERQUE DODGERS

Albuquerque, known primarily as the Dukes during its long baseball history, joined the Texas League in 1962. The club began a 47-year affiliation with the Los Angeles Dodgers the next year and adopted the Dodgers name from 1965 to 71. Although they were no longer the Dukes, their manager was former Dodgers great Duke Snider. The Dodgers played at Tingley Field, which opened in 1932 and had a capacity of 5,000 fans, but only seated 3,000 in its cozy concrete grandstand.

Albuquerque had several players who later spent time in the major leagues, though none became stars, including Charlie Hough (216 wins), Willie Crawford (.305, 21 homers), Luis Alcaraz (.328, 22 homers), Bill Sudakis (.293, 9 homers), and Ted Sizemore (.295, 5 homers). The Dodgers' typical starting lineup included:

C	Hector Valle
1B	Mel Corbo
2B	Luis Alcaraz
3B	Bill Sudakis
SS	Don Williams
RF	Kenneth Washington
CF	Willie Crawford (and LF)
LF	Ted Sizemore (and Catcher)

John Duffie (16–9, 2.40), Mike Kekich (14–4, 3.24), and Leon Everitt (15–13, 3.45), anchored the rotation. Charlie Hough, a 19-year-old Dodgers prospect, would have the best major league career among the pitchers,

Score book from game six.

but he spent most of 1967 in Single-A Santa Barbara and appeared in only a handful of games for Albuquerque. He did not pitch in the Dixie Series.

While the A's endured a summer-long pennant race with Montgomery and Evansville, the Dodgers played on the fringe for most of their schedule, then pulled the Texas League crown out of the fire in September. The Amarillo Sonics, a Houston Astros affiliate, spent most of the summer in first. On August 22, Amarillo was 72–50, while the third place Dodgers were 63–58 and 8.5 games out. *The Sporting News* conceded the inevitability of Amarillo's title, calling the club "the pennant-bound Amarillo Sonics."[37]

However, the Sonics collapsed and finished 3–15, while the Dodgers went 15–4 and won the title by three games. Duke Snider credited his team's sudden surge to playing in late-season doubleheaders:

A month ago, Albuquerque was struggling to stay above the .500 mark and, just 18 days before the end of the season, the Dodgers fell 9 and one-half games back by dropping a double-header at El Paso, 6–1 and 4-3…Albuquerque's miracle finish was accomplished in ten days. That's how long it took the Dodgers to close the gap and seize the lead for the first time since the opening day of the season…

"I never figured that we'd win a pennant on double-headers," Snider said after a 3–2, 4–3 sweep that kayoed El Paso, the night before Amarillo was eliminated. "You might say that the rain has been with us all year…not because of the postponements—but because we've been able to pick up on the clubs in the double-headers. We've had nine sweeps, we've split seven and we've lost two of them…we've played 18 double dips—and we didn't have one of them scheduled."[38]

Topps named six Dodgers as Double-A All-Stars: second baseman Luis Alcaraz, third baseman Bill Sudakis, shortstop Don Williams outfielder Willie Crawford, and pitchers John Duffie and Mike Kekich.[39]

THE DIXIE SERIES

The A's flew west on September 4. After a four-hour layover in Dallas, they finally arrived in Albuquerque and relaxed by watching the red-hot Dodgers win their final league game against the El Paso Sun Kings.[40] In a Series preview, columnist Salo Otero of the *Albuquerque Journal* playfully mocked the A's sleeveless vest-style jerseys and bright colors:

> Birmingham will be decked out like a ladies softball team. Finley has clothed his team in the same three changes of uniform he has for his big club.

> The Steel City will wear their seafoam green road uniforms here with their white kangaroo shoes unless it's muddy. In the mud they change to tan shoes. They also have gold and the traditional white outfits for home games at storied Rickwood Field.[41]

Tickets for the games were relatively inexpensive: $1.75 for box seats, and $1.25 for general admission.

Game 1. Birmingham at Albuquerque
Tuesday, September 5, Tingley Field

Birmingham started Vern Handrahan, a tall 30-year-old veteran right-hander from Canada, who had also played with Kansas City's Triple-A affiliate in Vancouver during 1967. Leon Everitt, a 20-year-old righty, who was also tall, took the hill for the Dodgers. The A's took an early lead on catcher Dave Duncan's two-run home run after Reggie Jackson walked in the top of the first.[42] The Dodgers scored three in the bottom of the frame, but in the fourth, Stan Wojcik singled home Hoss Bowlin and Jackson to give the A's a 4–3 advantage, which they clung to through 8 innings.

In the ninth, Luis Alcaraz, Duke City's power hitting second baseman, drilled a home run into the dark desert night to tie the score at four and send the game into extra innings. Birmingham rebounded in the eleventh. Mickey Dobbins singled, and Arturo Miranda tripled him home to give the A's a 5–4 lead.

Handrahan pitched well as he struck out 13 in 10⅓ innings, but the A's seemed to have left their gloves back in Birmingham, as they committed four errors, two by Joe Rudi, and the Canadian starter surrendered four unearned runs. In the bottom of the eleventh, he finally tired and again gave up the tying run on hits by Mel Corbo, Alcaraz, and Ken Washington.

After chasing Handrahan, the Dodgers loaded the bases against reliever Marcel Lachemann. With one out, Dodgers shortstop Don Williams hit a grounder to short, which was cleanly fielded by Miranda, but a defensive miscue finally cost Birmingham the game. Miranda made an error on his throw home to Duncan and Alcaraz scored. Reliever Norman Dermody got the win for the Dodgers, 6–5.[43]

The loss did not concern A's manager John McNamara, who bluntly said, "We're one down now, but not discouraged. We feel we've got the better club."[44]

Game 2. Birmingham at Albuquerque
Wednesday, September 6, Tingley Field

The second game was a matchup of aces. Dodgers manager Duke Snider handed the ball to John "Stretch" Duffie, a 21-year-old right-hander, who was one of the tallest players in organized baseball at 6-feet-7.[45] John McNamara sent 20-year-old right-hander George Lauzerique to the mound. Lauzerique was from Havana, Cuba, and was lanky himself at 6-feet-1. Pitching in Birmingham and Kansas City, he had a career-best 2.30 ERA over 184 combined innings and struck out 135.[46]

Through five innings under the lights, Game 2 lived up to its billing as a pitching duel between Duffie and Lauzerique: neither surrendered a run. In the bottom of the sixth, Corbo reached first base and the dangerous Alcaraz stepped to the plate. Alcaraz repeated his Game 1 heroics and crushed a home run to right-center field to give the Dodgers a 2–0 lead.[47]

The Dodgers added an insurance run in the eighth on a wild pitch by Marcel Lachemann and won, 3–0. Duffie pitched a complete game, striking out five while only surrendering 6 hits. "Stan Wojcik was the only Athletics batter to reach second…but Wojick injured his ankle sliding into second and had to leave the game."[48] Wojick did not appear in another game in the Dixie Series, but not because of his ankle; he flew home to Buffalo, New York, to get married.[49] With or without Wojick, the Dodgers had taken a commanding 2–0 lead in the Series.

McNamara remained unshaken, stating, "we've had our backs to the wall before, and fought back. If we win the final game tonight, we'll win the Series."[50]

Game 3. Birmingham at Albuquerque
Thursday, September 7, Tingley Field

The A's and Dodgers met for the final time in New Mexico the following evening. Continuing the theme, both starters were over 6 feet tall. Birmingham started reliable right-hander Mike Olivo. The Dodgers countered with 22-year-old lefty Mike Kekich, the second-best starter on the staff behind Duffie.[51] The contest had a season's worth of drama.

The Dodgers knocked Olivo out of the game in the first inning when a scalding line drive off the bat of Bill Sudakis struck his shin, sending him to the hospital for X-rays.[52] McNamara inserted yet another 6-footer into the game, reliever Nicky Curtis. Although the Dodgers scratched an unearned run, Curtis escaped further damage and shut them down through 6 innings. Meanwhile, Birmingham scored twice in the third inning and added another run in the top of the seventh to take a 3–1 advantage.

With two on and two out in the bottom of the seventh, McNamara stuck with Curtis to try to get the final out of the inning. He did not. Shortstop Don Williams doubled to right field to drive in Hector Valle and Larry Eckenrode to tie the score. After a single by Sudakis, a walk to Corbo, and three more hits by Alcaraz, Washington, and Sizemore, the Dodgers took a 7–3 lead.

In the top of the ninth, with the score still 7–3, the A's were facing the prospect of returning to Birmingham trailing three games to none. But the baseball gods were not done with their fun.

Norman Dermody, who relieved Kekich in the eighth, took the mound to close out the game. A's center fielder Wayne Norton opened the ninth with a ground ball to short, which caromed off a rock for a single over Williams' head. Mickey Dobbins, who had committed an error in each of the first three games, then singled. Santiago Rosario pinch hit for reliever Marcel Lachemann and hit a flare past Sudakis at third scoring Norton. After Dobbins scored on a fielder's choice by Allan Lewis to make the score 7–5, Miranda doubled to put two runners in scoring position. Snider ignored the fans' cries to remove Dermody; the reliever hit Bowlin to load the bases with one out.[53] Catcher Dave Duncan then came to the plate.

Duncan had hit 13 homers in 1967, which tied Rudi for second on the A's behind Jackson. He had already

homered once in the Series. Duncan "ran the count to 3–2 then blasted Dermody's fastball far over the left field wall to snatch apparent victory away from Albuquerque," reported the *Albuquerque Journal*. Of his grand slam, Duncan said, "It was a low fastball on the outside corner. I was guessing change. I just got lucky."[54] Although Duncan batted only .231 during the Series, his three homers and 7 RBIs led the A's.

McNamara then called on Rollie Fingers to pitch the bottom of the ninth, his first appearance in the series. The future closer made short work of the Dodgers, striking out one and allowing no baserunners in the 9–7 win. The A's trailed the Dixie Series, 2–1, but had renewed confidence as they left for the Magic City.

Game 4. Albuquerque at Birmingham
Saturday, September 9, Rickwood Field

After an off day, the series resumed at Birmingham's 57-year-old ballpark. McNamara announced veteran Handrahan, who had started Game 1, as his starter. Snider originally planned to use a three-man rotation of Everitt, Duffie, and Kekich for the Series. After the A's comeback win, he had second thoughts. There was speculation he would hand the ball to James Roberts, a righty from Dora, Alabama.[55] Before the game, Snider announced right-hander Ray Lamb would start.[56] However, when Saturday night arrived, he scrapped his new plan and Everitt took his place on the hill.[57]

Game 4 was the only game in the Series which was never in doubt. The A's pounded Everitt and three relievers for 15 hits, as Birmingham won, 9–1.[58] Every A's starter had a hit. Norton went 4-for-4 with a home run. Even Handrahan went 3-for-4 as the pitcher drove in a pair of runs. In the seventh inning, Duncan slugged a mammoth homer to dead center, which the *Albuquerque Journal* reported as having traveled 430 feet.[59] Alf Van Hoose of *The Birmingham News* contended the blast had "banged against the outer concrete wall right over a painted X which marks the spot Walt Dropo hit his mightiest blow in 1948. Dropo's homer measured 457 feet. Duncan's must have gone 462."[60]

Handrahan pitched a complete game for the victory, as he struck out three and allowed one run on 7 hits. This time his defense did not let him down, as the A's did not make an error for the first time in the Series. The Dodgers made three. The Series was now tied, but the momentum (and the home field advantage) was Birmingham's.

Game 5. Albuquerque at Birmingham
Sunday, September 10, Rickwood Field

On Sunday afternoon, McNamara started 21-year-old

Rollie Fingers, a 6-foot-4 right-hander, one of Kansas City's best pitching prospects. Fingers had signed with the Athletics in 1964, before the advent of the amateur draft, and pitched well as he progressed through Kansas City's minor league system. He had pitched one inning three days earlier in Albuquerque but was the best choice to get the ball with the Series tied.

Snider's decision was easy and this time he did not waver. He called on Duffie, who had thrown 9 shutout innings against the A's in Game 2. The young South Carolinian rewarded him with another masterful performance. Through 10 innings, Duffie held the A's scoreless. He allowed only two singles, both to Dobbins, and hit two other batters. He struck out four, walked none, and breezed through the A's powerful 4-5-6 hitters—Duncan, Rudi, and Jackson—who combined to go 0-for-9.

Fingers struggled to match Duffie's dominating performance, although he pitched well. Late in the game, he faced adversity twice. Sudakis led off the eighth inning with a double and Corbo's ground ball moved him to third. Alcaraz grounded to Bowlin, who held Sudakis and threw across the diamond to nip the speedy infielder at first. Washington then grounded out to Miranda to end the inning.[61] In the tenth, the Dodgers loaded the bases, as Washington, Sizemore, and Valle reached on weak singles. With two outs and the game in the balance, Snider decided not to pinch hit for Duffie. Fingers struck him out.[62] After dueling with Duffie for ten innings, Fingers had also thrown a shutout as he scattered 6 hits, while striking out 7 and walking none.

In the eleventh inning, McNamara lifted Fingers because he had reached his pitch limit.[63] He called on Dick Joyce, a 6-foot-5 southpaw from Maine, who had started 7 games during the summer. Joyce faced the top of Albuquerque's lineup, but did not allow a baserunner.

In the bottom of the inning, Duffie's wall of invincibility finally cracked. Allan Lewis led off with a double to left center and advanced to third on a bunt by Miranda. After throwing two strikes past Bowlin, Duffie threw a wild pitch, which "zoomed off the top of Hector Valle's mitt and Lewis scored" the winning run for the A's.[64]

Van Hoose compared the 1-0 win to the Birmingham Barons' unlikely triumph over Dizzy Dean and the Houston Buffaloes at Rickwood in the 1931 Dixie Series, and gushed in his praise for Duffie, writing:

Now there's another 1-0 Dixie Series classic grand old Rickwood can stack in memory alongside that historic beauty ancient Ray Caldwell

snatched from swaggering Dizzy Dean in 1931. The last one won't soon be forgotten either. … Rollie Fingers and Dick Joyce presently went out with young arms, live arms, to do to the Texas League champs what Ray Caldwell did to Dean and Houston 37 short years ago. Moreover, they may have licked a fellow named John Duffie who'll probably win more games in the majors than a fellow named Dean.[65]

The A's needed only one more win to clinch the Dixie Series.

Game 6. Albuquerque at Birmingham
Monday, September 11, Rickwood Field

On Monday night, the Dodgers and A's treated fans at Rickwood to another great pitching matchup. Game 2 starter George Lauzerique started for the A's and faced Mike Kekich, who had started Game 3 for the Dodgers. In a 10-inning contest, Lauzerique surrendered only 6 hits and walked two. Kekich allowed 9 hits and walked four but constantly pitched out of trouble during his 7 innings of work. The A's left 12 runners on base, which was the most for either team in the Series.

The game was scoreless through three frames. In the fourth, Williams singled to lead off the inning for the Dodgers. With one out, Corbo walked, and Alcaraz singled to drive Williams home. With two on and only one out, Lauzerique got out of the jam, but the Dodgers led, 1-0.

In the bottom of the seventh, with the score still 1-0, Lauzerique doubled off Kekich. Lewis's single brought him home to tie the game. In the eighth, Snider walked to the mound and called on Dermody to relieve Kekich. Snider got into an argument with home plate umpire Jake O'Donnell, who tossed the manager out of the game.[66] Van Hoose noted in his scorecard, Snider "refused to go." He later reported, "The moody ex-big leaguer took his sweet time about leaving, however. O'Donnell finally called Officer 'Bill' Williams and Snider went out peacefully."[67]

Dermody shut the A's out for two innings. In the tenth, Miranda and Bowlin grounded out. Duncan, who had hit a grand slam off Dermody in Game 3, then doubled. Dermody issued an intentional walk to Reggie Jackson. Rudi's single to left-center scored Duncan and ended the Dixie Series with a 2-1 Birmingham win.[68] Lauzerique got the complete game victory for the A's.[69]

A jubilant McNamara exclaimed, "We went for everything, the pennant and the Series, and we brought it all home. This is a great bunch of kids. They would never panic early when Evansville ran off so fast, nor

Sportswriter Alf Van Hoose's scorecard from game six of the 1967 Dixie Series.

when Montgomery got the hex going on us, nor when we got two down in this series."[70] The A's celebrated in Rickwood's clubhouse with champagne. Reggie Jackson, wearing a huge smile, took center stage in a photo that appeared in *The Birmingham News*.

In 1974, three of the A's who played in the Dixie Series, Reggie Jackson, Joe Rudi, and Rollie Fingers, played in the World Series against the Los Angeles Dodgers, which Oakland won four games to one with Fingers winning the MVP. Only Willie Crawford played in both the Dixie Series and World Series for the Dodgers.

SERIES STATS

Mickey Dobbins (.391, 5 runs), Allan Lewis (.381, 3 runs, 4 RBIs), Wayne Norton (.360, 4 runs), and Dave Duncan (.231, 5 runs, 3 homers, 7 RBIs) paced the A's hitters in the series.

Albuquerque's Ted Sizemore led all hitters with a .435 average and 10 hits. However, the future 1969 NL Rookie of the Year had little impact on the games. Nine of his hits were singles, and he only scored one run and collected two RBIs for the entire Series. Luis Alcaraz (.269, 2 homers, and 8 RBIs) and Don Williams (.259, 3 runs and 3 RBIs) were the most productive hitters for the Dodgers.

John Duffie was the best pitcher in the series, as he had an 0.47 ERA over 19 innings. The 1967 season was Duffie's best performance as a professional; after throwing 229 innings, he never lived up to Alf Van Hoose's comparison with Dizzy Dean. He would be out of baseball by 1969. Mike Kekich also had a

productive Series for the Dodgers, as he punched out 12 batters in 14 innings and had a 2.57 ERA.

Birmingham's pitching staff was largely a three-headed monster in the Series. Handrahan had a 1.40 ERA over 19⅓ innings, striking out 16. Lauzerique also pitched well with a 1.65 ERA and 16 strikeouts in his 16⅓ innings of work. Fingers pitched 11 innings, allowing no runs.

Baseball historian Bill James ranks the 1967 A's as one of the best minor league clubs of the 1960s.[71] Using James's complex Win Shares formula, of the players who appeared in the final Dixie Series, Birmingham's players would generate 887 win shares in the major leagues, which is far ahead of the 371 win shares the formula attributes to Albuquerque's future big leaguers.[72]

THE SECOND FAREWELL OF THE DIXIE SERIES

Attendance for each Dixie Series game was better than the averages the A's and Dodgers drew for each game in the regular season in 1967, but poor compared to past Series. The Dodgers drew 7,393 fans (2,464 per game) for the three games at Tingley Field. The A's sold just 6,949 tickets (2,316 per game) for the three games at Rickwood Field. Series attendance was even lower than the six-game Series in 1958 (18,000-plus). Relative to the overall season attendance in each league in 1958 and 1967, the Dixie Series was arguably better attended in 1967.

Despite poor ticket sales and high travel costs, the Southern League directors met in Birmingham on October 24 and voted to continue the Series in 1968.[73]

In December, Southern League President Sam Smith reiterated the two leagues planned to bring back the Series.[74] The optimism was short-lived. In February 1968, the Southern League directors voted to end the Dixie Series.[75]

COULD THE DIXIE SERIES EVER RETURN?

In 1971, the Southern and Texas Leagues each had seven franchises, which made scheduling impossible. The leagues created an awkward three-division "Dixie Association" with interleague play. The Association's eastern border was in Charlotte, North Carolina, and stretched to Albuquerque, New Mexico, to the west. Columnist Bob Quincy observed "[t]he only thing Charlotte and Albuquerque have in common is taxes."[76] The teams in the Association played an interlocking schedule, although the Texas and Southern Leagues had separate All-Star Games, one in Birmingham and the other in Albuquerque.[77] The four playoff teams were the Charlotte Hornets against the Asheville Tourists in the Southern League and the Arkansas Travelers against the Amarillo Giants in the Texas League. The Hornets ultimately won a 5-game series over the Travelers in the Association's Championship series. After one-year, the Dixie Association disbanded.

In the author's opinion, regardless of semantics, the 1971 championship series was not a return of "the Dixie Series" for two principal reasons. First, the Dixie Association had intraleague play during the regular season, while the original Dixie Series was a series between champions of truly distinct leagues. Second, the original Dixie Series, much like the World Series, was a best-of-seven series, while the Dixie Association series was a best-of-five.[78]

In the 1980s, Bobby Bragan, the former president of the minor leagues' governing body, the National Association of Professional Baseball Leagues, met with Carl Sawatski, the president of the Texas League. Bragan wanted to bring back the Dixie Series; Sawatski had no interest in the idea.[79]

It is doubtful the Dixie Series will ever return. The Series has now been gone for over 50 years, even longer than it existed in its original incarnation.

These days an evening at a minor league game is an experience in baseball-related entertainment, which has replaced the simple joy of watching a game. Intro music, between-innings-promotions, and cheap beer nights have replaced the civic pride of following the standings, watching the out-of-town scoreboard, scoring a game, and poring over box scores in a newspaper. Major league clubs have a much stronger grip on minor league affiliates than they did in the 1950s and 60s. The big leagues have hundreds of millions invested in players and the primary purpose of Double-A baseball is their development, not playing for championships.

Fans' appetites have also changed since turnstiles spun wildly at Rickwood during the '48 Dixie Series. Most sports fans in the South seem to lose interest in baseball once college football begins. On September 15, 2013, the Birmingham Barons won their most recent Southern League title beating the Mobile Bay-Bears at Regions Field in the fifth game of the SL Championship Series, 4–2. The actual attendance that Sunday night seemed much smaller than the announced crowd of 3,093, which included season ticket holders, many of whom did not bother to attend. Even the official attendance of Game 5 was about half of a regular season Barons game in 2013.

Major league owners and fans appear unified in an unspoken agreement. Neither is particularly interested in minor league baseball after Labor Day. Based on ticket sales, this was also true in 1967, albeit for different reasons. But for a magical week in September that year the A's and Dodgers made the last Dixie Series memorable for the fans who attended. ∎

Acknowledgments

The author is grateful to Mike Maddox for his comments and memories of 1967. Joe DeLeonard answered questions and provided copies of newspaper articles. Art Black provided helpful editorial assistance, and a copy of his completed scorecard from Game 6. Clarence Watkins dug through the archives at Rickwood and located a wonderful cartoon commemorating the A's title, which ran in *The Birmingham News*. Former sportswriter Wayne Martin generously allowed the author to copy Alf Van Hoose's scorecards from Games 4, 5, and 6, and April 22.

Notes

1. Blackie Sherrod, "Player Melon in Dixie Series Close to Tops," *The Sporting News*, October 13, 1948: 23.
2. "Dixie Series Draws 56,254 at Gate, $94,025 Receipts," *The Sporting News*, October 20, 1948: 23.
3. "Vols Would Skip Dixie Series Unless Indemnified by Loop," *The Sporting News*, March 26, 1958: 26.
4. Marshall Wright, *The Southern Association in Baseball, 1885–1961* (Jefferson, N.C.: McFarland, 2002), 516.
5. Harold V. Ratliff, "Negro Pitcher Wins Second for Dallas," *The Shreveport Journal*, April 24, 1952, 2B.
6. "Dixie Series Threatened by Race Segregation Law," *The Sporting News*, September 3, 1958: 35.
7. "Dixie Series Status Clouded by Color Bar in Birmingham," *The Sporting News*, September 24, 1958: 41.
8. Frank McGowan, "Corpus Christi Club Agrees to Use Only White Players in Games at Birmingham," *The Sporting News*, October 1, 1958: 54.
9. "Texas Loop Refuses to Cut Playoff, Dixie Series Ended," *The Sporting News*, February 12, 1959: 26.
10. Bill Rives, "Officials Ask More Help From Majors," *The Sporting News*, June 30, 1958: 36; and "Final Official Attendance Count," *The Sporting News*, October 28, 1959: 11.

11. "Final Official Attendance Count," *The Sporting News*, October 28, 1959: 11.
12. Harold Harris, "Ex-Sally Shows Optimism Under Southern Label," *The Sporting News*, January 25, 1964: 14.
13. Bill O'Neal, *The Southern League: Baseball in Dixie, 1885–1994* (Austin, Tex.: Eakin Press, 1994), 141.
14. Harris, 14.
15. Carlos Salazar, "Boss Burris Goals: 8-Club Texas Loop, Dixie Series Revival," *The Sporting News*, February 28, 1964: 26.
16. "Fisher's Streak Stopped," *The Sporting News*, August 1, 1964: 35.
17. "Texas and Southern Plan Revival of Dixie Series," *The Sporting News*, November 26, 1966: 40.
18. "Junior Series Hopes Fade, But Dixie May Be Revived," *The Sporting News*, December 10, 1966: 28.
19. "Southern Goes With Six Clubs," *Alabama Journal* (Montgomery, AL), Jan. 6, 1967: 12; "Dixie Series Revived; Knoxville Back In SL," *The Montgomery Advertiser*, January 6, 1967: 13.
20. "Texas, Southern Loops To Renew Dixie Series," *The Sporting News*, August 19, 1967: 42.
21. At the third annual Rickwood Classic in 1998, the Birmingham Barons donned the '67 A's uniforms. Posters sold at the Classic featured Willie Mays leaping against a psychedelic background with the event featuring a pun-inspired title, "The Summer of Glove" at the bottom of the poster. https://rickwood.com/product/summer-ofglove.
22. Finley was apparently not interested in purchasing Rickwood Field, however, as Belcher retained the title to the ballpark. After initially drawing no interest from the City of Birmingham and Jefferson County, Belcher put the ballpark, its contents, and its real estate on the auction block. In a 10-page brochure for the auction, which was scheduled for April 27, 1966, Belcher offered the ballpark in its entirety as a going concern, but also suggested the stadium could be razed and the land repurposed as an industrial site. Fortunately, the City of Birmingham purchased Rickwood. See Ben Cook, *Good Wood* (Birmingham, Alabama: R. Boozer Press, 2005), 90.
23. In the interim, Belcher attempted to sell Rickwood Field, but found no buyers. He decided to auction the ballpark on April 27, 1966, and created a 12-page brochure for the event. The brochure reported the park was in good condition and could be operated as a baseball facility immediately. However, Belcher hedged his bets and ominously offered to sell the ballpark in pieces so the land could be redeveloped. Fortunately for baseball fans everywhere, the City of Birmingham purchased the ballpark, which survives to this day. "Finley Returns Southern Farm Club to Birmingham," *The Sporting News*, December 1966, 1966: 32.
24. Paul Bryant, Jr. is the son of the University of Alabama's legendary head football coach, Paul "Bear" Bryant. He was also the general manager of the Birmingham Barons from 1964–65 before the team rebranded as the A's.
25. Alf Van Hoose, "Sublime to Ridiculous—That's Olivo," *The Sporting News*, Aug. 19, 1967: 35; and O'Neal, 147.
26. Joe Grzenda pitched on the last Birmingham Barons team to win the Southern Association and the Dixie Series in 1958 winning 16 games. He later appeared in 9 games for the Barons in 1961 in the final year of the Southern Association. In 1964, he returned to play for the reconstituted Birmingham Barons in the first season of the Southern League. He then pitched for the Mobile A's in 1966 and the Birmingham A's in 1967. No other player appeared on the rosters of both iterations of the Barons and both cities for the A's. In addition, although he did not pitch in the 1967 Dixie Series, he is the only player whose club won the Series in both the Southern Association and the Southern League.
27. O'Neal, 147; Bill James, *The New Bill James Historical Baseball Abstract* (NY, NY: The Free Press, 2001), 268.
28. Alf Van Hoose, "Ready Reggie rocks Rickwood," *The Birmingham News*, April 23, 1967: C-1.
29. Van Hoose, "Ready Reggie..."
30. Alf Van Hoose, "Jackson joins cycle gang," *The Birmingham News*, September 9, 1967: C-1.
31. Wayne Martin email correspondence with author, March 4, 2019.
32. "Minors Drew Over 10 Million For Fourth Straight Season," *The Sporting News*, Jan. 13, 1968: 37. By contrast, the Texas League's six clubs drew 609,890. Ibid. However, it is notable that the Southern Association's attendance in 1959 was nearly three times the SL's 1967 attendance, albeit with two more clubs.
33. "Dixie Series Doubtful Unless A's Take Flag," *The Sporting News*, September 2, 1967: 43; Leroy Bearman, "Renewal of Dixie Series Hinges on Birmingham Win," *Albuquerque Journal*, August 13, 1967:42; and *Birmingham Barons 2018 Media Guide*: 90.
34. Frank McGowan, "A's Birmingham Farm Clinches Southern Crown," *The Sporting News*, Septtember 9, 1967: 35.
35. "Six Star Spots To Albuquerque In Topps Voting," *The Sporting News*, October 28, 1967: 21.
36. "Southern Sparks," *The Sporting News*, Sept. 16, 1967: 46. Following the Dixie Series, the A's promoted Hoss Bowlin to Kansas City, where he got his first and only major league hit on September 16, 1967, against the Angels.
37. "Dixie Series Doubtful Unless A's Take Flag," *The Sporting News*, September 2, 1967: 43; and Birmingham Barons 2018 Media Guide: 90.
38. Carlos Salazar, "A-Dodgers Give TL Bum's Rush, Clinch Pennant," *The Sporting News*, September 16, 1967: 44.
39. "Six Star Spots To Albuquerque In Topps Voting," *The Sporting News*, October 28, 1967: 21.
40. Photo Caption, *Albuquerque Journal*, Sept. 5, 1967: C-1; and "Dixie Series Starts In Albuquerque Tonight," *Alabama Journal* (Montgomery, AL), September 5, 1967: 12.
41. Salo Otero, "Famed Dixie Series Opens Tonight," *Albuquerque Journal*, September 5, 1967: C-1.
42. "A's Defeated On Error In Dixie Series Opener," *Alabama Journal* (Montgomery, AL), September 6, 1967: 17.
43. Ibid; "Game of Tuesday, September 5," *The Sporting News*, September 23, 1967: 39.
44. Alf Van Hoose, "A's gift Dodgers to win in 11, 6–5," *The Birmingham News*, September 6, 1967: 32.
45. www.ricketsonfuneralhome.com/obituaries/John-Duffie/#!/Obituary.
46. Lauzerique pitched professionally until 1976, including four seasons in the major leagues, mostly as a reliever, but never lived up to the promise he displayed in the summer of '67.
47. "A's Ace Falls; Trail Dixie Series by Two," *Alabama Journal* (Montgomery, AL), Sept. 7, 1967: 32; "Game of Wednesday, September 6," *The Sporting News*, September 23, 1967: 39.
48. "A's Ace Falls; Trail Dixie Series by Two," *Alabama Journal* (Montgomery, AL), Sept. 7, 1967: 32; "Game of Wednesday, September 6," *The Sporting News*, September 23, 1967: 39.
49. Frank Maestas, "Rally in Ninth Trips Bums," *Albuquerque Journal*, September 8, 1967: 45.
50. Alf Van Hoose, "Mac says A's 'just got beat'," *The Birmingham News*, September 8, 1967: 23.
51. In 1973, Kekich would achieve notoriety when he swapped places with fellow pitcher Fritz Peterson, going to live in Peterson's house with his wife and children, and Peterson taking up residence in Kekich's.
52. Frank Maestas, "Rally in Ninth Trips Bums," *Albuquerque Journal*, September 8, 1967: 45.
53. Maestas, "Rally in Ninth..."
54. Maestas, "Rally in Ninth..."
55. Alf Van Hoose, "Dave saves 'our' A's," *The Birmingham News*, September 8, 1967: 8.
565. "Bums After Third Win," *Albuquerque Journal*, September 9, 1967: 19.
57. "Dodgers Beaten on 7-Hitter, 9–1" *Albuquerque Journal*, September 10, 1967: 19.
58. "Game of Saturday, September 9," *The Sporting News*, September 23, 1967: 39.
59. "Game of Saturday, September 9."
60. Alf Van Hoose, "Heroes aplenty as A's even Dixie Series 2–2," *The Birmingham News*, September 10, 1967: C-1. *The Sporting News* also reported that the ball traveled 462 feet.
61. "Duffie Loses Heartbreaker," *Albuquerque Journal*, September 11, 1967: 15.

62. "Duffie Loses Heartbreaker."
63. "Game of Sunday, September 10," *The Sporting News*, September 23, 1967: 39.
64. "Duffie Loses Heartbreaker.".
65. Alf Van Hoose, "Dean Missed Rickwood and he's poorer, too," *The Birmingham News*, September 11, 1967: C-11.
66. "Birmingham Wins Dixie Series Title," *Albuquerque Journal*, September 12, 1967: 15.
67. Alf Van Hoose, "Time was ripe, our A's struck," The *Birmingham News*, September 12, 1967: C-6-8.
68. Van Hoose, "Time was ripe..."; "Birmingham Wins Dixie Series Title," *Alabama Journal* (Montgomery, AL), September 12, 1967: 14.
69. "Game of Monday, September 11," *The Sporting News*, September 23, 1967: 39.
70. "Time was ripe, our A's struck,": C-8.
71. James, 267–68.
72. A's: Reggie Jackson (444), Rollie Fingers (188), Joe Rudi (173), Dave Duncan (71), Marcel Lachemann (7), George Lauzerique (2), Vern Handrahan (1), Santiago Rosario (1), Dick Joyce (0), Don O'Riley (0), Allan Lewis (0), and Hoss Bowlin (0). Dodgers: Ted Sizemore (130), Willie Crawford (123), Bob Stinson (49), Bill Sudakis (47), Mike Kekich (17), Luis Alcaraz (5), Hector Valle (0), Leon Everitt (0), and John Duffie (0). Ray Lamb, who almost started Game 4, and did not appear in the Dixie Series, had 26 win shares in the major leagues. Charlie Hough, who also did not pitch in the Series, is credited with 233 win shares during his career.
73. Frank McGowan, "Southern League Drafts Plans for 1968 Season," *The Sporting News*, November 4, 1967: 46.
74. Stan Isle, "Vet Richardson Back at Helm of Eastern League," *The Sporting News*, December 9, 1967: 34.
75. Frank McGowan, "Southern Cancels Dixie Series in Plans for '68," *The Sporting News*, February 17, 1968: 26.
76. Bob Quincy, "Hefner Boosts Illini," *The Charlotte Observer*, September 19, 1971, 9D.
77. "In Unique Dixie Association: Two 'Star Games Set," *The Montgomery Advertiser*, April 11, 1971: 13.
78. "Dixie Association series," *The Delta Democrat-Times* (Greenville, MS), August 29, 1971: 12; "Bragan Sets Dixie Series," *Victoria Advocate* (Victoria, TX), August 28, 1971, 15.
79. O'Neal, 165.

SABR BioProject Team Books

In 2002, the Society for American Baseball Research launched an effort to write and publish biographies of every player, manager, and individual who has made a contribution to baseball. Over the past decade, the BioProject Committee has produced over 6,000 biographical articles. Many have been part of efforts to create theme- or team-oriented books, spearheaded by chapters or other committees of SABR.

THE 1986 BOSTON RED SOX:
THERE WAS MORE THAN GAME SIX
One of a two-book series on the rivals that met in the 1986 World Series, the Boston Red Sox and the New York Mets, including biographies of every player, coach, broadcaster, and other important figures in the top organizations in baseball that year. .
Edited by Leslie Heaphy and Bill Nowlin
$19.95 paperback (ISBN 978-1-943816-19-4)
$9.99 ebook (ISBN 978-1-943816-18-7)
8.5"X11", 420 pages, over 200 photos

THE 1986 NEW YORK METS:
THERE WAS MORE THAN GAME SIX
The other book in the "rivalry" set from the 1986 World Series. This book re-tells the story of that year's classic World Series and this is the story of each of the players, coaches, managers, and broadcasters, their lives in baseball and the way the 1986 season fit into their lives.
Edited by Leslie Heaphy and Bill Nowlin
$19.95 paperback (ISBN 978-1-943816-13-2)
$9.99 ebook (ISBN 978-1-943816-12-5)
8.5"X11", 392 pages, over 100 photos

SCANDAL ON THE SOUTH SIDE:
THE 1919 CHICAGO WHITE SOX
The Black Sox Scandal isn't the only story worth telling about the 1919 Chicago White Sox. The team roster included three future Hall of Famers, a 20-year-old spitballer who would win 300 games in the minors, and even a batboy who later became a celebrity with the "Murderers' Row" New York Yankees. All of their stories are included in Scandal on the South Side with a timeline of the 1919 season.
Edited by Jacob Pomrenke
$19.95 paperback (ISBN 978-1-933599-95-3)
$9.99 ebook (ISBN 978-1-933599-94-6)
8.5"x11", 324 pages, 55 historic photos

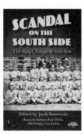

WINNING ON THE NORTH SIDE
THE 1929 CHICAGO CUBS
Celebrate the 1929 Chicago Cubs, one of the most exciting teams in baseball history. Future Hall of Famers Hack Wilson, '29 NL MVP Rogers Hornsby, and Kiki Cuyler, along with Riggs Stephenson formed one of the most potent quartets in baseball history. The magical season came to an ignominious end in the World Series and helped craft the future "lovable loser" image of the team.
Edited by Gregory H. Wolf
$19.95 paperback (ISBN 978-1-933599-89-2)
$9.99 ebook (ISBN 978-1-933599-88-5)
8.5"x11", 314 pages, 59 photos

DETROIT THE UNCONQUERABLE:
THE 1935 WORLD CHAMPION TIGERS
Biographies of every player, coach, and broadcaster involved with the 1935 World Champion Detroit Tigers baseball team, written by members of the Society for American Baseball Research. Also includes a season in review and other articles about the 1935 team. Hank Greenberg, Mickey Cochrane, Charlie Gehringer, Schoolboy Rowe, and more.
Edited by Scott Ferkovich
$19.95 paperback (ISBN 9978-1-933599-78-6)
$9.99 ebook (ISBN 978-1-933599-79-3)
8.5"X11", 230 pages, 52 photos

THE TEAM THAT TIME WON'T FORGET:
THE 1951 NEW YORK GIANTS
Because of Bobby Thomson's dramatic "Shot Heard 'Round the World" in the bottom of the ninth of the decisive playoff game against the Brooklyn Dodgers, the team will forever be in baseball public's consciousness. Includes a foreword by Giants outfielder Monte Irvin.
Edited by Bill Nowlin and C. Paul Rogers III
$19.95 paperback (ISBN 978-1-933599-99-1)
$9.99 ebook (ISBN 978-1-933599-98-4)
8.5"X11", 282 pages, 47 photos

A PENNANT FOR THE TWIN CITIES:
THE 1965 MINNESOTA TWINS
This volume celebrates the 1965 Minnesota Twins, who captured the American League pennant in just their fifth season in the Twin Cities. Led by an All-Star cast, from Harmon Killebrew, Tony Oliva, Zoilo Versalles, and Mudcat Grant to Bob Allison, Jim Kaat, Earl Battey, and Jim Perry, the Twins won 102 games, but bowed to the Los Angeles Dodgers and Sandy Koufax in Game Seven
Edited by Gregory H. Wolf
$19.95 paperback (ISBN 978-1-943816-09-5)
$9.99 ebook (ISBN 978-1-943816-08-8)
8.5"X11", 405 pages, over 80 photos

MUSTACHES AND MAYHEM: CHARLIE O'S THREE TIME CHAMPIONS:
THE OAKLAND ATHLETICS: 1972-74
The Oakland Athletics captured major league baseball's crown each year from 1972 through 1974. Led by future Hall of Famers Reggie Jackson, Catfish Hunter and Rollie Fingers, the Athletics were a largely homegrown group who came of age together. Biographies of every player, coach, manager, and broadcaster (and mascot) from 1972 through 1974 are included, along with season recaps.
Edited by Chip Greene
$29.95 paperback (ISBN 978-1-943816-07-1)
$9.99 ebook (ISBN 978-1-943816-06-4)
8.5"X11", 600 pages, almost 100 photos

SABR Members can purchase each book at a significant discount (often 50% off) and receive the ebook edtions free as a member benefit. Each book is available in a trade paperback edition as well as ebooks suitable for reading on a home computer or Nook, Kindle, or iPad/tablet.
To learn more about becoming a member of SABR, visit the website: sabr.org/join

Considerable Excitement and Heavy Betting

Origins of Base Ball in the Dakota Territory

Terry Bohn

When the Yankton Treaty was signed in 1858, the United States government acquired a large parcel of land: the northernmost part of the Louisiana Purchase of 1803, much of which had been Sioux Indian land. In 1861, the area was incorporated as the Dakota Territory. Its borders changed over the next decade, at one time including parts of present day Montana and Wyoming, but eventually shrank to what is now North and South Dakota. The first territorial capital was established in Yankton (the far southeast corner), but was later moved to Bismarck (now North Dakota) in 1883. In 1889 the territory was split in half at the forty-sixth parallel when President Benjamin Harrison signed legislation making North and South Dakota the thirty-ninth and fortieth states in the Union.

White settlers in the territory followed the transportation routes: first rivers via steamboat, then wagon trails, and later the railroads. Two of the earliest communities were Yankton and Vermillion, both located on the Missouri River in the southeast corner of the territory. The Yankton band of the Dakota (Sioux), for which the city is named, occupied the site of the city when Lewis and Clark stopped there in 1804. Yankton was incorporated as a city in 1869 and became an important steamboat stop, especially after gold was discovered in the Black Hills a few years later. French fur traders first visited the city of Vermillion in the eighteenth century and named it after a red pigment made from the mineral cinnabar that local Indians used as paint. The Dakota name for the town translates to "The place where vermillion is obtained." Vermillion, which sits east of Yankton, was founded in 1859 and incorporated in 1877.

The author has previously established that the earliest recorded base ball game in Bismarck occurred in 1873.[1] Other historians have documented that soldiers in the Seventh Cavalry at the US Army post at Fort Abraham Lincoln formed the Benteen Base Ball and Gymnastics Club around the same time.[2] Within a short time a second club had been formed, and the two nines played base ball while on the Black Hills

Expedition in 1874. Four members of the post's base ball teams suffered gunshot wounds at the Little Big Horn in 1876 and one ballplayer died with Custer in the battle. But the Benteens were not the first base ball club in the Dakota Territory. This essay traces the first known base ball clubs and match games in the southern part of the Dakota Territory through the decade of the 1870s.

> The White Caps went to bat and made 23 runs in the first inning, enough to discourage any club, but the Coyotes went to the bat not one bit discouraged. They scored 12 runs. At the end of the 3rd innings, the Coyotes stood 40, the White Caps 30.
>
> —*Yankton Press and Dakotaian*
> October 27, 1870

In 1869, the first fully professional base ball team was formed in Cincinnati, Ohio. The "Red Stockings" traveled across the country on the new transcontinental railroad and rang up a perfect record of 64 wins and no losses.[3] That spring, the April 3, 1869, issue of the *Dakota Republican* of Vermillion, Dakota Territory, reported that the Star of the West Base Ball Club, probably named for a saloon of the same name in the city, was reorganizing for practice for the coming season. The term "reorganizing" implied that there may have been an earlier version of the club, but this is the first known written record of a base ball club in the territory. A match game between the Star of the West and the Excelsiors of Bloomingdale was scheduled for September 1 of that year, but no record of the result of the contest could be found.

The following year, several clubs organized in the area. When they organized in March 1870, the Coyote Base Ball Club of Yankton boasted of having, "...material enough to make a nine that can scoop anything this side of the Mississippi."[4] The Frontier Base Ball Club organized in Vermillion that summer and later changed their name to the "Spotted Tails." An estimated 2,500 people gathered on July 4 in Vermillion as the Spotted Tails beat the "Shoo Flys" of Star Prairie, 36–6, in five innings. The first nine of the Young Americans squared off against the Lincoln Clippers at the Independence Day celebration in Lincoln, and the White Caps of Sioux City, Iowa, defeated the "Railroad" club of Cherokee, 76–41, at another July 4 event in the area.

Organizational structure of these clubs was similar to those formed in other parts of the country. The Spotted Tails published a list of the members, elected a slate of officers, adopted a Constitution and By-Laws, and formed committees on Finance and Grounds. At an August meeting of the Spotted Tails club, the following rules were adopted:

1. The first nine shall meet every Saturday at 2PM on the grounds and play a practice game of at least two hours and a half.
2. All members of the Club who cannot furnish a reasonable excuse for absence at all practice games shall be fined $2.50 and expelled for the second offense.

Contests between clubs were called match games as distinct from practice games and were arranged by a representative of the club, usually the president, who issued a written challenge in the local newspaper. This communication included details such as the date, time, and location of the match, along with any specifics about rules and the amount of any wager. The challenged club then issued their response in writing, either agreeing to the terms set forth or suggesting an alternative. Below is the communication between the presidents of the Spotted Tails of Vermillion and the Coyotes of Yankton, printed in the July 7 and July 14, 1870, issues of the *Dakota Republican*. It is not known if a mutually agreeable date was found.

A CHALLENGE YANKTON, July 6, 1870

To Dr. J. G Lewis, President Spotted Tails Base Ball Club: Sir: – The 1st nine of the "Coyote Base Ball Club" to play a match game of Base Ball at Vermillion, or any place that the latter may designate, on the 22d of July, 1870; game to commence at 2 o'clock P.M. The game to be governed by the rules and regulations of the National Base Ball Association.

C. H. Edwards, President
Morris Taylor, Secretary.

Vermillion, July 13, 1870

C. H. Edwards, President, Coyote Base Ball Club, Yankton; Dear Sir:-Individual engagements on the part of the members of the Spotted Tails Base Ball Club, will prevent us playing you on the 22d inst., as proposed; but we will play you a single game any time during the month of September, most convenient to you. Game to be governed by the new Base Ball regulations.

J. G. Lewis, President
E. D. Baker, Secretary.

The Missouri River, the route Lewis and Clark took to explore the area in 1804–06, bisects the Dakota Territory from the southeast to the northwest. The US Army built several forts along the river, stretching from Fort Randall, located on the south side of the river near the present-day South Dakota-Nebraska border, to Fort Buford near the Canadian border. Fort Randall was established in 1856 for the purpose of controlling the Teton Sioux Indians in the area and protecting the settlers moving west on the overland route known as the Oregon Trail.

At Fort Randall, Lieutenant Thomas O'Reilly of the Twenty-second Infantry formed a base ball club at the post in 1870. They played three games against another team formed at the fort, the Trotters of the Fourteenth Infantry. The report of one contest between the teams played on July 9 was the first time a box score appeared in a newspaper in the Dakota Territory.[5] The Trotters held a 29–19 lead after seven innings, but the O'Reilly's rallied for twenty-five runs in the final two innings to take a 44–30 win. The box score was simple and concise in its design. It listed the name of the umpire (along with a comment about his judgment and impartiality) and the names and positions of the players. The only statistics after the players' names were an "O" and an "R" for outs and runs. Then, as today, the two most important elements in determining who wins baseball games were outs and runs.

After his team defeated the Trotters, O'Reilly issued a challenge to the Yankton Coyotes to play a match game at the fort in early August and wagering a new bat and ball. Traveling in carriages and crossing the Missouri River by boat, the Coyotes took two days to traverse the 60 miles west to the fort. The host O'Reilly's believed they had secured a win when they scored 17 runs in their half of the ninth inning, but the Coyotes came back with five runs of their own, winning 49–48 with the deciding run scoring on a muff by

The box score of the July 9, 1870 Trotters–O'Reilly's match, the first known in a Dakota Territory newspaper, Dakota Republican, *July 14, 1870.*

the O'Reilly's right fielder. Betting, which was common among the spectators at games, was said to be "spirited." The newspaper account also noted that wagers were not confined to men, saying, "...even the ladies who were present took such an interest in the game that they promised each other certain articles in the dry goods line if such and such should come to pass."[6]

After a lunch break and rest period in which participants indulged in lemonade and "such," the Coyotes took on the post's other team, the Trotters. The Coyotes, "petered out through overexertion" (or drinking "such") dropped the game to the Trotters, 28–12, in five innings. Holding a club to a dozen runs in five innings was considered a strong pitching performance at the time. Hence, the Trotters' hurler Lieutenant W.H. Bowers, who also umpired the first game and "rendered entire satisfaction by his prompt and fair decisions," was singled out for his ability to pitch the ball with lightning speed. Bowers—also said to catch and bat well—displayed this prowess despite having lost his left arm in battle, presumably during the Civil War.

The Coyotes, along with O'Reilly, Bowers, and other officers of the Twenty-second and Fourteenth Infantries, then retired to the post dining room "decorated with American flags and fitted up in a gay and festive manner" for a grand dinner. The table was reportedly "ladened [sic] with all the solid delicacies of the land, backed up with supplies from eastern and southern markets." After dinner,

Corks began to 'pop' but most singular to relate not one of the contestants were wounded or disabled during the entire action, which was spirited

and lasted until an early hour. The Coyotes were too much fatigued to hold up their side of the game with success, so far as speeching [sic] and singing was concerned, but at drinking lemonade they showed a remarkable capacity and solid judgment.[7]

This last was likely a comment on their ability to hold their liquor. After spending the night, the Coyotes, despite being a trifle tired and sleepy, started for home the next morning "happy and gay."

After a tune-up game in which they defeated the Spotted Tails, 52–20, the Coyotes issued a challenge to another strong team in the vicinity, the White Caps of Sioux City, Iowa. The White Caps accepted, and a home-and-home series was scheduled for mid-October with the first game to be played in Sioux City. On Saturday October 15, the White Caps beat the visiting Coyotes, 35–17, in a game called after eight innings due to darkness. The Sioux City paper said the Coyotes "took their defeat with good right grace"[8] and although the report in the Yankton paper stopped short of making any excuses (the Coyotes were playing without three of their first nine), the reporter did say that a cold, blustering northwest wind "had such an effect on them they never played so poorly since the club was organized."[9]

An unnamed writer in the *Yankton Press* summed up the base ball fever taking place in the region by editorializing the following:

Base Ball in the United States has gained a national celebrity, so much that every city, town, and village in the country has one or more base ball clubs. They have become almost as much of a necessity as newspapers and it is a question of about equal merits. Which is the best advertisement for a town—a first class newspaper, or a first class base ball club? For our part, we are inclined to one is as good as the other and a little better. Sioux City and Yankton, not to be outdone by their sister cities, have what they term, first rate clubs—clubs that have, to use a slang expression "cleaned up" everything in their respective localities and who have long felt a desire to cross bats with each other for the championship of the Northwest.[10]

The White Caps then traveled by stage coach to Yankton the following week to resume their series. Arriving late Thursday night, they stayed at the St. Charles Hotel and were greeted by the proprietor, M.A. Sweetser.[11] He reportedly showed them to their rooms and provided them "something called 'a night cap,' (an article of clothing you will understand)."[12] The teams gathered on the grounds the next morning and again played in a chilly north wind, but the Coyotes "retrieved their lost laurels and covered themselves all over with base ball glory"[13] by squaring the series with a 56–25 win.[14] After the game, the White Caps returned to the St. Charles where Sweetser, "extended hospitalities in the shape of something calculated to warm our chilled blood and raise our depressed spirits."[15]

That night, the Coyotes staged a ball at the Stone (School) Hall in honor of their guests (and their ladies) and even invited their rivals, the Spotted Tails, to come over from Vermillion for the event. The citizens of Yankton raised $300 to ensure the Coyotes could properly entertain their guests. The *Yankton Press and Dakotan* said of the event,

> The Hall was beautifully decorated with flags and at the east end of the Hall, over the stage, were the words WELCOME WHITE CAPS AND SPOTTED TAILS in large letters… the music was splendid, and lovers of the dance very numerous. Over 50 persons were on the floor every set. It was, without an exception, the grandest and most festive occasion ever held in Yankton.[16]

The *Yankton Press* noted, "The members of the visiting clubs were as gentlemanly and social a body of men it has ever been our good fortune to meet, and we hope the day is not distant when they will be called again to come this way."[17]

Daylight peeped through the windows before the festivities were over, but at some point during the evening it was decided to gather at the grounds at 10AM the next morning for a third and deciding game of the series. The wind was blowing again, and because of the way the grounds were laid out, the wind blew in the face of the pitcher and favored the batters. This yielded predictable results. The White Caps scored twenty-three first inning runs, but the Coyotes battled back and eventually won the six-hour marathon, 99–77. As was customary, they were awarded the championship ball and declared themselves the champion base ball team of the Northwest.[18] The White Caps were gracious in defeat saying of their opponents, "…they deserve it for a more gentlemanly, entertaining, and courteous set of boys we have never met than the Coyotes of Yankton."[19]

Members of the champion Coyotes came from all walks of life. Outfielder William Gould was a riverboat pilot; third baseman Thomas Duff operated a meat market; and first baseman Al Wood ran a jewelry store in Yankton. Arthur Linn, who was the starting pitcher in the second game of the Sioux City series, was a newspaperman. He had arrived in Yankton that spring from Iowa, took charge of the editorial department of the *Yankton Press and Dakotaian*, and eventually bought controlling interest in the paper. Nothing is known about Linn's background in base ball, but he was described as "…an intelligent, honest, and upright man, and a true Republican."[20] The Coyotes' most talented player may have been teenage outfielder Charlie Delamater, was often singled out in game stories for his wonderful ability as a "fly catcher." He died less than three years later, at age 19, of consumption.

The Spotted Tails organized again in April 1871, but later in the summer changed their name to the Red Caps. In June, a second base ball club that had been started in Vermillion, the "Early Risers," challenged the Red Caps to a match game on the Fourth of July. The challenge was accepted and the game, "witnessed by a very large concourse of both ladies and gentlemen," was won by the more experienced Red Caps, 52–16.

Interestingly, the Vermillion paper listed base ball as one of the many vices encroaching on an otherwise civilized society:

> Dakota has improved vastly in advancing and ennobling influences during the last year or two. Now it is well known that certain institutions are invariably concomitants of highly civilized and cultivated communities, and they never go beyond them, and that where society is nearest its highest perfection, there do they most abound. We speak of gambling houses, brothels, base ball, horse racing, billiard matches, seduction, divorces, prize fights, murders, and similar institutions.[21]

The Red Caps challenged the Reserves of Minnehaha to a game in Sioux Falls later in 1871 and the journey, described in great detail in the *Dakota Republican*, provided an example of hardships encountered during overland travel at the time. The "jolly crew" set off from Vermillion early on Monday, August 7, in two wagons, their singing attracting the attention of passersby looking for their homesteads. After a break at 3PM to eat dinner and rest the horses, the party set off again and estimated they had covered about 30 miles before stopping for the night around 10PM. They spread blankets, bison robes, and coats on the prairie grass, but swarming mosquitoes made it impossible for anyone to sleep. They set off again a couple of hours later, reached the small town of Canton around sunrise and, after stopping for breakfast, pushed on the final fifteen miles to Sioux Falls, arriving at 3:00 the next afternoon.[22]

Following a good night's rest at the Hotel de Sioux Falls, the group went to the grounds that afternoon where the Reserves edged the Red Caps, 37–36. The Red Caps then challenged the Reserves to a match at their grounds in Vermillion for September 28. The Red Caps turned the tables, defeating the Reserves, 71–35, and afterward, the Red Caps offered to play the Reserves the next day, and "victory again perched upon the banners of the Red Caps," again winning, 61–33. The Dakota Republican wrote, "The best of feeling existed between the clubs during both entire games, and they parted on as excellent terms as they met."[23]

Having beaten the Sioux Falls club two of three games and "every other club they have played in a match game," the Red Caps laid claim to the championship of the Northwest. The Coyotes of Yankton, the previous year's champion, also claimed to have gone undefeated, including wins over the Red Caps. The Vermillion paper acknowledged as much, but argued because those Yankton wins were when the team was still called the "Spotted Tails" early in the season, technically, the Coyotes had not defeated the Red Caps. Further, the Red Caps claimed that every time they challenged the Coyotes to a match game, they failed to accept, which, to their minds, counted as a win for them and a loss for the Coyotes.[24]

Over the next three years the Yankton Coyotes, the Vermillion Red Caps, and a number of other clubs continued to operate, but the respective cities' newspapers provided little coverage of the teams. Clubs in the area came up with some colorful nicknames. Two nines, presumably soldiers, named the "Dirty Stockings" and the "Government Socks," played a match at Fort Sully (near present-day Aberdeen, South Dakota) in 1870. Over the next couple of years a second club, the "Black Hillers," formed in Yankton and the Clay County "Plow Boys," the "Sleepies" of Maple Grove, and the "Hole in the Stockings" of Lincoln Center had match games. A few years later, in another matchup between military nines, the "Hard Scrables" [sic] defeated the "Never Sweats," 43–22.[25]

By the mid-1870s, both members of base ball clubs in the Dakota Territory and their fans became more knowledgeable about the game. The Yankton Press and Dakotaian printed scores of games of the National League, a professional major league formed in 1876 among cities in the eastern United States. The scores

of these games were much lower than local games where teams routinely scored forty or fifty runs, so they began to equate low scores with better, more skilled play. The result of a Yankton game in 1873 was reported as a ratio, saying the score was 3–1 when actually it was 45–15. The relatively low score in a 17–2 win by Yankton over the Black Hillers prompted the game report to comment, "…the play of both clubs was very good, as the small score will show."[26] The summary went on to emphasize that Yankton only committed six errors in the contest.

> A couple of steamboat rooters got into a dispute this morning over the relative merits of the Yankton and Vermillion base ball clubs, and supplemented the argument with a rough and tumble fight, in which hands, feet, teeth, and stones were used, and a considerable amount of blood spilled.
>
> —Yankton Press and Dakotaian
> July 3, 1875

In July 1875, the Yankton Press and Dakotaian caught wind of an item in the Sioux City Journal stating that the Sioux City club had "frightened all base ball nines [including, it was implied, the home town Yanktons] by their play." That report called for a response from Yankton, who dared Sioux City to issue a challenge. Sioux City promptly did and Yankton immediately accepted. Plans were made for three games, the first of which was to be played at Yankton on July 22. The Yankton Base Ball club quickly put together a social party to host the Sioux City club when they arrived, and took the unusual step of selling $1 tickets to defray expenses.

The visitors arrived by freight train on the day of the game and immediately went to the Douglas Avenue grounds, the home field of the other club in Yankton, the Black Hillers. "A large and fashionable attendance, a large proportion of which were ladies…"[27] saw Yankton beat Sioux City, 29–17. Although the Yankton Press was complimentary of their opponent's skill and gentlemanly behavior, they did comment that the score was as close as it was only because the Sioux City club was a picked nine, made up of the best players in the city. Two weeks later Sioux City called off a return game claiming their grounds were in poor condition due to the presence of weeds. The Yankton paper pointed out that this state of disarray contradicted an earlier statement in the Journal which said, "Our ball tossers [Sioux City] claim to have the best grounds west of Boston. They are located near the foundry. The runs between the bases have all been leveled by the removal of sod."[28]

The two teams were again scheduled to meet in early September at a base ball tournament held during the Vermillion Harvest Festival.[29] Rain fell the morning of the game and, according to one member of the Sioux City club, when they arrived at the grounds they found them "...in fair condition without a particle of water standing thereon." The Yankton club's assessment was different, saying that the grounds were "covered with two inches of water" and they convinced the festival committee to postpone the game until the next day. Sioux City could not stay in Vermillion another day, so Yankton played and beat Springfield, another team entered in the tournament, 23–5, to take home the $75 first prize.

The goodwill and friendship that had existed between the two clubs a few years earlier was now strained by the incident in Vermillion. According to the Sioux City players, the "lack of pluck" in the Yankton club caused the failure to play the game. Yankton

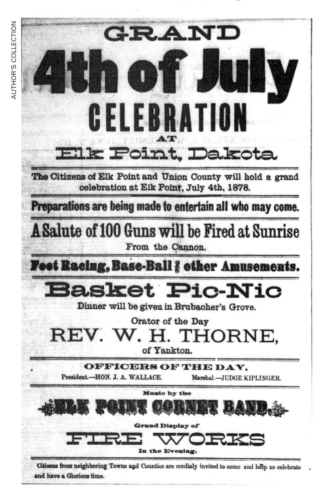

Base ball was one of the events at early July 4 celebrations in the Dakota Territory, Union County (D. T.) Courier, June 26, 1878.

countered that Sioux City failed to pay their entry fee for the tournament and "came up here almost unannounced and stood around in the rain all day." They went on to say that Sioux City's refusal to play was a pretext to "get out of their contract and sneak away to their homes." The Dakotaian added, "They [the Sioux City club] are about as contrary and unreasonable a set as the other Sioux on the reservation."[30]

Despite the hard feelings, the teams made one more effort to play again when Yankton challenged Sioux City to a match game to be played at Vermillion in early October, and upped the ante by suggesting they play for any amount from $100 to $500 a side, provided the clubs play with the same nine men they entered at the tournament. Sioux City was not willing to accept those terms because it was rumored that they had brought in a professional pitcher from the east.[31] In their detailed response, Sioux City essentially said that the original agreement was for a three game series with the first game held in Yankton, the second in Sioux City, and the third, if necessary, at a neutral site in Vermillion. Their denial went on to say that if Yankton wanted to come to Sioux City, they would gladly play them, but they had no intention of going back to Vermillion after what had happed there during the Harvest Festival tournament. No record could be found of any more games between Yankton and Sioux City that year, nor in any subsequent seasons in the decade.

Earlier that summer, in June of 1875, three companies of the Seventh Cavalry were sent to Fort Randall "to be actively employed guarding the entrance routes to the gold fields," while the remaining six companies stayed back at Fort Abraham Lincoln. Two base ball clubs, the McDougals and the Benteens, were among the members of the Seventh Cavalry, sent to Fort Randall.[32] According to one report, while there, each played a game against the post team, the Randalls.[33] The report also implied that these were the first games between teams of the two army forts.[34] The Benteens returned to Fort Randall again in September and easily beat a picked nine of the Seventh Cavalry 39–6. The writer, Theodore Ewert (who signed his article T.O.D.), remarked, "...neither club played up to their high standards owing to the high wind."[35] A few days later the Benteens dropped a game, umpired by Ewert, to a picked nine at Fort Randall, 12–9, but Ewert said, "It is hoped that these two nines will meet again soon as a large amount of money will probably change hands at such an event."[36]

Later that summer the Randalls changed their name to the Lugenbeels, in honor of Pinkney Lugenbeel, commander at the post. After racking up a series of wins against area rural nines, and after the Yankton–Sioux City series fell through, the Lugenbeels challenged Yankton to a game to decide the championship of the Northwest. The soldiers had to schedule games around their military duties, so when they informed Yankton of available dates, Yankton told them they had planned a tour through Sioux City, Omaha, and Council Bluffs during the proposed dates, so they would be unavailable. It was later learned that Yankton had no such tour scheduled, which resulted in accusations they were ducking the Lugenbeels. They finally agreed to a match game October 28, 1875, but there is no record of the game having taken place.

"A base ball game played yesterday at the foot of Third Street between two steamboat nines—the "Galoots" of the C.K. Peck and the "Lunch Grabbers" of the Nellie Peck. James Spargo was scorer. The result of five innings gave the "Galoots" 37 and the "Lunch Grabbers" 11."

Yankton Press and Dakotaian
August 25, 1877

The Yanktons and Red Caps of Vermillion continued to field teams over the next few years. The Coyotes noted that they had secured the services of some eastern players that would make the strongest nine they had ever had, but no record could be found of the two clubs facing each other. By the end of the decade, the Lugenbeels of Fort Randall emerged as the top nine in the region with their main rival being Springfield, another small community on the Missouri River. They faced off on July 4, 1879, in Springfield with the Lugenbeels scoring nine runs in the seventh inning and four more in the eighth to take a 20–13 victory. On the trip back to the fort, the wagon carrying the Lugenbeel players overturned and right-fielder Harris sustained a broken leg. Upon arriving at the post hospital, the army surgeon amputated the leg, but Harris died the next day.

Throughout the decade of the 1870s, box scores gradually added more details. The summary of an early Yankton–Sioux City match included the names of fielders participating in double plays and a count of the number of "fly catches" for each fielder, possibly an indication of the difficulty and rarity of those events in early base ball. The box score for the Lugenbeel–Springfield match described above added an inning-by-inning line score, and the names of the players making first base hits and second base hits. In addition to "R" and "O" (runs and outs) tallies for each player, a

A box score from the Lugenbeel–Springfield game July 4, 1879, including the ill-fated Harris, batting third for the Lugenbeels, Yankton Press and Dakotaian, *July 17, 1879.*

"B" (presumably for bases), and an "A" and "E" (assists and errors) were added. Springfield was charged with twenty errors in the game while the winning Lugenbeel squad only committed seventeen.

The Lugenbeels next defeated a club from Niobrara (across the Missouri River in Nebraska), 29–18, and then won a return match in Niobrara a few weeks later. In addition to the usual compliments about hospitality and goodwill that accompanied game stories, the reporter felt the need to add that if the two clubs met again, "…your [Niobara's] windy pitcher should practice and be able to deliver the ball from below the hip and from the shoulder,"—implying that he had used an illegal overhand delivery. Nonetheless, the *Yankton Press and Dakotaian* said of the Lugenbeels, "In the base ball line, they are the best in Dakota."

A devastating Missouri River flood in the spring of 1881 wiped out much of the cities of Vermillion and Yankton, and consequently little base ball was played over the next couple of years. However, the game had gained a foothold, and as new settlements sprang up with the expansion of the railroad, scores of communities in the Dakota Territory boasted base ball teams by the mid-1880s. By then, base ball was well established in the mining camps in the Black Hills of present-day South Dakota. The ball club from Aberdeen traveled all the way to St. Paul, Minnesota, for a game in 1883, and the 1887 Watertown "Invincibles," who were said to employ five outside players, considered themselves the undisputed champions of the Dakota Territory.

Although the population has always been too small to support professional baseball except in the lower rungs of the minor leagues, since its origins in the 1870s, semipro and amateur baseball has been played with as much interest and enthusiasm in North and South Dakota as anywhere in the country. ∎

Notes

1. Terry Bohn, "Many Exciting Chases After the Ball: Nineteenth Century Base Ball in Bismarck, Dakota Territory, *Baseball Research Journal*, Society for American Baseball Research (SABR), Volume 43, Issue 1.
2. See Tim Wolter, "Boots and Saddles: Baseball with Custer's Seventh Cavalry," *The National Pastime*, Society for American Baseball Research (SABR), Number 18, 1998, Larry Bowman, "Soldiers at Play: Baseball on the American Frontier," *Nine: A Journal of Baseball History and Culture*, Volume 9, University of Nebraska Press, January, 2000, and John M. Carroll and Dr. Lawrence A. Frost, *Private Theodore Ewert's Diary of the Black Hills Expedition of 1874*, CRI Books, Piscataway, NJ, 1976.
3. https://www.baseball-reference.com/bullpen/1869_Cincinnati_Red_Stockings
4. "B B Club," Yankton (D. T.) *Press and Dakotaian*, March 10, 1970.
5. "The Boys in Blue and the National Game," *Dakota Republican*, Vermillion, D. T., July 14, 1870.
6. "Base Ball," Yankton (D. T.) *Press and Dakotaian*, October 19, 1870.
7. "Base Ball at Fort Randall, the Games and the Result," *Yankton* (D. T.) *Press and Dakotaian*, August 11, 1970.
8. "Base Ball," *Sioux City* (IA) *Journal*, October 16, 1870.
9. "Base Ball," Yankton (D. T.) *Press and Dakotaian*, October 19, 1870.
10. "Base Ball—Sioux City vs. Yankton—The Latter Victorious," *Yankton* (D. T) *Press and Dakotaian*, November 2, 1870.
11. Sweetser was often selected to umpire local games. One report (*Yankton Press and Dakotan*, September 7, 1870) indicated that he was an old base ballist, having been an active member of the Olympics of Washington, DC for two or three years. No other documentation could be found to substantiate that claim.
12. "The 'White Caps' at Yankton, Base Ball Championship!, The Coyotes Hold the Championship of the North-West!!!, The White Caps Defeated," *Dakota Republican*, Vermillion, D. T., October 27, 1870.
13. "Base Ball," Yankton (D. T.) *Press and Dakotaian*, October 26, 1870.
14. *Yankton* (D. T.) *Press and Dakotaian* of October 27, 1870, had the score 56–23.
15. "The 'White Caps' at Yankton," *Dakota Republican*, Vermillion, D. T., October 27, 1870.
16. "The 'White Caps' at Yankton," *Dakota Republican*, Vermillion, D. T., October 27, 1870.
17. "The 'White Caps' at Yankton," *Dakota Republican*, Vermillion, D. T., October 27, 1870.
18. Usually, just one ball was used in match games. The tradition was for the winning team to take possession of the ball.
19. "Base Ball—Sioux City vs. Yankton—The Latter Victorious," *Yankton* (D. T.) *Press and Dakotaian*, November 2, 1870.
20. *Yankton* (D. T.) *Press and Dakotaian*, April 7, 1870.
21. "Civilization," *Dakota Republican*, Vermillion, D. T., June 15, 1871.
22. "A Trip to Sioux Falls," *Dakota Republican*, Vermillion, D. T., August 17, 1871.
23. "Base Ball," *Dakota Republican*, Vermillion, D. T., October 5, 1871.
24. *Dakota Republican*, Vermillion, D. T., October 19, 1871.
25. *Yankton* (D. T.) *Press and Dakotaian*, July 10, 1879.
26. "For the Championship," *Yankton* (D. T.) *Press and Dakotaian*, July 16, 1875.
27. "29 to 17, But Unfortunately the Large Figures Adorn the Yankton's Club Score, The Uncertainty of Base Ball as Exemplified at Yankton Yesterday", *Sioux City* (IA) *Journal*, July 23, 1875.
28. "Base Ball Grounds," *Yankton* (D. T) *Press and Dakotaian*, July 31, 1875.
29. Early harvest festivals, like the one held in Vermillion, would eventually evolve into county fairs.
30. "NOW STOP YOUR TALK, Or Come Forward and Cover the Little Sum Dedicated to the S. C. B. B. Club," *Yankton* (D. T) *Press and Dakotaian*, October 4, 1875.
31. *Yankton* (D. T.) *Press and Dakotaian*, October 10, 1875.
32. Army teams were usually named after the captain, or the highest ranking officer on the team.
33. The author of the article signed it T. O. DORE, no doubt Theodore Ewert.
34. "From Randall, Custer's Cavalry to Do Police Duty Instead of Searching for More Hidden Treasure—Base Ball Notes," *Yankton* (D. T.) *Press and Dakotaian*, June 7, 1875.
35. *Yankton* (D. T) *Press and Dakotaian*, September 6, 1875.
36. "For Randall, A Good Game of Base Ball," *Yankton* (D. T.) *Press and Dakotaian*, September 10, 1875.

First Base Among Equals

Prime Ministers and Canada's National Game

Stephen Dame

It could be argued that the most famous sentence ever written by a Canadian author is W.P. Kinsella's, "If you build it, he will come." That ghostly utterance may only be matched by Christina McCall's and Stephen Clarkson's equally phantomic line about Pierre Trudeau: "he haunts us still." Being interested in both political and baseball history, I find myself exploring the relationship between Canada's first ministers and our first *national game*. That's right: from our earliest days—until cheap and reliable indoor refrigeration changed how we ate and played sports—baseball was referred to as Canada's national game.

Canada's baseball historian Bill Humber has made this point repeatedly in print and various public presentations.[1] *The Globe* called baseball our national game during the summer of 1891.[2] University of Windsor Professor Craig Greenham wrote that during the period before the First World War, "baseball was the game of import in Canada—not the British game of cricket nor the Native Canadian game of Lacrosse."[3] A baseball-playing soldier in the First World War explained in a trench newsletter that he was thrilled to be "playing the national game behind the lines in France." Baseball, our original national game, has been an everyday part of outdoor life in Canada since at least the 1830s and probably long before. So, it makes perfect sense that the people running for Canada's highest office have tossed ceremonial pitches, crashed Little League championships, and been depicted both striking out and going deep in a century's worth of editorial cartoons. The story of baseball and Canadian prime ministers is rich with adventure and anecdote.

We should start at the beginning. The origins of baseball are, of course, misty and indistinct. Starting at the beginning of Canadian prime ministers is a clearer course. Baseball, though ubiquitous in Confederation-era Canada, was not loved by all. Shortly after John Alexander Macdonald became Canada's first prime minister in 1867, the *Ottawa Journal* looked down its nose at the game. "Baseball is not played in centres of civilisation and art," the paper opined, "but in remote Ontario towns, it is still played. With the opening up of colonization roads, it is supposed the people of those parts will become more civilized and gradually be divorced from their rude pastimes."[4] It was probably best not to mention divorce around Canada's fourth PM, John Thompson. As a converted Catholic, he was quite devout and madly in love with his progressive and vigorous wife, Annie. When the couple decided to vacation in Ontario's Muskoka region during the summer of 1894, Thompson became the first Prime Minister to witness a baseball game while in office. Two teams of sportsmen representing Barrie and Orillia played games of lacrosse and baseball as part of the annual Bracebridge Picnic.[5] The Thompsons watched the lacrosse game in full, but left the baseball game early, one presumes, to beat the traffic.[6]

In October 1899, Prime Minister Wilfrid Laurier traveled via rail to the Windy City as US President McKinley's guest of honor. Laurier was feted in the streets during a city-wide parade. The *Chicago Tribune* noted "the fact that Sir Wilfird's carriage, like that of President McKinley's, was drawn by four horses, while each of the others had but two, was notice to the crowds that he was someone of special prominence."[7] The parade concluded at the West Side Park grandstand. The Chicago Orphans played a doubleheader that day. "Sir Wilfrid Laurier, to quote from the baseball reporter, made an excellent impression upon the grandstand, and was compelled frequently to doff his hat."[8]

Laurier later made history as the first prime minister to throw a ceremonial first pitch. Travelling to Red Deer, Alberta, as part of a pre-election tour of the west, Sir Wilfrid was invited to toss the ball before a game between Red Deer and Alix on August 12, 1910. "I thank God that I am in perfect health," he said from the mound. "I don't know that I have ever felt better in my life."[9] He may have felt better blowing a heater past an unsuspecting batter the following summer. While touring Nova Scotia during the 1911 election campaign, Laurier arrived at Stellerton. Baseball clubs there were engaged in "a life and death struggle for the baseball championship of Pictou County"[10] when

Laurier and his finance minister William Fielding arrived at the diamond. The ballplayers urged Laurier to throw a pitch. "With a hearty laugh, the PM consented, thereby rendering eighteen men supremely happy."[11] Laurier asked Fielding to be his catcher, and had a batter dig into the box. "Sir Wilfrid knew where to stand too, having pitched a ball at one of the games in the west on his trip out there. Laurier didn't wind up and his pitch looked curiously easy. Even still, the batter missed it by five feet."[12] Thus Wilfrid Laurier retired from organized baseball with his balls to strikes percentage sitting firmly at 100% strikes.

Prime Minister Robert Borden, elected in 1911, watched Canadian soldiers play baseball in France during the First World War. When he witnessed the Canadian Corps championship in a specially constructed stadium packed with 70,000 army enthusiasts, he told the *Toronto Globe* that it was "the greatest day of his life."[13] Back home, he and Laurier put aside their political differences when they sat together on Parliament Hill and watched the annual Parliamentary Press Gallery vs. Members of Parliament softball game. Author Allan Levine explained that "after only three innings the journalists were losing 33 to 7 and the game was called for cocktails."[14]

William Lyon Mackenzie King, prime minister for more than two decades, often used baseball as a drawing card for his political rallies and picnics.[15] In 1925, nearing the end of his first term, he spoke at a "mammoth picnic" between games of baseball being played at Richmond Hill, Ontario. He even used the opportunity to announce the date of the next federal election.[16] In 1926, amid rumors of a Canadian entry into the senior circuit (just 43 years premature), Prime Minister King was invited to address the National League Golden Jubilee Dinner.

One year after he took office, Prime Minister John Diefenbaker took part in the 1958 Parliamentary Security Service vs. Members of Parliament game on The Hill. The Chief played catcher while Governor General Roland Michener pitched. The executive battery prepared for the debut of a fearsome batter from Toronto, the Leader of the Opposition, Lester Pearson. Pearson was a ringer, having played semi-pro baseball in Guelph before moving on to more mundane pursuits such as winning the Nobel Peace Prize. His Excellency tossed a ball so far outside the strike zone that Diefenbaker could not corral it. But Pearson swung like a screen door and missed by a country kilometre. Dief howled with laughter, while Lester B demanded the Vice Regal throw him another, more hittable, pitch. Michener obliged and Pearson smacked the ball well

out into the Parliamentary lawn. The game itself, won 13-5 by the M.P.s, was more of a farcical than hard-fought affair. The *Ottawa Citizen* described the scene thus: "[T]he security staffers, most viewers agreed, had six men on the bases when M.P. Warner Jorgenson caught an infield fly while resting flat on his back. The six or so runners scampered in all directions, the M.P.'s peppered the ball from base to base to base and umpire M.P. Murdo Martin shut his eyes in horror. There were cries of 'Order, Mr. Speaker!' and several requests for a new federal election."[17]

New elections would be called of course, and in 1963, victory belonged to a ballplayer. No politician ever made baseball a more successful part of their political brand than did former second baseman Lester Pearson, whose escapades are detailed in the article that begins on page 62. He made scheduled and unscheduled campaign stops at Little League games during all of his election tours. When asked about what he felt was his greatest contribution to Canada while serving in the First World War, he answered, "My home run at Bramshott (base) which helped defeat a team of Americans."[18] He stopped his campaign caravan in Kingston, Ontario, when he spotted a group of boys playing a game in the yard at St. Patrick's Catholic School. As reported by the *Toronto Daily Star*, "The Liberal leader showed some of the old diamond ability as he got ahold of a pitch. It proved to be one of the most heart-warming receptions of his election tour. When he turned to leave he was given a burst of applause by the children."[19] In Winnipeg, a reporter noted how Pearson's speeches were peppered with references to his baseball past. "All through his tour so far, Mr. Pearson has been dogged by snide references to his party's record during its 23 years as the government. Mr. Pearson's experience in handling difficult questions at international councils and his youthful experience as a baseball player (to which he frequently refers) stands him well in these instances."[20]

Pierre Trudeau took over from Pearson, becoming prime minister in the spring of 1968. Trudeau's father Charles had been an owner of the Montreal Royals three decades earlier. Pierre's son Justin once explained his father's attachment to the game. "Baseball was his sport and it was really important for him to bring us to games," he told author Jonah Keri. "As a kid, it was one of those things that he had bonded with his dad over. Baseball was all part of family lore for us. So for my father, baseball was really important."[21] Pierre Trudeau took his sons to Exhibition Stadium in Toronto in April of 1978. After the prime minister threw out the first pitch, the Trudeau clan watched the Blue Jays beat the White Sox and then ventured into the Jays clubhouse. Blue Jays manager Roy Hartsfield hid a bottle of beer under his desk. The rest of the team were not so concerned about exposing the children to vice. One of the Jays gifted 6-year-old Justin his very own pack of chewing tobacco.[22] A year later, outside the same stadium, the *Toronto Star* asked departing fans if they had heard of Trudeau's political rival Joe Clark. "No," answered one fan, "does he play for the Blue Jays?"[23] Before his retirement, Pierre Trudeau addressed baseball executives at the Commissioner's luncheon that preceeded the All-Star Game at Montreal's Olympic Stadium. The PM confessed, "it's tough to be a prime minister in a country when you know Gary Carter could be elected tomorrow. There are 24 million people in Canada. Most of them are Expo fans, the rest go around lighting candles for the Blue Jays.[24]

By the time those Blue Jays' prayers were answered, Brian Mulroney was prime minister, having won the job in 1984. He and US President George H.W. Bush had jointly thrown the ceremonial first pitch to open the Blue Jays 1990 season.[25] They again appeared together at the 1991 All-Star Game in Toronto. The two events were known as the Hot Dog and All-Star Summits, respectively.[26] Mulroney invited the 1992 Blue Jays to Ottawa after their World Series triumph that year. Grant Fuhr, the celebrated Edmonton Oilers goaltender, told the *Globe and Mail* that he and his championship teammates felt slighted. They had never been invited anywhere, he declared. In fact, his only interaction with Mulroney's government came when Revenue Canada sent him an assessment on one of his taxable benefits: a Stanley Cup ring.[27]

Kim Campbell, Canada's first female prime minister, scheduled a brief stop at Heather Park Field in Prince George, British Columbia, during her 1993 election campaign. It was to be a twenty minute photo opportunity. Instead she spent more than two hours amongst the 14- and 15-year-old ballplayers and their families. Campbell played catch, watched the finals of the Babe Ruth Provincial championships, and basked in the positive energy and media coverage during what was one of her best days of an otherwise ill-fated campaign.[28] When Campbell lost the election to Jean Chrétien just two days after Joe Carter walked-off the 1993 World Series, editorial cartoonist Bruce Mackinnon of the *Halifax Chronicle-Herald* could not resist conflating the current events. He sketched an image of Campbell, a beleaguered pitcher on the mound, wearing Mitch Williams's "wild thing" jersey, watching the electoral ball go over the fence.

Jean Chrétien played baseball in his youth and even credited the game with advancing his political career. Chrétien told TVO in 2013: "In those days we had an annual softball game between the M.P.s and the press gallery. I pitched for the M.P.s team. Pearson was the manager. We won the game, and that was the day I earned my seat in the cabinet."[29] Chrétien also recounted a fantastic baseball story in his most recent memoir. While visiting a remote fishing village on Nova Scotia's Cape Breton Island, attention turned from politics to baseball:

> While we were eating, a television station was broadcasting a World Series baseball game (Orioles/Reds), and everyone had an eye on it. Suddenly a torrential rain poured down on the village, and the power went out. The game was being hotly contested, and the sports fans were very disappointed. Someone came up with a battery-operated radio and tuned in a station to catch the rest of the game. But the only station he found was describing the game in French from Iles de la Madeleine. And so I instantly became a sports commentator, as I was the only francophone in the room who could understand and describe in English what was going on in the World Series.[30]

Chrétien later discussed double plays and player salaries with US Presidents Bill Clinton and George W. Bush. Later in his term, when policy differences such as softwood lumber trading or the war in Iraq arose, Chrétien considered his "personal relations with George W. Bush to be very cordial."[31] Chrétien wrote, "I was the only person of all the G8 leaders who could talk baseball with him."[32]

Chrétien retired in December 2003 and was succeeded by Paul Martin, a shipping magnate and son of a cabinet minister, who grew up playing ball in Windsor, Ontario. Martin played baseball internationally before he played politics on the world stage. As is still the case with teams today, his Windsor-based squad of young ballplayers would routinely cross the border to play teams in Detroit, Michigan. Long after he'd left office, when President Donald Trump stated that the undefended Canadian border was dangerous, Martin joked on the CBC that he didn't realize he and his border-crossing teammates had been such security threats.[33] While he was prime minister, Martin made a habit of inviting the Canadian-based teams competing in the Little League World Series to a Parliamentary reception on The Hill each year. The East Nepean Eagles were fêted in 2004 with a grand reception in the large Commonwealth Room in the Centre Block of Parliament.[34]

A hockey man occupied the prime minister's office in 2006. Stephen Harper spoke often of Canada's other game, and even wrote a book on the subject. During the spring 2011 election, *Toronto Life* magazine decided to rank the candidates for Canada's top job based on their fondest baseball memories. "During election campaigns, it is time honoured tradition for the media to analyze every scrap of data that it gets from party leaders," the magazine wrote. "In honour of the Jays home opener we asked both Prime Minister Stephen Harper and Opposition Leader Michael Ignatieff about their favourite baseball games ever."[35] Harper answered, "when Joe Carter hit his game winning home run off Mitch Williams to win the 1993 World Series for the Blue Jays."[36] A home run of an answer for a politician. Ignatieff grounded softly to the pitcher when he answered the same question with, "I actually watched, on a crackly, black and white TV, Don Larsen pitch his perfect [1956 World Series] game, and Yogi Berra running right up to the mound like that."[37] For baseball nerds, his response was a clarion call, a true fan seeking the top job. Yet, for average Canadians, who already wondered if Ignatieff had spent too much time in, and still too often thought about, the United States, it was a blunder. "Hey, points for originality and for sounding like a flesh-and-blood person," the magazine commented. "The problem is the reference is obscure enough to anyone who isn't a baseball fan that it still sounds like Ignatieff can't help but tell us he's the smartest guy in the room. We get it already."[38] When the Blue Jays were again competitive, Harper was fighting for his political life in the 2015 federal election. The 42nd Canadian federal campaign was the longest in history. It began just days after the non-waiver trade deadline and did not end until the Blue Jays were ready to play in the ALCS. On August 31, Prime Minister Harper made an unofficial campaign stop at Rogers Centre. "Conservative leader Stephen Harper seems like the latest to jump on the Blue Jays bandwagon,"[39] reported the CBC. Harper attended batting practice and was toured around the infield and introduced to players and coaches by Jays legend Roberto Alomar. Harper and his children stayed to watch the Blue Jays vs. Cleveland game.

The Jays, in the midst of a hotly contested playoff race, lost with Harper in attendance. They had done the same when New Democratic Party leader Thomas Mulcair attended a game two weeks earlier. When Liberal leader Justin Trudeau appeared at a game in September and the Jays also lost, scribes began to wonder:

> Since prime minister Stephen Harper dissolved Parliament on August 2 to kick off the longest federal election in modern Canadian history, the Blue Jays have lost just six times in 29 games. If you showed up to a game in the last five or so weeks, you had a nearly 80-per-cent chance of seeing them win. And yet the Jays are 0-3 in games attended by a federal party leader. NDP leader Thomas Mulcair was the first to visit on August 14, watching as the Jays' 11-game win streak was snapped by the New York Yankees. Then on Monday, Harper stopped by to see the Jays fall to Cleveland. On Friday night it was Liberal Leader Justin Trudeau's turn to mess with the team's karma.[40]

When Jose Bautista hit his legendary "bat flip" home run in game five of the American League Division Series, he was sending the Blue Jays to the next level only six days before Canadians decided to elevate Justin Trudeau. The proximity of historical events inspired two separate cartoonists to independently design the same cartoon. Both Michael de Adder and Terry Mosher depicted Trudeau as the triumphant batter, and Harper as the discarded bat.

While being welcomed at a White House State Dinner held in his honor, Prime Minister Trudeau heard US President Barack Obama remark, "Our work as nations remains rooted in the friendship between our peoples, and we see that reflected all along our shared border." The president continued, "At the baseball diamond in Coutts, Alberta, if you hit a home run, there's a good chance the ball will land in Sweetgrass, Montana."[41] In 2017, as part of an official address on the occasion of July 30 being declared Canada Baseball Day, Prime Minister Trudeau reflected on the game that meant so much to his family. "I remember as a kid, my dad taking us to the Big O to watch our beloved Expos. Gary Carter, Tim Raines, Andre Dawson, these were heroes for me. It was an opportunity for me to connect with my dad as well, as he loved baseball. For us it was a big family outing. It was an opportunity to sit back, watch my dad eat hot dogs and mostly enjoy a great summer pastime."[42]

Wilfrid Laurier threw strikes, Mackenzie King promoted games, and Lester Pearson hit home runs. All three, as well as many of their contemporaries, went to baseball games in order to find crowds of voters during election seasons. Contemporary campaigns are no different. A seemingly endless stream of political ads aired during the Canadian broadcasts of the 2019 Major League Baseball playoffs. Conservative leader Andrew Scheer claimed to have "socked a dinger" during the French-language leaders' debate.[43] The game of baseball, as it has from Macdonald to Trudeau, will continue be an enduring facet of Canadian life. In fact, if we could look across the historical span of this paper, we would not see many aspects of life in Canada remaining constant from 1867 to 2020. Yet, as long as there has been a Dominion, strong and free, stretching from sea to sea to sea, and as long as that place has been governed by prime ministers, there has been baseball. May it forever be so. ∎

Notes

1. William Humber, "What Was Early Canadian Hockey and What Does it Owe to Others." *Seneca College.* (2017): 1.
2. "Sport," *The Globe*, August 29, 1891, 5.
3. Craig Greenham, "On The Battlefront: Canadian Soldiers, an Imperial War, and America's National Pastime." *American Review of Canadian Studies*, vol. 42 (2012): 3.
4. "The Baseball Season," *London Advertiser*, May 3, 1887, 5.
5. "Picnic at Bracebridge," *The Globe*, August 10, 1894, 1.
6. "Premier in Muskoka," *Montreal Gazette*, August 1, 1894, 4.
7. "Procession," *The Chicago Tribune*, October 8, 1899, 1.
8. "Sir Wilfrid in Chicago," *The Globe*, October 11, 1899, 12.
9. "Keep Up Standard of Canadian Life," *The Globe*, August 11, 1910, 1.
10. "Tremendous Crowd at New Glasgow Gave Liberal Leader a Fine Reception," *The Toronto Daily Star*, September 1, 1911, 3.
11. "Tremendous Crowd," 3.
12. "Tremendous Crowd," 3.
13. Canadian Press. "Dominion Day At The Front," *The Globe*, July 6, 1918, 7.
14. Allan Levine. *Scrum Wars: The Prime Ministers and the Media.* Toronto: Dundurn Press, 1996.
15. "Liberal Chiefs Draw Big Crowd at The Stadium," *The Globe*, August 16, 1920, 1.
16. "Liberals To Meet At Richmond Hill," *The Globe*, August 22, 1925, 11.
17. Greg Connolley, "Crazy Man, Crazy! What A Game!" *The Ottawa Citizen*, July 24, 1958, 21.
18. Connolley, "Crazy Man, Crazy!" 21.
19. "Pearson Demonstrates Baseball Skill, Thrills Children," *The Toronto Daily Star*, March 29, 1958, 3.
20. William Kinmond, "Transition," *The Globe and Mail*, March 6, 1958, 23.
21. Jonah Keri, "Jonah Keri sitdown with Justin Trudeau," CBS Sports, last modified April 24, 2017, https://www.cbssports.com/mlb/news/ jonah-keri-sitdown-with-justin-trudeau-canadas-prime-minister- talks-sports-immigration-montreal-and-more.
22. Paul Patton, "Triple Play and Two Homers Help Jays Beat Chi-Sox," *The Globe and Mail*, April 24, 1978, S6.
23. Victoria Stevens, "Clark Roasts Trudeau at Tory Barbecue," *The Toronto Star*, June 29, 1978, A3.
24. "Glib PM Regales All-Stars With Humorous Barbs," *The Globe and Mail*, July 14, 1982, S1.
25. Michelle Lalonde, "Security at SkyDome Tight For Bush's Baseball Visit," *The Globe and Mail*, April 9, 1990, A12.
26. Tim Harper, Bruce Campion Smith, "Cheerful Leaders Have All Star Fun," *The Toronto Star*, July 10, 1991, A2.
27. David Shoalts, "Having A Ball At The Public Trough," *The Globe and Mail*, December 18, 1992, C10.
28. Andrea Johnson, "Sign Of The Times," *Prince George Citizen*, July 23, 2014, 1.
29. Steve Paikin. "Fifty Years Ago This Week, Lester Pearson Became Prime Minister." *Television Ontario*, last modified April 10, 2013, https://www.tvo.org/article/fifty-years-ago-this-week-lester- pearson-became-prime-minister-part-i.
30. Jean Chrétien, *My Stories, My Times.* Toronto: Random House, 2018: 181.
31. Chrétien, *My Stories, My Times*, 193.
32. Ryan Remiorz, "Gifts Tell Story of Chrétien's Reign," *The Toronto Star*, April 14, 2012, A19.
33. Power and Politics. "Interview With Paul Martin." June 6, 2018. *Canadian Broadcasting Corporation*.
34. Government of Canada. "Prime minister to meet little league baseball champions." Media Advisory. Last modified, November 2, 2004. https://www.canada.ca/en/news/archive/2004/11/prime-minister- meet-canadian-little-league-baseball-champions.html.
35. John Michael McGrath, "What do Harper, Ignatieff and Layton's favourite baseball moments say about their characters?" *Toronto Life*, April 4, 2011.
36. McGrath, "What do Harper..."
37. McGrath, "What do Harper..."
38. McGrath, "What do Harper..."
39. McGrath, "What do Harper..."
40. Brendan Kennedy, "Blue Jays Drop Ball in Defeat to Orioles," *The Toronto Star*, September 5, 2015, S2.
41. Government of the United States of America. "Remarks by President Obama and Prime Minister Trudeau." *Media Advisory*. Last modified, March 10, 2016. https://ca.usembassy.gov/remarks-by-president- obama-and-prime-minister-trudeau-of-canada-at-arrival-ceremony.
42. Sportsnet. "Message from the prime minister on Canada Baseball Day." *News*. Last modified July 20, 2017. https://www.sportsnet.ca/baseball/mlb/message-prime-minister- canada-baseball-day.
43. Stephen Dame, "The storied links between prime ministers and baseball," *The Kingston Whig Standard*, October 22, 2019, A5.

Addtilonal Sources

Baseball Obscura Blog. Accessed via: medium.com. Available at: https://medium.com/@BaseballObscura/that-time-toronto-almost- joined-thena tionalleague-in-1886-30c4fd46c306.

Borins, Sara, ed. *Trudeau Albums*. Penguin. Toronto, 2000.

Boyko, John. *Cold Fire: Kennedy's Northern Front*. Knopf Canada. Toronto, 2016.

Canadian Broadcasting Corporation. Accessed via cbc.ca. Available at: https://www.cbc.ca.

Calgary Herald. Accessed via newspapers.com. Available at: https://www.newspapers.com.

Chrétien, Jean. *Reflections on my Years as Prime Minister*. January 30, 2008. Accessed via myshx.ca. Available at: https://www2.myshx.ca/polilcal-sci- ence/refleclons-my-years-prime-minister

Cohen, Andrew. *Extraordinary Canadians: Lester B. Pearson*. Penguin. Toronto, 2008.

Columbia Broadcaslng System Sports. Accessed via cbssports.com. Available at: https://www.cbssports.com

Dame, Stephen. *Batted Balls and Bayonets: Baseball and the Canadian Expe- ditionary Force, 1914–1918*. Available at: http://baseballresearch.ca/wp-content/uploads/2018/03/Dame17.pdf.

Diefenbaker, John. *One Canada: Memoirs of The Right Honourable John G. Diefenbaker*.

Lester B. Pearson

Canada's Ballplayer Prime Minister

Stephen Dame

The first real job I had after university was working in politics on Ottawa's Parliament Hill. The job title was "legislative assistant to a Member of Parliament," but really, I was a grunt. I answered the mail, prepared the propaganda, and greeted visitors to the office. The best part of the gig was the location. As a political history nerd, I was thrilled to be working in and around the century-old Centre Block, the massive gothic-revival home to Canada's bicameral legislature. Leading tours of visiting constituents around that space quickly became one of my favorite duties. A certain visit, on each tour I gave, was to the statue of a fellow baseball fan, Prime Minister Lester B. Pearson. Lester B. sits just outside the House of Commons. Unlike his other immortalized contemporaries, Pearson is depicted seated in his office chair.

Tour guide lore states that Lester B. Pearson's statue is placed so that he appears to be watching the softball and baseball games played in front of Centre Block.

His statue is angled ever so slightly to stage left. There he sits, overlooking the vast lawns of Parliament Hill. His monument was constructed this way (according to tour guide lore) so that he could watch over the softball and baseball games played on the greenery in front of Centre Block.

Indeed, that spot hosted more than a century of bat and ball games. Members of the press played Members of Parliament in an annual softball affair there. Teams composed of security staffers, federal police, mail clerks, Parliamentary assistants, and even M.P.s skipping out on votes, have all shuffled around the bases in the shadow of the Peace Tower. Pearson was such a baseball nut that those who honored him thought it appropriate his statue be able to observe these baseball games forever. Today Lester B. patiently waits for a game to break out on the very spot where he himself, both as Leader of the Opposition and later as Prime Minister of Canada, played ball. His middle initial stands for "Bowles," but it may as well have stood for "baseball." No other prime minister in Canadian history so loved the game or made it such a resonant part of his political brand.

The connections between Pearson and Canada's original national game are myriad. Just five pages into Pearson's three volume autobiography, the man himself details an early baseball memory. It is an anecdote in the vein of W.P. Kinsella, wherein grown men link their affection for baseball to the men they loved:

Grandfather Pearson had a particular passion for baseball, a passion inherited by his son, my father, and his grandsons. My last outing with him was on Dominion Day in 1913. He had retired from the ministry; he was frail, aging, and his eyesight had almost gone. The Toronto baseball team, in the old International League, was to play two games, morning and afternoon, on that holiday at the Ball Park at Hanlan's Point, across Toronto Bay. Grandfather was determined to go, and his son, my uncle Harold, with whom he was then living, agreed. I was happy and excited to escort. I remember we had good seats. It was a good game and my grandfather, who could hardly see the players, let alone the ball, enjoyed it as much as I did.[1]

The following year, Pearson was playing second base in Hamilton's City Baseball League while he was working for the municipality. Then, as he put it, his world ended when the world went to war. Pearson enlisted first as a medical orderly with the University of Toronto medical unit. While stationed in Salonika, Greece, he played baseball with his fellow soldiers there. "He was a natural leader, good at baseball," said his roommate William Dafoe.[2] As the war went on, and especially after the arrival of the American troops, baseball became a more and more prominent part of a soldier's daily life. Teams were organized by battalions, military hospitals, groups of officers, and even prisoners of war. Baseball was played regularly by Canadian soldiers at more than 90 known locations throughout Europe.[3] Canadians played on their rest and reserve rotations, sometimes within meters of exploding German shells.[4] Games between Canadian and American troops took on a naturally competitive nature. At soccer stadiums and cricket pitches, thousands of locals and servicepeople paid money to watch military men play baseball.[5] When asked during an interview for an External Affairs position what his greatest contribution to the war had been, Pearson deadpanned, "My home run at Bramshott [base]" which helped defeat a team of Americans.[6]

While on leave in London, Pearson looked the wrong way crossing the street and was hit by a bus. He survived the double-decker hit and run, and as a result may have survived the war. He was invalided home. Healed up by the summer of 1919, Pearson was at a loss in terms of direction. "What then, to do? I was restless, unsettled, and had no answers. But it was early summer and I loved baseball. I went to Guelph, the home of not only my parents, but also of a team in the Inter-County League, a very good semi-professional organization."[7] Pearson knew two players on the team from his days playing ball in Hamilton. He walked into the ballpark and walked onto the team. He was given a job at the Partridge Tire and Rubber Company where he "punched the clock and did odd jobs when not playing baseball."[8] When Pearson determined that his path through baseball would not take him to the majors, he began to study for entry into the foreign service. By 1943, he was working for the Canadian government in Washington, DC. In his memoirs, Pearson wrote of the serious nature of baseball games played between the Canadians and Americans in the US capital:

The baseball games which really mattered—apart from those of the Washington Senators in the American League, which I loved to watch whenever I could—were those between the Canadian Embassy and the State Department. We had a reasonably good team, thanks to a few experts from the Canadian military mission. Our diplomatic worry was that we might prejudice our good relations with the [US] State Department by beating them too easily. At the same time national pride would permit no defeat by the foreigner. So we worked out a unique and ingenious way of handicapping. We placed a jug of martinis and a glass at each base and agreed that whenever a player reached a base, he had to drink a martini. This ensured a record number of men stranded on third base and, if anyone did try to make home plate, he could easily be tagged.[9]

Pearson distinguished himself in the foreign service and at the United Nations. While in New York, he had a "life pass to Ebbet's Field" to watch the Brooklyn Dodgers play ball.[10] In 1957, after leading the peace process to defuse a potential nuclear war over the Suez Canal, he received the Nobel Peace Prize. While breaking the news to the country, *The Globe and Mail* referred to him not as a professor, diplomat, or potential Liberal Leader, but as "a 60-year-old baseball fan."[11] Baseball, from the very beginning, was a large part of Pearson's political identity.

Pearson won the Liberal leadership in January 1958. That spring, he mixed politics with baseball for the first time as Leader of the Opposition. He and Prime Minister John Diefenbaker took part in the Parliamentary Security Service vs. Members of Parliament game on The Hill, as detailed in the preceding article ("First Base Among Equals: Prime Ministers and Canada's National Game" on page 57).

When the election came later in 1958, Pearson barnstormed the country like all politicians, but made a few more stops along the way. His handlers were well aware that his baseball skill could make the bowtie-wearing policy wonk seem more leaderlike. He stopped his campaign caravan in Kingston when he spotted a group of boys playing a game in the yard at St. Patrick's Catholic School. "Once a semi-pro baseball player, the Liberal leader showed some of the old diamond ability as he got ahold of a pitch. It proved to be one of the most heart-warming receptions of his election tour. When he turned to leave he was given a burst of applause by the children."[12]

In Winnipeg, a reporter noted how Pearson's speeches were peppered with references to his baseball past. "All through his tour so far, Mr. Pearson has been dogged by snide references to his party's record during its 23 years as the government. Mr. Pearson's experience in handling difficult questions at international councils and his youthful experience as a baseball player (to which he frequently refers) stands him well in these instances."[13] Pearson lost the election, but it was only his first strike.

The *Toronto Star* ran a photo puzzle game shortly after the election whereby the word "Pearson" appeared as a possible answer below a photo of boys playing baseball.[14] While praising Canada's democracy post-election (turnout was 80%), Robert Turnbull wrote in *The Globe and Mail* that "dictators simply aren't sportsmen," before praising Dwight Eisenhower, Harold MacMillan, and Lester Pearson for their athletic pasts. Incorrectly assuming Lester B was done after his 1958 loss, Turnbull wrote, "Lester Pearson's thrills will now come primarily from watching baseball."[15]

The 1962 campaign saw the continued baseball branding of Lester Pearson. At Barry's Bay, the talk of baseball turned to action on the local diamond. Pearson "missed his first pitch at bat with a Little League baseball team, but blasted the second ball into centre field, over the heads of the 400 district residents, striking the window of a parked car. The window remained in one piece."[16]

One of Pearson's star candidates in 1962 was hockey star Red Kelly. At Coronation Park in Oakville, Ontario, Pearson and Kelly staged a photo-op on the baseball diamond. A stage-managed moment for the cameras occurred when Kelly and Pearson just happened to drop in on the St. Dominic's junior team as they began a practice. "Terry Houghton, 10, pitched three balls, Mr. Pearson hit one fly, which was dropped, bunted once into a crowd of photographers and was caught by the pitcher on the third ball."[17] The campaign stop was a success. A photo of Pearson up to bat, while Kelly played catcher behind him (both men in full suits) was picked up by newspapers across the country. It became clear during the Oakville stop that Pearson would not be able to make it back to Maple Leaf Stadium in time for his scheduled ceremonial first pitch. "I am not throwing out the first ball in Toronto," he said. "But it's not who throws out the first ball, but who hits the last one that really counts."[18] A staffer was asked by a reporter if the op-position leader could afford to miss an appearance before such a crowd. "Mr. Pearson was disappointed. It's not that he minds so much missing the political opportunity," said a Liberal spokesperson, "but he is mad about baseball."[19]

Pearson made yet another stop at a baseball diamond during the '62 campaign, this time in Kingston, Ontario. He pitched to Little Leaguers and again succeeded in getting his picture in the papers—what political types call "earned media" today. When he was asked there about his close relationship with US President John Kennedy, Pearson relayed that he had just returned from Washington where he met the president. The meeting was an undeniable political favor from Kennedy. A reporter then asked if the Canadian election was of any importance to Washington. Pearson replied, "The election is of as much consequence as the fact that the Washington Senators have just suffered their 13th straight loss."[20] The baseball-branded Pearson succeeded in dismantling John Diefenbaker's historic majority in 1962, but did not win enough seats to become prime minister. A year later, another election was called, and 1963 marked the most significant year for baseball and Canadian prime ministers. Baseball would prove to strengthen the relationship between Canada and its largest trading partner, the game factored into an election again, a certifiable baseball nut finally became prime minister and a film of the PM watching a World Series game was deemed too politically damaging to show on television.

The 1963 campaign began, of course, with more baseball messaging from Lester Pearson. On Prince Edward Island he broke out the ballgame metaphors while criticizing Diefenbaker: "Mr. Pearson accused the government of avoiding decisions in an effort to avoid making mistakes. 'I don't like a baseball game with no hits, no runs and no errors.'"[21] Later in the campaign, a *Globe and Mail* endorsement noted Pearson's athletic past: "A man who once played semi-professional baseball, and still retains a lively interest in all competitive sport, doesn't fit the picture of a scholar loaded down with honours, a Nobel Prize winner." The editorial went on to note how Pearson grabbed a handful of snow the previous day, packed it tightly, "reared back and pitched it over the heads of the photographers."[22] The *Toronto Star* endorsement from the '63 campaign did not shy away from portraying Pearson as a baseball man:

Pearson's love of baseball, as a fan long after he ceased to play, is the basis of song and story in the External Affairs department. As head of the department, Mr. Pearson had to make frequent trips to Europe. If these journeys happened to coincide with the World Series, he would somehow manage to arrive at a certain capital in Europe where the Canadian ambassador could always be relied upon to have short wave reception of the games.[23]

All of the baseball ballyhoo finally paid off. Pearson's Liberals won the 1963 election. A few weeks after taking office, Pearson was invited to join President Kennedy at his family's summer estate in Hyannis Port, Cape Cod. The two men, acquainted with each other thanks to a White House dinner held for Nobel Prize winners in 1962, "got along like schoolboys."[24] "The President had been told by the American Ambassador, Walton Butterworth, that baseball was a great hobby of mine," Pearson wrote in his memoirs. "The President may have treated this information sceptically." What followed was a command performance by Pearson. "The White House Press Corps said they'd never seen anything like it," wrote the *Vancouver Sun*. "Pearson talked baseball and radiated confidence and good humour."[25] Pearson himself wrote:

Lester B. Pearson at his desk.

[Kennedy's aide, Dave] Powers was famous for his statistical infallibility on baseball. We discussed batting and earned run averages back and forth with Powers throwing a few curves at me. My answers showed that I knew something about the sport.[26]

One key exchange in particular led Pearson to bring up the name of Mets reliever Ken MacKenzie. Pearson later explained to reporters that his knowledge of seemingly obscure relief pitchers was augmented by the fact that MacKenzie, "was a Canadian who lived in my constituency. Indeed, I had helped to get him into professional baseball."[27] Pearson wasn't sure if the Americans and their President had been impressed by his grasp on North American or International Affairs, but he was certain they were impressed by his knowledge of baseball.[28] Kennedy and Pearson went on to have—although tragically brief—the best camaraderie between any President and prime minister of the twentieth century.

Pearson not only impressed Kennedy and Powers, he thoroughly won over the American media during his visit. The AP thought Pearson had stolen the show.[29] When reporters asked Pearson about his baseball fandom, apparently unaware that he shared a love

of the Red Sox with Kennedy, Pearson quipped about his newfound position of power. "I was in the opposition for a long, long time and I developed a certain sympathy for the underdog," recorded journalist Bill Galt. "Then he flashed a wide grin and added: 'Now I'm a Yankee fan.' The press corps roared with laughter."[30] Canada's ambassador to the United States, Charles Ritchie, thought Pearson's trip south was "tinged with euphoria."[31]

The *Indiana Gazette*, of all papers, ran a small blurb about the Hyannis Port Summit. They may have taken Pearson's baseball joke literally. "Canada's Prime Minister Lester Pearson is, it turns out, quite a baseball fan. He is a fan of the New York Yankees, but the prime minister confided that a generation ago, he liked the Boston Red Sox—Kennedy's favourite."[32] Back in Ottawa, the prime minister was happy to compete in the press gallery vs. M.P.s softball game. Pearson batted leadoff, connecting for "a solid smash," and helped the Members of Parliament defeat the press by a score of 9–7.[33]

Halfway through his term in office, Pearson was asked by *Maclean's Magazine* what he would be doing had politics not panned out, he replied that "his ambition had been to become a major league baseball manager."[34] During this time, the Liberal Party also

ARCHIVES OF CANADA

Talking baseball with US president John F. Kennedy was effective diplomacy for Pearson.

agreed to allow a film crew to document the life of the prime minister. The CBC agreed to air the documentary in prime time. The project was conceived as a way to promote the PM ahead of the next election. Instead it turned into a public relations disaster, with baseball playing a very prominent role. "A shoulder camera and microphone followed the prime minister for days producing some intimate shots of Mr. Pearson's unguarded moments."[35] One of these moments included Pearson intently watching a midday baseball game. The film showed Pearson with his feet up on a chair, eating lunch and watching a World Series game on October 7, 1963. The Yankees were playing the Dodgers. The sounds of the Star Spangled Banner, and later Vin Scully's voice, could be heard echoing through the prime minister's office. When cabinet minister Allan J. MacEachen entered to speak with the PM, Pearson was clearly distracted by the game, even apologizing for such. According to the producer of the film, the CBC broadcast was scuttled by disapproving Liberal staffers, a charge Pearson had to vigorously deny in the House. The national broadcaster stated that the film did not meet its standards for quality.[36] The film didn't air on television until after Pearson had left office.

When it came time to retire, Pearson provided us a link between Canada's baseball prime minister, and *Shoeless Joe*, Canada's baseball book:

When Prime Minister Lester Pearson announced he would retire, one of the first telegrams came from *New York Times* columnist James Reston,

who cabled: 'say it isn't so, Mike.' Pearson met Reston here last night and the writer asked if the Prime Minister had gotten the allusion. Reston said it was the lament of a little boy to Babe Ruth, when the home-run king announced he was hanging up his spikes. Pearson, an old baseball fan, corrected Reston: 'It's what a little boy said to Shoeless Joe Jackson in 1919.'[37]

"Politics isn't always sporting," Pearson said in an exit interview to the *Globe and Mail*. "You know the man who said 'nice guys finish last?'" he asked reporter Dick Beddoes. "Leo Durocher?" responded the scribe. "Yes, Durocher," continued the outgoing PM. "Well two years after that he finished last, and he was gone from the Dodgers."[38]

John McHale, general manager and vice president of the new Montreal team in the National League, was the first to offer Pearson a retirement gift. The *Toronto Star* reported that the former Prime Minister was to be named honorary president of the Montreal Voyagers.[39] While they had the name of the team wrong, they were correct on the position. Amid rumours in 1968 that he would be taking over the World Bank, Lester Pearson was named honorary president of the Montreal Expos instead. He did in fact take a role with the bank later that year, but it was the baseball job which he mentioned to journalist Frank Jones. "As a boy, I wanted to get into big league baseball, and now I'm honourary president of the Montreal baseball club."[40] On April 14, 1969, it was Pearson, before 29,000 fans at Jarry Park, who went to the mound to toss the first ceremonial pitch in Expos history.[41]

Nearer the end of his life, Pearson was still attending baseball games:

The Pearsonian sense of humour would be on display in 1970, after he had an eye removed because of a malignant tumor. Pearson went to a Montreal Expos game and met umpire Al Barlick before the contest. "How are you?" asked the ump. "I'm fine," Pearson replied. "But I've recently had an operation that qualifies me for your business… I had my eye out."[42]

More than fifty years since Pearson left office, Canada is down to one major league club, but sandlots, gravel infields, and beautifully manicured diamonds continue to fill each summer with young ballplayers eager to hit, throw, and catch. On the lawn in front of Centre Block, Frisbee and soccer kick-arounds are more common now, but the occasional game of catch can still be observed. Remaining among us, from sea to sea to sea, are those who share Lester Pearson's passion for the game of baseball. And if, by chance, you ever find yourself in Ottawa, walking across the old baseball grounds known as Parliament Hill, be sure to stop by and tip your cap to the statue of Lester B. Pearson, Canada's ballplayer prime minister. ■

Bibliography

Baseball Obscura Blog. Accessed via: medium.com. https://medium.com/@BaseballObscura/that-time-toronto-almost-joined-the-national-league-in-1886-30c4fd46c306.

Borins, Sara, ed. *Trudeau Albums*. Penguin. Toronto, 2000.

Boyko, John. *Cold Fire: Kennedy's Northern Front*. Knopf Canada. Toronto, 2016.

Canada, Government of. Media Advisory. *Prime Minister to Meet Canadian Little League Champions*. November 2, 2004. Accessed via Canada.ca. https://www.canada.ca/en/news/archive/2004/11/prime-minister-meet-canadian-little-league-baseball-champions.html.

Canadian Broadcasting Corporation. Accessed via cbc.ca. https://www.cbc.ca/.

Calgary Herald. Accessed via newspapers.com. https://www.newspapers.com.

Chicago Tribune. Accessed via newspapers.com. https://www.newspapers.com.

Chrétien, Jean. *Jean Chrétien; My Stories My Times*. Random House. Toronto, 2018.

Chrétien, Jean. *Reflections on my Years as Prime Minister*. January 30, 2008. Accessed via mystfx.ca. Available at: https://www2.mystfx.ca/political-science/reflections-my-years-prime-minister.

Cohen, Andrew. *Extraordinary Canadians: Lester B. Pearson*. Penguin. Toronto, 2008.

Columbia Broadcasting System Sports. Accessed via cbssports.com. https://www.cbssports.com.

Dame, Stephen. *Batted Balls and Bayonets: Baseball and the Canadian Expeditionary Force 1914–1918*. http://baseballresearch.ca/wp-content/uploads/2018/03/Dame17.pdf.

Diefenbaker, John. *One Canada: Memoirs of The Right Honourable John G. Diefenbaker, Volume 1: The Crusading Years*. Macmillan. Toronto, 1975.

Donaldson, Gordon. "Breaking The Mould" in *Maclean's Magazine*. April 6, 1998.

Eastern Morning News. Accessed via newspapers.com. https://www.newspapers.com.

The Evening Standard. Accessed via newspapers.com. https://www.newspapers.com.

Finkel, Alvin and Conrad, Margaret, eds. *History of the Canadian Peoples—1867 to the Present*. Cultural Currents in the Industrial Age. Addison, Wesley, Longman, Toronto, 2002.

Finkel, Alvin and Conrad, Margaret, eds. *History of the Canadian Peoples—1867 to the Present*. Interwar Culture. Addison, Wesley, Longman, Toronto, 2002.

Francis, R. Douglas and Smith, Donald B, eds. *Readings in Canadian History—Post Confederation. Idealized Middle Class Sport For a Young Nation*. Nelson. Calgary, 2002.

The Globe and Mail. Accessed via Toronto Public Library Archive. https://www.torontopubliclibrary.ca/detail.jsp?Entt=RDMEDB0057&R=EDB0057.

Gwyn, Richard. *John A.: The Man Who Made Us. The Life and Time of John A. Macdonald*. Random House. Toronto, 2007.

Indiana Gazette. Accessed via newspapers.com. https://www.newspapers.com.

The Iodine Chronicle. "Play Ball." June 15, 1916.

Levine, Allan. *King: A Life Guided by the Hand of Destiny*. Dundurn Press. Toronto, 2012.

Levine, Allan. *Scrum Wars: The Prime Ministers and the Media*. Dundurn Press. Toronto, 1996.

London Advertiser. Accessed via the British Newspaper Archive. https://www.britishnewspaperarchive.co.uk.

Long Branch Daily Record. Accessed via newspapers.com. https://www.newspapers.com.

Martin, Lawrence. *Chrétien*. Lester Publishing. Toronto, 1995.

Martin, Paul. Quoted on "Power and Politics" on the Canadian Broadcasting Corp. June 6, 2018.

Montreal Gazette. Accessed via newspapers.com. https://www.newspapers.com.

New York Tribune. Accessed via newspapers.com. https://www.newspapers.com.

Ottawa Citizen. Accessed via newspapers.com. https://www.newspapers.com.

Ottawa Journal. Accessed via newspapers.com. https://www.newspapers.com.

Paikin, Steve. "Fifty Years Ago This Week, Lester Pearson Became Prime Minister." April 10, 2013. Accessed via tvo.org. https://www.tvo.org/article/fifty-years-ago-this-week-lester-pearson-became-prime-minister-part-i.

Pearson, Lester B. *Mike: The Memoirs of the Rt. Hon. Lester B. Pearson, Volume One 1897–1948*. University of Toronto Press. Toronto, 1973.

Pearson, Lester B. *Mike: The Memoirs of the Rt. Hon. Lester B. Pearson, Volume Three 1957–1968*. University of Toronto Press. Toronto, 1973.

Prince George Citizen. Accessed via newspapers.com. https://www.newspapers.com.

Province of Canada. Accessed via provinceofcanada.com. https://provinceofcanada.com.

Sportsnet. Accessed via sportsnet.ca. https://www.sportsnet.ca.

Stewart, J.D.M. *Being Prime Minister*. Dundurn Press. Toronto, 2018.

Toronto Life Magazine. Accessed via torontolife.com. https://torontolife.com/city/toronto-politics/harper-ignatieff-baseball-moments.

Toronto Star. Accessed via Toronto Public Library Archive. https://www.torontopubliclibrary.ca/detail.jsp?Entt=RDMEDB0111&R=EDB0111.

Total Pro Sports. Accessed via totalprosports.com. https://www.totalprsembassy.gov. https://ca.usembassy.gov/remarks-by-president-obama-and-prime-minister-trudeau-of-canada-at-arrival-ceremony.

Vancouver Sun. Accessed via newspapers.com. https://www.newspapers.com.

The Windsor Star. Accessed via newspapers.com. Available at: https://www.newspapers.com.

Notes

1. Lester B. Pearson, *Memoirs of the Right Honourable Lester Pearson. Vol 1*. Toronto: University of Toronto Press, 1972: 5.
2. Peter C. Newman, "Pearson: A Good Man In a Wicked Time," *Toronto Daily Star*, December 16, 1967, B7.
3. Stephen Dame, "Batted Balls and Bayonets: Baseball and the Canadian Expeditionary Force 1914–1918." Centre for Canadian Baseball Research. Last modified November, 2017. http://baseballresearch.ca/wp-content/uploads/2018/03/Dame17.pdf.
4. Dame, "Batted Balls and Bayonets."
5. Dame, "Batted Balls and Bayonets."
6. Dame, "Batted Balls and Bayonets."
7. Lester B. Pearson, *Memoirs of the Right Honourable Lester Pearson. Vol 1*. Toronto: University of Toronto Press, 1972: 40.
8. Pearson, Memoirs.
9. Pearson, Memoirs.
10. Ken McKee, "Pearson the fan, Player," *Toronto Daily Star*, December 15, 1967, 16.
11. Canadian Press, "Pearson Says Award Tribute To Canada," *The Globe and Mail*, October 15, 1957, 10.
12. "Pearson Demonstrates Baseball Skill, Thrills Children," *The Toronto Daily Star*, March 29, 1958, 3.
13. William Kinmond, "TransiRon," *The Globe and Mail*, March 6, 1958, 23.
14. "Sample Puzzle No. 3," *Toronto Daily Star*, May 14, 1959, 19.
15. Robert Turnbull. "Political Gamesmanship," *The Globe and Mail*, January 3, 1959, A11.
16. Walter Gray, "Hundreds Cheer Pearson in PC Stronghold," *The Globe and Mail*, May 26, 1962, 9.

17. Stanley Westall, "Kelly Outdraws Fastest Liberal Gun," *The Globe and Mail*, May 10, 1962, 10.
18. Westall, "Kelly Outdraws Fastest Liberal Gun."
19. "Maple Leafs Fan Pearson," *The Globe and Mail*, May 9, 1962, 1.
20. "Caroline Puzzled," *The Globe and Mail*, May 1, 1962, 9.
21. Bruce Macdonald, "Pearson or Paralysis, Liberals Note," *The Globe and Mail*. March 21, 1963, 1.
22. Ralph Hyman, "Still a Reasonable Man," *The Globe and Mail*, April 10, 1963, 7.
23. John Bird, "The Bird View," *Toronto Daily Star*, April 22, 1963, 7.
24. John Boyko. *Cold Fire: Kennedy's Northern Front*. Toronto: Knopf Canada, 2016, 156.
25. Bill Galt, "Pearson Scores a Homer," *The Vancouver Sun*, May 11, 1963, 1.
26. Lester B. Pearson, *Memoirs of the Right Honourable Lester Pearson. Vol 1*. Toronto: University of Toronto Press, 1972: 101.
27. Pearson, *Memoirs*, 101. Pearson's memoirs contain a much-repeated anecdote that he, Kennedy, and Powers discussed a game "in Detroit" in which Canadian Ken MacKenzie pitched in relief. Since MacKenzie was with the Mets, Detroit seems an unlikely location for the game. The anecdote is repeated often without questioning this erroneous detail.
28. Pearson, *Memoirs*, 101.
29. Bill Galt, "Pearson Scores a Homer," *The Vancouver Sun*, May 11, 1963, 1.
30. Galt, "Pearson Scores a Homer,"
31. John Boyko. *Cold Fire: Kennedy's Northern Front*. Toronto: Knopf Canada, 2016, 156.
32. Newspaper Enterprise Association, "Baseball's Lure Beyond U.S. Borders," *The Hagerstown Daily Mail*, May 25, 1963, 14.
33. United Press International, "A Hit!" *Long Branch Daily Record*, August 5, 1963, 8.
34. Peter C. Newman, "The Unhappy Warrior," *The Ottawa Journal*, March 23, 1965, 7.
35. Canadian Press, "Lester Pearson, his Life and Times," *The Windsor Star*, December 28, 1972, 18.
36. "Lester Pearson, his Life and Times."
37. Robert Reguly, "It Wasn't So: Pearson Puts Record Straight," *Toronto Daily Star*, December 29, 1967, 2.
38. Dick Beddoes, "Pearson Outdistances His Rivals," *The Globe and Mail*, April 6, 1968, 41. Pearson engaged in a bit of political hyperbole there: The Dodgers never finished last under Durocher.
39. "Montreal Voyages Into Baseball," *Toronto Daily Star*. August 14, 1968, 16.
40. Frank Jones, "Pearson letter to bank's chief led to new job," *Toronto Daily Star*. August 20, 1968, B1.
41. Elizabeth Swinton, "This Day In Sports History: First MLB Game Played Outside Of The U.S.," *Sports Illustrated*, last modified April 14, 2020, https://www.si.com/mlb/2020/04/14/thisday-sports-history-first-mlb-game-played-outside-us-montreal
42. J.D.M. Stewart. *Being Prime Minister*. Toronto: Dundurn Press, 2018, 159.

The Last Thousand-Hundred Man

Douglas Jordan, PhD

INTRODUCTION

If you pick the baseball milestone carefully enough, you can always reduce to one the number of players that qualify. For example, the only player to hit more than 72 home runs in a season is Barry Bonds. He hit 73 dingers in 2001. Second on the list is Mark McGwire with 70 in 1998. The selection of 72 as a specific cutoff leaves Bonds as the only qualifier. But choosing a cutoff this way is suspect because it's arbitrary. Sufficiently large round numbers may seem just as arbitrary as qualifying values, but getting 3,000 hits means a batter has had a great career. Three hundred wins is a great career for a pitcher.

It's not unusual to combine round numbers as qualifying criteria. The question that sparked the idea for this paper is this: how many players have appeared in 1,000 games and have thrown 100 complete games? Individually, neither of these milestones is unique. About 1,600 position players have played in at least 1,000 games and almost 400 pitchers have thrown at least 100 complete games. But to get to 1,000 appearances as a pitcher is much more difficult. Cy Young pitched for 22 years and appeared in only (!) 906 games as a pitcher. That's why almost all of the 16 pitchers who have appeared in more than 1,000 games are modern relief pitchers. Jesse Orosco heads the list with 1,252 games

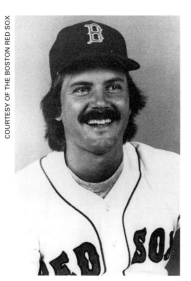

Dennis Eckersley joined the Red Sox in 1978.

COURTESY OF THE BOSTON RED SOX

played. But relief pitchers, by definition, don't throw complete games. So in order to appear in 1,000 games, and throw 100 complete games, a pitcher had to have a successful (and lengthy) career as both a starting pitcher and a relief pitcher. Give some thought to who you think might qualify in both categories.

There are actually a number of players who meet these criteria, but most of them had a career path that began as a pitcher and later transitioned to position player rather than starter turned reliever. The most famous of the group is Babe Ruth. Ruth appeared in 2,503 games in his career, mostly as an outfielder. But he came up as a pitcher and threw in 163 games. He went 94–46 and had a career ERA of 2.28 with 107 complete games. There are five nineteenth century players who followed a similar pattern of starting as a pitcher and switching to a position player. These players include Kid Gleason (1,968 games, 240 complete games), John Ward (1,827 games, 245 complete games), Cy Seymour (1,529 games, 105 complete games), Elmer Smith (1,237 games, 122 complete games), and Dave Foutz (1,136 games, 202 complete games). More recently, over his 25-year career (1959–1983) Jim Kaat pitched in 898 games and completed 180 games. Kaat also appeared in 106 additional games only as a pinch hitter or pinch runner, bringing his total number of appearances up to 1,004.

But beside Kaat (who needed over 100 non-pitching appearances to get there), the only starter turned reliever to meet the 1,000 appearance and 100 complete game standard is Dennis Eckersley. The purpose of this article is to celebrate Eckersley's accomplishments. He is almost certainly the last pitcher who will accomplish this twin feat since it is becoming increasingly uncommon for starting pitchers to complete games. All data in this article are from Baseball-Reference.com.

OTHER STARTERS TURNED RELIEVER

Are there other pitchers who could possibly qualify? One player that immediately comes to mind when thinking of starters who later pitched as relievers is John Smoltz. Smoltz had a great 21-year career that culminated with his election to the Hall of Fame in 2015. But his time as a starting pitcher was mostly during the 1990s or later, when it became less common for starters to go nine innings. And he pitched as a reliever for only four years. Smoltz wound up with 723 appearances, 53 complete games, and 154 saves. Tom Gordon is another starter who turned into a reliever. He spent ten of his 21 years as a starter or swingman, but compiled only 18 complete games. He spent 11 years as a reliever earning 158 saves and a total of 890 appearances. Bob Stanley also pitched in both roles during his career. He wound up with 637 appearances and 21 complete games in his 13-year career. Kerry Wood finished his 14-year career with 446 appearances, 11 complete games, and 63 saves. Finally, Rick Honeycutt pitched in 797 games and compiled 47 complete games during his 21-year career. The data for these other dual-role pitchers put Eckersley's accomplishment into perspective. It's *very* difficult to pitch 100 complete games and appear in over 1,000 games.

ECKERSLEY CAREER SUMMARY

Eckersley started his major league career with the Cleveland Indians in 1975 at 20 years of age. He was an All-Star for the Tribe in 1977 and threw a no-hitter that year before being traded to the Red Sox in 1978. In his debut year with Boston he went 20–8 with a 2.99 ERA. He made another All-Star appearance with the Red Sox in 1982. The Cubs were looking for pitching help in 1984, so the Red Sox traded Eckersley and Mike Brumley to Chicago in exchange for Bill Buckner. This is how Buckner got to the Red Sox before making his infamous error during the 1986 World Series. Eckersley developed some arm problems during his three-year tenure with the Cubs and was traded to the Oakland A's before the 1987 season.

Given the arm problems that Eckersley had been having, A's manager Tony La Russa decided to use him out of the bullpen instead of as a starter. Over the course of about two seasons, Eckersley's role evolved

to where he became one of the first relievers to be used as a one-inning closer. He thrived in the role. Eckersley won both the Cy Young award and the MVP award in 1992 when he had 51 saves and a 1.91 ERA. He pitched for Oakland for nine years earning a total of 320 saves in 525 games with a 2.74 ERA. Eckersley went to St. Louis in 1996 where he earned 66 more saves in two years before finishing his career at age 43 back in Boston in 1998. He was inducted into the Hall of Fame in 2004. Since the end of his playing career, he has worked in broadcasting with the New England Sports Network (working Red Sox games) and TBS.

THE NUMBERS, FIRST HALF OF CAREER

Eckersley's career divides neatly into two halves. He was a starting pitcher 1975–86 and almost exclusively a reliever 1987–98. This makes it natural to divide his career accomplishments into these two portions of his career. The numbers show that he was an above-average starter before transitioning to one of the best relievers of all time. Table 1 shows selected statistics from when he was a starting pitcher.

In order to put the starting pitcher portion of his career into perspective, a group of starting pitchers was selected that had the same career ERA+ as Eckersley did during the first half of his career. The statistic ERA+ is superior to pure ERA because it accounts for both league ERA and the ballpark the player pitched in. Eckersley's ERA+ as a starter was 111. This means that, on average over the course of his career, the league ERA was 11 percent higher than his ERA. However, it is more intuitive to think of the inverse of ERA+. The inverse of 111 multiplied by 100 is 0.901. This means that all of the pitchers in Table1 had a career ERA that was about 90 percent of the league ERA, on average. They are all better than average pitchers over the full course of their careers.

Although there are 312 pitchers who have a career ERA+ above 111, the accomplishments of the pitchers in Table 1 are still impressive. Gooden and McDowell

Table 1: Dennis Eckersley Selected Starting Pitcher Data and Comparisons

	Yrs.	W	L	ERA	G	SV	IP	SO	BB	ERA+	WHIP
Dennis Eckersley	12	151	128	3.67	376	100	2496	1627	624	111	1.212
Tommy John	26	288	231	3.34	760	162	4710.1	2245	1259	111	1.283
Dwight Gooden	16	194	112	3.51	430	68	2800.2	2293	954	111	1.256
Sid Fernandez	15	114	96	3.36	307	25	1866.2	1743	715	111	1.144
Josh Beckett	14	138	106	3.88	335	12	2051	1901	629	111	1.232
Jack McDowell	12	127	87	3.85	277	62	1889	1311	606	111	1.302

ERA+ is 100*[leagueERA/ERA] adjusted to the player's ballpark(s)
WHIP is Walks and Hits per Inning Pitched

both won a Cy Young Award. Beckett was the MVP of the 2003 World Series and the 2007 ALCS. Eckersley's two All-Star appearances (as a starting pitcher) are in line with the others. Fernandez had two, Beckett and McDowell had three, and Gooden and John had four All-Star appearances.

From a numerical perspective, Table 1 shows that Eckersley's WHIP is better than all but Fernandez. This is a good indication of his control. He didn't walk too many batters. Most germane to this article is his 100 complete games. Of modern pitchers, John has 62 more complete games, but it took him 26 years (the second longest career ever for a pitcher, after Nolan Ryan. Ryan pitched for 27 years!) to get that many. During his first two years with Boston (1978 and 1979), Eckersley had consecutive seasons of 16 and 17 complete games. These represent 46 percent and 52 percent respectively of his starts those two seasons. In old-school style, he liked to finish what he started. To summarize, even though his career as a starting pitcher was not Hall of Fame worthy, his starting career ERA +, and these comparisons, show that he was a very good starting pitcher. Finally, it is interesting to note that Randy Johnson also finished his career with exactly 100 complete games in the 618 games he pitched in. Johnson's career ERA + was 135.

THE NUMBERS, SECOND HALF OF CAREER

Eckersley got even better after his age 31 season in 1986. Not only did he manage to pitch for an additional 12 years as a relief pitcher, but his pitching numbers improved dramatically even though he was older. Table 2 is similar to Table 1 except that it only includes his statistics for the second half of his career as a relief pitcher. Pitchers in Table 2 after Eckersley are listed in order of career saves.

During the second half of his career, Eckersley lowered his ERA from 3.67 to 2.96, his WHIP from 1.212

to 0.999, and improved his ERA + from 111 to 136. The improvement in ERA + means that on average he had an ERA about 74 percent (1/1.36) of the league ERA for those 12 years. His control improved dramatically, too. As a starter he walked a batter every 4.0 innings (2496/624) but as a reliever he walked a batter only every 6.9 innings (790/114). His strikeout to walk ratio went from 2.6 as a starter to 6.8 as a reliever. Even taking into account the different styles of pitching required to be a starter versus being a reliever, these are significant improvements as he got older.

This level of pitching performance moves him from being a better than average starting pitcher to one of the all-time great relief pitchers. Even though he was only a closer for only about 12 years, he is seventh on the all-time list in saves. The six pitchers who have more saves then he does are included in Table 2. All six of them pitched as a reliever for at least 16 years to exceed the 387 saves Eckersley accumulated in just 12 years. Because he had such good control of his pitches during this period, he walked few batters which resulted in a WHIP of 0.999. This figure is essentially equivalent to the WHIP that Mariano Rivera put up (WHIP of 1.000) over his outstanding career. Rivera also had a career ERA + of 205 (the best ever for pitchers who pitched at least 1000 innings). This means that his average ERA over the course of his career was 49 percent (1/2.05) of the league average. Rivera's best year in terms of ERA + was 2008 when his ERA + was 316. This means his ERA was 32 percent (1/3.16) of the league average that year. That's a pretty amazing season, even for a closer who pitched just 70.2 innings total that year. But as we will see next, Eckersley had a season better than this in terms of ERA + even though his ERA + overall during these 12 years were not as good as Rivera's record-setting career performance.

As great as Rivera was, he never managed the feat that Eckersley did in 1992. That year Eckersley led the

Table 2: Dennis Eckersley Selected Relief Pitcher Data and Comparisons

	Yrs.	W	L	ERA	G	CG	IP	SO	BB	ERA+	WHIP
Dennis Eckersley	12	46	43	2.96	695	387	789.2	774	114	136	0.999
Mariano Rivera	19	82	60	2.21	1115	652*	1283.2	1173	286	205*	1.000
Trevor Hoffman	18	61	75	2.87	1035	601	1089.1	1133	307	141	1.058
Lee Smith	18	71	92	3.03	1022	478	1289.1	1251	486	132	1.256
Francisco Rodriguez	16	52	53	2.86	948	437	976	1142	389	148	1.155
John Franco	21	90	87	2.89	1119	424	1245.2	975	495	138	1.333
Billy Wagner	16	47	40	2.31	853	422	903	1196	300	187	0.998
Jonathan Papelbon	12	41	36	2.44	689	368	725.2	808	185	177	1.043
Eckersley (total career)	**24**	**197**	**171**	**3.50**	**1071**	**390**	**3285.2**	**2401**	**738**	**116**	**1.161**

*All-time career record

Eckersley in action as starting pitcher at Fenway.

majors in saves with 51, had a 1.91 ERA, a WHIP of 0.913 and an ERA+ of 195 (his ERA was 51 percent (1/1.95) of league average) in 80 innings pitched. With this outstanding performance, he was awarded both the AL Cy Young award and the AL MVP award. Only nine other pitchers have won both awards in the same year since the Cy Young award was established in 1956. And yet, from a numerical perspective, 1992 wasn't even Eckersley's best year. In 1990 Eckersley had 48 saves, a 0.61 ERA, a WHIP of 0.614, and an incredible ERA+ of 603 (his ERA was 17 percent (1/6.03) of league average!) in 73.1 innings. He gave up only five earned runs and walked just four batters that entire season.

It also helps to put his second half ERA+ of 136 into perspective. Two very well-known pitchers finished their careers with ERA+ marks at, or close to, 136. Christy Mathewson had a career ERA+ of exactly 136 and Cy Young finished his career at 138. Admittedly, this is not a perfect comparison because Eckersley's overall career ERA+ is 116. But he was keeping pace with all-time greats during the latter half of his career.

As with life, athletic careers have ups and downs. Although this article highlights many of the positive aspects of Eckersley's career, he is arguably most well-known for one of his mistakes. This is the danger of performing on the national stage: when things go poorly, everybody remembers it. In one of the most famous moments in baseball history, an injured Kirk Gibson came to bat against Eckersley in the bottom of the ninth inning of Game 1 during the 1988 World Series. Gibson hit his famous home run (and made his also famous right arm pump after rounding first base) to give the Dodgers a walk-off victory. Eckersley says he's been asked about the pitch he threw to Gibson constantly for the past 30 years.

CONCLUSION

Dennis Eckersley is one of only two pure pitchers to have appeared in over 1,000 games (1071 total) and to have thrown 100 complete games (he finished with exactly 100). To achieve these milestones, he needed to be effective and durable, as both a starting and relief pitcher. The skills required to meet this standard are so rare that he will likely be the last pitcher to ever do it. The purpose of this article is to make these facts known to a broader public, and to celebrate the baseball career of a man who went from being an above-average starting pitcher, to one of the best relief pitchers of all time. ■

Acknowledgments

My sincere thanks to two anonymous reviewers for taking the time to carefully read the paper and provide feedback. Their comments substantially improved the paper and corrected the omission of players who are now included in the article.

Source

Portions of the career summary are taken from the SABR Baseball Biography Project; https://sabr.org/bioproj/person/98aaf620#sdendnote2anc.

Maris and Ruth

Was the Season Games Differential the Primary Issue?

Brian Marshall

This article discusses Roger Maris's 1961 season from a new perspective. This is not a comparison of each home run hit by Maris in 1961 with those hit by Babe Ruth in 1927, but rather proposes a method to compare the Maris performance with the Ruth performance on a near-equivalent basis. Though there exists the "low hanging fruit" of a nominal eight game difference in the two seasons, the method proposed here involves comparing the two players' plate appearances (PA). Because each player had a large number of PA and their totals only differ by seven, the two performances can be considered essentially equivalent. This makes PA a much better number to be used for comparison purposes than the number of season games. PA is superior to at bats (AB) because it is inclusive of all appearances at the plate, therefore representing every "opportunity" to make a hit, get on base or advance a runner(s). We will discuss the infamous ruling by Ford Frick in 1961 not only because the difference in the number of season games forms the basis for the article, but also for perspective.

1927 SEASON NOTES

On Friday, September 30, 1927, the New York Yankees played Washington at Yankee Stadium in the 154th and penultimate game of the season.[1] It was a clear day with the temperature in the low to mid 80s at game time, a 3:00 PM start.[2] The score was tied at 2–2 heading into the bottom of the eighth inning, with the top of the Yankee order coming to bat. First up was the center fielder Earle Combs, who grounded out. Next up was the shortstop Mark Koenig, who tripled. The next to bat was the right fielder, George Herman "Babe" Ruth, who took his position at the plate with a reddish colored bat that was named "Beautiful Bella" and weighed about 42 ounces.[3] Pitching for the Senators was the veteran Tom Zachary, who threw a first-pitch strike to Ruth. The next pitch was high for a ball. The third pitch Zachary served up was low, fast, and inside. The Babe stepped into it and Beautiful Bella met the ball with a loud crack that sent the ball into the right field bleachers about halfway up.

Zachary, of course, wasn't happy; he threw his glove to the ground in a display of anger, yelled that it was a foul ball, and argued with the umpire as Ruth slowly jogged around the bases.[4] Later, in the clubhouse, Ruth shouted, "Sixty, count 'em, sixty! Let's see some other son of a bitch match that!"[5] Ruth's 60th home run scored two runs, and the Yankees won by a score of 4–2. That great example of five o'clock lightning set a single season record, breaking his own record of 59 set in the 1921 season.

1961 SEASON NOTES

The 1961 season will always be remembered as the year that Roger Maris of the New York Yankees hit 61 home runs to set a new single-season home run record. It was a monumental achievement by Maris at the time—one that few, if any, would have predicted from the unassuming outfielder, and one that he would not duplicate. His previous season best was the year prior when he hit 39 homers, and his season best after 1961 was only 33. That being said, you just never know in sport when a player, or a team, can come out of nowhere and surprise everyone on a given day or in a given season. That is exactly what Maris did. To top it off, Maris was the polar opposite of Ruth both from a personality and from a career home run perspective. While Ruth relished the limelight and had 714 career home runs to his credit, Maris shied away from attention and would end his career with 275.

It was also an expansion year in the American League. The Washington Senators moved to Minnesota to become the Twins, and new franchises were formed in Washington and Los Angeles to bring the league's team count to ten. To accommodate the additional squads, the schedule was increased to 162 games. Each AL team would play the other nine teams 18 times, nine games at home and nine games on the road, to comprise 162 games. In comparison, the 1927 New York Yankees played the other seven AL teams 22 times, 11 games at home and 11 games on the road, to make up the 154-game schedule. (The author did not compare the quality of pitchers and pitching between the 1927 and 1961 seasons as it was not part of the scope of this article.)

FRICK RULING

As the 1961 season progressed it became apparent that two New York Yankees, Maris and Mickey Mantle, were going to go head to head for the home run title, not just for that season, but for all time. The Maris/Mantle home run battle and the nominal eight game differential stimulated MLB Commissioner Ford C. Frick to make the following ruling on July 17, 1961:

> Any player who may hit more than sixty home runs during his club's first 154 games would be recognized as having established a new record. However if the player does not hit more than sixty until after his club has played 154 games, there would have to be some distinctive mark in the record books to show that Babe Ruth's record was set under a 154-game schedule and the total of more than sixty was compiled while a 162-game schedule was in effect.[6]

There were two problems, and one issue, with the Frick ruling that apparently were unbeknownst to him at the time of the ruling. The first major problem was that the wording "some distinctive mark" did not define what the distinctive mark would be, leaving it open to interpretation. That is exactly what the media did; they interpreted the "distinctive mark" wording to mean an asterisk, as the following quotation states:

> FORD FRICK, the baseball commissioner, ruled rightly when he decreed that no successor to Ruth would be recognized unless he hit 60 or more homers within the 154-game schedule on which the Babe operated. The new 162-game schedule would offer too great a target. Frick has added that any man who surpassed Ruth's 60 in the added eight games, would have to be content with entry in the record book under an asterisk.[7]

The second major problem with the Frick ruling was that he created a situation where the fans would be focused on the first 154 games with great anticipation and meaning and the remaining eight games would effectively be rendered less meaningful. That situation wasn't owner-friendly or good for business, as owner Bill Veeck put it: "What he did, in that one brilliant stroke, was build the interest up to that 154th game and throw the final eight games out in the wash

with the baby. What he did was to turn what should have been a thrilling cliff-hanger lasting over the full final week of the season into a crashing anti-climax."[8]

Then there was the issue that Frick considered himself a friend of Ruth's. As a sportswriter for the William Randolph Hearst-owned *New York American* newspaper, Frick had covered the New York Yankees beginning in 1922.[9] He had also been a ghost writer for Babe Ruth's newspaper columns.[10] The *Los Angeles Times* lampooned Frick's friendship with Ruth and its relationship to the matter of the asterisk as follows:

> Once upon a time there was this nice man. His name was Ford Frick and he was president of the National League which was a nice job because all he had to do was what Branch Rickey told him.
>
> One day a committee came to him and said "How would you like to be Czar of all baseball?"
>
> So they made him Czar of all baseball ....
>
> And one day the Czar said, "Look can't I do ANYTHING around here?!" and his subjects said "Sure!' You can call off any World Series where the field is wet enough, Just check with Walter O'Malley first." And he said, "I don't mean THAT! Anybody knows enough to come in out of the rain. I want to do something about baseball!" This puzzled them.
>
> "What do you want to do?" they asked suspiciously. "I want to put an asterisk after Roger Maris' name!" he screamed. "After all, Babe Ruth was a friend of mine!"[11]

ANALYSIS

Using the number of scheduled games as the standard to evaluate the legitimacy of Maris's home-run record may have been the perceived best approach at the time but was it? Although there is an eight-game differential in Maris's favor, the number of games do not necessarily equate to opportunity. Did Maris have five percent more opportunity than Ruth? To compare the Maris in 1961 and Ruth in 1927 performances on a more equivalent basis it becomes necessary to use a metric with a lower degree of variation: plate appearances.

PA is the sum of a player's at-bats (AB), walks (BB), sacrifice hits (SH), sacrifice flies (SF), reached base on interference, and being hit by a pitch (HBP). The PA totals for Maris in 1961 and Ruth in 1927 were nearly equal, differing by only seven, or a differential of a mere one percent (see Table 1 below).

Table 1. Determination of PA[12]

Metric	Babe Ruth 1927	Roger Maris 1961
AB	540	590
BB	137	94
HBP	0	7
SH	14	0
SF	0	7
PA	691	698

Table 1 indicates that the HBP, SH, and SF can effectively be negated with respect to the two players since the sum of the three metrics in each case is 14 which results in a difference between the two amounting to the BB differential. The plate opportunity ceases to be a true hitting opportunity if the batter is intentionally walked. Both Ruth in 1927 and Maris in 1961 typically batted third, so a pitcher had to pick his poison. In the case of the 1927 Yankees, the pitcher could choose to walk Ruth and face Lou Gehrig, and in 1961 the pitcher had a choice between Maris and Mantle. Ruth was in fact walked 43 more times than Maris.

Maris's final three home runs were hit after the 154th game, but for each of home runs number 59 and 60, Maris hit them when he'd had fewer PA than Ruth (see Table 2 below).

Table 2. Home Runs with Respect to Game Number and PA Number[13]

			PLAYER			
	Babe Ruth			Roger Maris		
HR #	Date	Game #	PA #	Date	Game #	PA #
58	9/29/27	153	679	9/17/61	152	655
59	9/29/27	153	682	9/20/61	155	666
60	9/30/27	154	687	9/26/61	159	684
61	N/A	N/A	N/A	10/1/61	163	696

N/A = Not Applicable

Regarding the famous number 60 home run hit by Ruth, it was during game number 154 and PA #687 while the 60th home run hit by Maris was during game number 159 and PA #684. Maris hit his 60th home run five games later than Ruth hit his 60th home run but Maris managed to do it a full three plate appearances ahead of Ruth. This fact clearly indicates that the Game Number wasn't as key as it was perceived to be during the 1961 season. The graphs of the Average PA for both Ruth and Maris, over the course of the respective seasons, is depicted in Figure 1. It is clear that the two graphs are distinct in that they do not touch at any point other than for the first game of the season, nor do they cross at any point. It is also clear that the average PA for Babe Ruth is greater than that for Roger Maris throughout the whole season.

Figure 1. Graph of Average PA

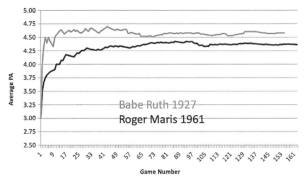

The ratios of PA/GP (Games Played) and PA/HR (Home Runs) are displayed in Table 3, showing that those for Maris are less than Ruth's. Maris had less opportunity on a per-game basis than Ruth, and on average hit a home run per slightly fewer plate appearances. The PA/GP are those depicted in Figure 1 as the final values for each of Ruth and Maris. Even though Maris played in more games and had seven more PAs, his PA/GP ratio was lower than Ruth's over the course of the season. It is for this reason that it can be said that Ruth had more opportunities, on average, per game.

Table 3. Determination of Player PA Ratios

Player	GP	HR	PA	PA/GP	PA/HR
Babe Ruth	151	60	691	4.58	11.52
Roger Maris	160	61	698	4.36	11.44

The raw data for Tables 2 and 3 and Figure 1 were derived from the Baseball-Reference.com web site, specifically the team batting table on the team pages, the standard batting table on the player pages, the game-by-game logs on the game log pages, and the play-by-play table on the game boxscore pages.[12] The PA/GP listed in Table 3 are those depicted in Figure 1 as the final values for each of Ruth and Maris.[13]

Table 3 states that the number of games played by Maris in 1961 was 160, while Maris's Baseball-Reference.com page lists him as playing in 161 games. There were three games during the 1961 season when Maris did not record any PA: May 22, July 29, and September 27. Maris was in the lineup for the May 22 game at Yankee Stadium, and took his position in right field, but he came out due to an eye irritation.[14] (Yogi Berra, who had been behind the plate, went to right field and Johnny Blanchard went in to replace Berra as

Roger Maris played a longer season in 1961 than Ruth did in 1927, but because he had fewer plate appearances per game throughout the season, in the end Ruth had only 7 fewer PAs.

catcher.) Maris was only in the game for a few minutes during the top of the first inning, and never made a plate appearance in the game. For the game on July 29, Maris was never in the lineup because he was sidelined with a pulled muscle in his left leg.[15] (Berra again played right field.) On September 27, Maris was given the day off as detailed in *The New York Times*: "Maris, who had hit his sixtieth homer on Tuesday night, said he was 'too bushed' to play. When Roger asked permission to skip yesterday's game, manager Ralph Houk readily consented."[16]

THE END OF THE SEASON: NO ASTERISK

When the final official AL batting statistics were released for publication by MLB on December 17, 1961, there was no asterisk, nor any other mark/indication, associated with Maris's statistics. John Drebinger pointed out in *The New York Times* that there wasn't any "star, asterisk or footnote attached to the listing" of the notation that Maris had set a record for hitting the most home runs in a single season.[17] Remember that at the time when Maris hit his 59th home run, the asterisk had seemed assured, as evidenced by this September 21 *Times* article, whose headline blared Maris was "resigned" to the mark:

> Maris, surrounded and half-pinned to the dressing room wall at Memorial Stadium, even conceded to Commissioner Ford Frick's asterisk.

The commissioner, it will be recalled, had ruled that if Maris was to match or break Babe Ruth's record of sixty homers in a season, he would have to do it within 154 games. Any mark beyond that, Frick insisted, would get an asterisk in the record book.[18]

Frick maintained that he never stated there should be an asterisk, saying: "As for that star or asterisk business, I don't know how that cropped up or was attributed to me, because I never said it."[19]

Frick effectively was his own worst enemy in the asterisk matter. However, after all the dust had settled, the official AL statistics didn't include a mark beside Maris's feat. Down the road, any baseball historian or researcher would know and understand there was a difference in the number of AL games in the 1927 and 1961 seasons because it is low-hanging fruit. Less obvious is the fact that Maris had fewer opportunities per game on average, and ultimately hit his record-tying 60th home run in three fewer PAs than Ruth.

CONCLUSIONS

The thought of employing an asterisk, or any other mark, in the record book solely based on the difference in the number of scheduled regular season games was not the proper approach for Maris's 1961 accomplishment. The number of games doesn't necessarily equate to the degree of opportunity. Frick was too close to the situation due to his past affiliation with Ruth and may have been influenced by his personal feelings to a degree when he made his ruling, although I don't doubt that he felt he had the best interest of MLB in mind. He could have waited until the end of the season and made a decision after he had a chance to review all the statistics and the matter in detail.

Both the 1927 and the 1961 seasons were similar, from a team perspective, in that both teams won their respective pennants and won the World Series. The New York Yankees of 1927 were arguably one of the greatest teams in MLB history with a season record of 110 wins, 44 losses, and one tie. The New York Yankees of 1961 had a record of 109 wins, 53 losses, and one tie. Ruth in 1927 was involved in a home run race with his teammate Gehrig much as Maris in 1961 was with Mantle.

Both Ruth and Maris were similar from a player perspective in that they both batted left, played right field, and typically batted in the third position of the batting order. They also both typically hit their home runs in Yankee Stadium into the infamous "short porch" down the first-base line (and both hit more home runs on the road than at home).

On the surface, it appeared to be a no-brainer that Maris would have more opportunity to accomplish his feat than Ruth did to accomplish his. The fact is that Maris actually had less opportunity on a per game basis. This doesn't mean to imply that Maris was better than Ruth as a player or from a hitting perspective, but it does say that Maris in 1961 edged out Ruth in 1927, not merely in total number of home runs hit, but from a PA perspective as it relates to when a number of his HRs were hit. In summary:

a) The number of scheduled games differed by 8, a 5% differential.

b) The PAs for Maris are 698 and for Ruth are 691, a difference of 7, a 1% differential.

c) Maris had a lower Average PA/GP throughout the whole of the season.

d) Maris had a lower PA/HR.

e) Maris hit his 60th in PA #684 and Ruth hit his 60th HR in PA #687.

While the number of games can be greater, it doesn't necessarily equate to more opportunity. It is the opportunity that must be equal, or near equal, for the performances to be considered equivalent. Then a suitable comparison can be made. ■

Notes

1. The New York Yankees actually played 155 games in the 1927 season because there was a make-up game for the April 14 game with the Philadelphia Athletics that was tied after ten innings when the game was called due to darkness.
2. "The Weather," *The New York Times*, October 1, 1927, 39.
3. Harvey Frommer, *Five O'Clock Lightning: Babe Ruth, Lou Gehrig, and the Greatest Team in Baseball, the 1927 New York Yankees.* Hoboken, NJ: John Wiley & Sons, Inc., 2008, 145.
4. "Ruth Crushes 60th to Set New Record: Babe Makes it a Real Field Day by Accounting for All Runs in 4–2 Victory," *The New York Times*, October 1, 1927, 12.
5. Robert W. Creamer, *Babe: The Legend Comes to Life.* (The Penguin Sports Library, General Editor, Dick Schaap.) New York, NY: Penguin Books, 1986, 309.
6. "Ruth's Record Can Be Broken Only in 154 Games, Frick Rules," *The New York Times*, July 18, 1961, 20.
7. "This Morning with Shirley Povich: Mantle has Rare Chance to Beat Ruth's 60," *Washington Post*, July 25, 1961, A14.
8. "Commissioner Just a Traffic Cop to Veeck: Frick's 'Asterisk' Ruling on Maris Enough to Give Master Promoter Apoplexy," *Chicago Daily Tribune*, July 25, 1962, Part 4, 4.
9. "Ford Frick," Wikipedia, accessed September 2019. https://en.wikipedia.org/wiki/Ford_Frick
10. Warren Corbett, "Ford Frick," SABR Baseball BioProject, accessed September 2019. https://sabr.org/node/41789
11. Jim Murray, "A Czar is Born," *Los Angeles Times*, December 17, 1964, Part III, 2.
12. Standard batting tables from the player pages for Babe Ruth and Roger Maris on Baseball-Reference.com, accessed in September 2019. https://www.baseball-reference.com/players/r/ruthba01.shtml and https://www.baseball-reference.com/players/m/marisro01.shtml
13. The author compiled a separate table for each of Babe Ruth and Roger Maris that calculated the PA on a game-by-game basis then summed the PAs over the course of the season. Then for each of the games Ruth and/or Maris hit a home run the author documented the outcome for each individual PA during the game and numbered them incrementally. The author used the "Play by Play" information provided on Baseball-Reference.com to obtain the "outcome" information for each of the PAs. Naturally, the final PA numerical number had to match PA total listed for each of Ruth and Maris. The purpose of creating the individual PA Tables was to have a means to both identify and to "look up" an individual PA and associate it with a given home run and/or outcome for each of the games Ruth and/or Maris hit a home run. Baseball-Reference.com was accessed a number of times during the month of September 2019.
14. John Drebinger, "Yanks Overwelm Orioles After Being Retired in Order for First Five Innings," *The New York Times*, May 23, 1961, 50.
15. "Yanks Edge Birds, 5-4, On Berra's Homer in Eighth," *Baltimore Sunday Sun*, July 30, 1961, Sports section, 1.
16. John Drebinger, "Orioles Turn Back Yanks on Barber's Pitching and Gentile's 46th Homer," *The New York Times*, September 28, 1961, 52. The Yankees technically played 163 games in the season, as the second game of the doubleheader played on April 22 was called on account of rain when the score was tied. The game itself was replayed from the beginning as part of another doubleheader on September 19. The April game did not factor in the standings, but the personal statistics for the players in that rained-out contest did count.
17. John Drebinger, "Record of Maris Has No Asterisk," *The New York Times*, December 23, 1961, 18.
18. Louis Effrat, "Maris is Resigned to * in the Record Books: * Will Mean Record Was Set After 154 Games," *The New York Times*, September 21, 1961, 42.
19. "No * Will Mar Homer Records, Says Frick With †† for Critics: If Maris Surpasses Ruth 60, Feat Will Get Full Credit as 162-Game Standard," *The New York Times*, September 22, 1961, 38.

Cubic Players

Randy Klipstein

When Brandon Nimmo took his position in right field on September 26, 2018, in a game at Citi Field, he was wearing his usual number nine and would bat ninth in the batting order. It seemed to me that this was an interesting confluence of facts: a player whose uniform number matches his fielding position and his position in the batting order. I wondered about other players who have achieved this trifecta and become "Cubic Players."

Of course, fielding position and especially batting position can change daily for some, and players change numbers throughout their careers, so I set out to document the number of games for each player where their three numbers (uniform, batting order, and fielding position) were the same, in the history of baseball. I limited this study to the players in the starting lineup, at their starting fielding position. Pinch hitters, relief pitchers, defensive replacements, and fielding position changes were not considered. I looked at only regular season games for the ninety-year period of 1929–2018. The convention of players wearing numbers began in earnest in 1929, after a few brief experiments, and was completely phased in by the mid-1930s.

This is a very unlikely feat for pitchers. In fact, according to Retrosheet, only one starting pitcher batted leadoff in this period: Cesar Tovar, on September 22, 1968, the day he duplicated the Bert Campaneris feat of playing all nine positions in a game. He wasn't wearing number one, however, thus no pitcher (or anyone wearing number one or anyone batting leadoff) has ever been Cubic. Of course, we can also eliminate players wearing a number greater than nine, or less than one, and Designated Hitters.

I employed the Uniform Number Tracker database at the Baseball-Reference website. To identify games in which a player's batting order position matched his fielding position, I used Retrosheet's Game Log files, which provide starting lineups and initial fielding positions. Retrosheet and Baseball-Reference are wonderful resources and I am grateful that they make their information available for download free of charge. It would be beneficial, however, if there were a standard for player identification. For instance, Hank Aaron is identified as "aaroh101" by Retrosheet and "aaronha01" by Baseball-Reference (and by Sean Lahman's Baseball Database, another wonderful free resource). Checking to ensure that the files from the two sources were merged correctly added a lot of time and created an opportunity for errors. Cases like the two players named Abraham Nunez, who played concurrently, required careful handling.

METHODOLOGY

My results are not perfectly correct, though they are close as possible under the constraints. Here is why I could not achieve perfection:

1. I relied on Retrosheet and Baseball-Reference exclusively as the source of the data for this study (and again, I am forever grateful to them). Any errors or incomplete information, however, in either source, could have created errors in my results.

2. I already mentioned that the two sources use different IDs for players, creating opportunities for errors.

3. Baseball-Reference provides the numbers a player wore by year and team. It does not provide daily detail. If a player wore more than one number for the same team in the same year, I had no way to tell at what point during the season that the change was made. For instance, in 1972, Bobby Grich started the year wearing number sixteen, which he had worn since he first reached the majors in 1970. At some point during the year, he switched to number three, which he wore for the rest of his Oriole career. I considered these cases to be indeterminate and removed them, since I could not verify what uniform number such players wore on a particular day in those years.

4. No source that I am aware of tracks numbers worn by players to commemorate special occasions, such as Jackie Robinson Day, and I made no attempt to identify such days and the players who wore special numbers for a single game.

5. The final source of errors is me. I attempted to automate this to as great an extent as possible but could not do so entirely. Baseball-Reference's database provided player, team, uniform number, and year, but the downloaded data were not in a usable tabular format. I managed to reformat them into a table, but without the team. I merged the two source files by player and year. Then, for each player who appeared to satisfy the cubic criteria, I looked up their Baseball-Reference page to check that the player actually wore the right number for the right team. For instance, in 1979, Oscar Gamble wore number seven with the Rangers and number seventeen with the Yankees. His only games that year in left field, batting seventh, came with the Yankees, however. Thus, I had to remove those games. I spent a great deal of time checking these cases, but I can't be sure that errors weren't made.

Confucius said, "Better a diamond with a flaw than a pebble without." No, I don't think he was talking about baseball.

RESULTS BY POSITION

There have been 10,180 instances of a cubic player-game. This works out to be about 113 times per year. Only 335 players have played a cubic game.

As I'm sure you have realized, the frequency of this is vastly different by number. Looking at it through the lens of fielding position, it is far more likely to be accomplished by an infielder than an outfielder; and far more likely for an outfielder than a catcher, as shown in Table 1.

Table 1. Cubic Player-Games by Position Category

Catcher	Infielder	Outfielder
44	9,069	1,067

Breaking it down further, we see in Table 2 that among infielders, the feat is far more likely to be accomplished by fielders at the corners. In the outfield, the frequency declines as we move from left to right. Cubic right fielders are relatively new; the first one appeared in 1978. On June 1, 1920, right fielder Sammy Vick batted ninth in the Yankee lineup (pitcher Babe

Ruth batted fourth). It wasn't until the Designated Hitter rule was established that a right fielder would bat ninth again.

Table 2. Cubic Player-Games by Position

C (2)	IB (3)	2B (4)	3B (5)	SS (6)	LF (7)	CF (8)	RF (9)
44	3,450	987	3,841	791	758	246	63
<1%	34%	10%	38%	8%	7%	2%	1%

Of those 63 right field player-games, 61 occurred in the American League. Perhaps as National League managers bat their pitchers eighth, we'll see more cubic NL right fielders, joining Ryan McGuire and Brandon Nimmo.

When we look at the 335 cubic players by position, in Table 3, we see:

Table 3. Cubic Players by Position Category

Catcher	Infielder	Outfielder
7	189	142

Table 4 provides the position detail.

Table 4. Cubic Players by Position

C (2)	IB (3)	2B (4)	3B (5)	SS (6)	LF (7)	CF (8)	RF (9)
7	56	19	79	37	89	37	20
2%	16%	6%	23%	11%	26%	11%	6%

Careful readers will note that outfielders account for only about 10% of cubic player-games (Table 2), yet about 43% of the cubic players have been outfielders (Table 4). Infielders, and particularly first and third basemen, exhibit the opposite relationship. It's not unusual for a left fielder to bat seventh, for instance, in a particular game. But left fielders who bat seventh don't tend to have long careers. We will see that cubic records are driven by a few prolific players, and they are infielders, generally first or third basemen.

RESULTS OVER TIME

I had a hunch that this feat has become more unusual, for three reasons.

1. When uniform numbers were first assigned, they were often assigned based on the player's position in the batting order, thus creating a systemic link between two of the three figures.

2. Single digit numbers are being retired. Since numbers are seldom unretired, this factor will have an increasingly strong effect as time goes on. The Yankees have retired numbers one through nine, ensuring that no Yankee will ever

play a cubic game again. The last Yankee to do so was Tony Fernandez in 1995.

3. The use of set lineups seems to have become extinct, making it more unlikely for an individual player to amass a high number of cubic games (and perhaps also leading to more cubic players).

To check if this is actually true, I grouped the ninety years in the study into nine ten-year periods: 1929–38, 1939–48, etc. As I expected, I found that the number of cubic player-games, and ratio of cubic player-games to total games played (which is a more meaningful measurement as it normalizes for expansion and a longer regular season schedule), had been steadily declining. However, the trend has reversed and the frequency has increased in the two most recent decades, as shown in Table 5. I believe that the decade 1989–98 is the outlier. We've reached a relatively steady state of about 3% to 4% of games played over that last fifty years. By chance, in that one ten-year period, it seldom happened. Prolific cubic players, like the immortals, don't come around on a regular schedule.

Table 6 provides the number of cubic players in each decade.

Table 7 is a matrix of the number of cubic player-games by decade and number. It's interesting that most of the occurrences for first basemen and shortstops happened in the earlier years, while most of the occurrences for second basemen (due to one player who we will meet in the next paragraph) and outfielders happened in more recent years.

Table 5. Cubic Player-Games by Decade

	1929–38	1939–48	1949–58	1959–68	1969–78	1979–88	1989–98	1999–2008	2009–18
Cubic Player-Games	2,581	1,680	1,028	1,142	711	537	226	976	1,299
% of Total Games Played	21%	14%	8%	7%	4%	3%	1%	4%	5%

Table 6. Cubic Players by Decade

1929–38	1939–48	1949–58	1959–68	1969–78	1979–88	1989–98	1999–2008	2009–18
50	36	35	30	31	31	44	52	61

Table 7. Cubic Player-Games by Decade and Number

	1929–38	1939–48	1949–58	1959–68	1969–78	1979–88	1989–98	1999–2008	2009–18	Total
2	13	3	–	1	5	12	8	2	–	4
3	962	1,062	744	379	253	5	10	22	13	3,450
4	95	87	33	–	2	23	2	200	545	987
5	1,036	374	152	510	406	433	68	549	313	3,841
6	314	148	8	197	11	–	14	70	29	791
7	118	4	67	50	19	44	82	96	278	758
8	43	2	24	5	10	9	29	14	110	246
9	–	–	–	–	5	11	13	23	11	63
Total	2,581	1,680	1,028	1,142	711	537	226	976	1,299	10,180

PLAYER RECORDS

Brandon Phillips is the all-time leader in career cubic games played. Table 8 provides the top ten.

Table 8. Top 10 Leaders in Career Cubic Games

Brandon Phillips	700	Second Base
Brooks Robinson	668	Third Base
Pinky Higgins	541	Third Base
Mickey Vernon	466	First Base
Harmon Killebrew	439	First Base
Bill Terry	418	First Base
George McQuinn	366	First Base
David Wright	326	Third Base
Bob Horner	300	Third Base
Joe Kuhel	264	First Base

Appendix A shows the top ten players in lifetime cubic games at each number. In Appendix B you will find the top ten players in cubic games in each decade.

Pinky Higgins established the career mark in 1937 and held the record for thirty-three years, until Brooks Robinson eclipsed him in 1970. Robinson held the record for forty-six years until Brandon Phillips passed him in 2016.

The record for most cubic games in a single season is held by Bill Terry. In 1934 he played 153 cubic games (every game that the Giants played that year). The top ten seasons are shown in Table 9.

Table 9. Top 10 Single Seasons

Bill Terry	1934	153
Mickey Vernon	1954	148
Bill Terry	1935	143
Mickey Vernon	1953	141
Pinky Whitney	1932	137
Pinky Higgins	1936	129
Brandon Phillips	2013	127
Brooks Robinson	1969	125
Pinky Higgins	1935	124
Brandon Phillips	2009	122

Table 10 provides the single season records for each number.

Table 10. Single Season Leaders for each Number

2	Billy Sullivan Jr.	1938	13
3	Bill Terry	1934	153
4	Brandon Phillips	2013	127
5	Pinky Whitney	1932	137
6	Eric McNair	1935	98
7	David Murphy	2012	64
8	Joe Marty	1937	30
9	Jody Gerut	2004	12

Brooks Robinson holds the record for most years leading all of baseball: nine. Brandon Phillips led in eight years. No one else led in more than four years.

Brooks Robinson also holds the record for most years with at least one cubic game: seventeen. Harmon Killebrew had eleven such years, and Brandon Phillips had ten. No one else had more than eight.

FRANCHISE RECORDS

Table 11 provides the total player-games for each franchise. I've grouped the oldest sixteen and the fourteen later expansion teams separately.

Table 11. Number of Cubic Player-Games for each Franchise

Older Franchises		Later Expansion Franchises	
Orioles	1,182	Mets	394
Red Sox	1,137	Rangers	235
Twins	1,047	Padres	169
Reds	837	Mariners	117
Athletics	697	Nationals	110
Giants	582	Diamondbacks	80
White Sox	577	Angels	72
Pirates	524	Astros	55
Dodgers	429	Blue Jays	50
Indians	407	Marlins	39
Braves	404	Brewers	29
Phillies	327	Rays	28
Cubs	240	Royals	26
Tigers	152	Rockies	17
Cardinals	122		
Yankees	95		

It wasn't surprising to me that Yankees are last among the original franchises, given their proclivity for retiring single digit numbers. Incidentally, Babe Ruth was the first cubic Yankee, in 1931. It was his only cubic game.

For no systemic reason, 57% of the cubic player-games have been recorded by teams that were in the American League at the time. However, in the last four decades, 76% of the incidences have been by National League teams. As you've seen, one prolific cubic player can leave an imprint on the totals. As shown in Table 8, the top ten most prolific players account for 44% of all the cubic player-games.

Table 12 lists the leaders for each franchise. Notice that Brandon Phillips, the Reds second baseman for eleven years (2006–2016), and Brooks Robinson, the Orioles third baseman for more than two decades (1955–1977), are far ahead of everyone else. Pinky Higgins, next on the all-time list, amassed cubic games for the Athletics and Red Sox. Mickey Vernon, fourth on the list, tallied cubic games for the Indians and Senators.

Table 12. All-time Franchise Leaders

Angels	Bobby Grich	23
Astros	Pete Runnels	51
Athletics	Pinky Higgins	344
Blue Jays	Anthony Gose	15
Braves	Bob Horner	300
Brewers	B.J. Surhoff	15
Cardinals	Peter Bourjos	49
Cubs	Ripper Collins	137
Diamondbacks	Stephen Drew	61
Dodgers	Cookie Lavagetto	145
Giants	Bill Terry	418
Indians	Mickey Vernon	87
Mariners	Adrian Beltre	79
Marlins	Jorge Cantu	21
Mets	David Wright	326
Nationals	Sean Berry	29
Orioles	Brooks Robinson	668
Padres	Kevin Kouzmanoff	124
Phillies	Pinky Whitney	173
Pirates	Elbie Fletcher	110
Rangers	David Murphy	126
Rays	Matthew Michael Duffy	14
Red Sox	Jimmie Foxx	228
Reds	Brandon Phillips	700
Rockies	Seth Smith	8
Royals	George Brett	9
Tigers	Billy Rogell	81
Twins	Harmon Killebrew	439
White Sox	Joe Kuhel	264
Yankees	Jake Powell	73

ANOMALIES AND HALL OF FAMERS

There are nine players who have played a cubic game at more than one position, as shown in Table 13.

Table 13. Players who have played a Cubic Game at more than One Position

Travis Jackson	Third Base and Shortstop
Bob Bailey	First Base and Left Field
Michael Cuddyer	First Base and Third Base
David DeJesus	Left Field and Right Field
Chris Coghlan	Left Field and Center Field
Alex Presley	Left Field and Center Field
Eric Owens	First Base and Center Field
Ross Gload	First Base and Left Field
Jason Romano	Left Field and Center Field

There have been many players who played a cubic game for more than one team, but Hank Majeski is the only one who did it with four different clubs. Mark DeRosa and David DeJesus did it with three teams.

Many players have played a cubic game in each league.

Matt Duffy leads all active players with twenty-seven lifetime cubic games, again, through the 2018 season. Eduardo Escobar is a close second with twenty-five. So, Brandon Phillips's career record is safe for a while.

Nineteen Hall of Famers have played at least one cubic game, as shown in Table 14. Interestingly, many of them played cubic games at a position other than the one for which they are most renowned. I expect that Adrian Beltre and Albert Pujols will be added to this list.

Table 14. Cubic Games by Hall of Famers

Brooks Robinson	668	Third Base
Harmon Killebrew	439	First Base
Bill Terry	418	First Base
Jimmie Foxx	228	First Base
Joe Gordon	74	Second Base
Travis Jackson	55	43 at Shortstop and 12 at Third Base
Jim Bottomley	52	First Base
Johnny Bench	41	Third Base
Rogers Hornsby	11	Second Base
George Brett	9	Third Base
Lou Boudreau	6	Third Base
Hack Wilson	5	Second Base
George Kell	5	First Base
Joe Medwick	4	Left Field
Willie Stargell	3	Center Field
Charlie Gehringer	2	First Base
Babe Ruth	1	First Base
Arky Vaughan	1	Third Base
Tony Lazzeri	1	Shortstop

There have been many games where multiple players were cubic. For instance, the last one in the period occurred on April 9, 2018, the Rays versus the White Sox, both third baseman, Matt Duffy and Yolmer Sanchez, batted fifth and wore five. The record for most cubic players in a game is three, accomplished sixteen times. The most recent occurrence was a game on April 16, 1969, Baltimore at Boston. The three players were Brooks Robinson (5) for the Orioles, and George Scott (5) and Rico Petrocelli (6) for the Red Sox.

The record for most cubic players for one team in a game is also three. On July 20, 1949, in a game in which he singled, doubled, and was hit by a pitch in five plate appearances, the Indians all-star center-fielder Larry Doby was thrown out trying to steal home with the bases loaded and no outs. Doby was fined and benched for the next five games by player-manager Lou Boudreau.[1] In those five games, Cleveland's lineup included Mickey Vernon batting third, Joe Gordon batting clean-up, and Lou Boudreau batting fifth. These are the only five games where as many as three teammates were cubic.

COMING HOME

I suppose Babe Ruth was the greatest of all cubic players, but special mention should go to football star D. J. Dozier. He played just one season in the big leagues and appeared in twenty-five games, yet he tallied five cubic games in his fourteen starts.

Fewer than 2% of all major league players have played even one cubic game. The 335 who have form a special fraternity. A few are enshrined in Cooperstown; others didn't have much more than a cup of coffee. All are bound by this special trait, having played the game in perfect harmony. ∎

Acknowledgments

The author thanks the peer reviewers who made this a better article and welcomes requests for more information, such as a complete listing of cubic players.

The author can be reached at rbk65@optonline.net.

Note

1. "Doby Fined By Boudreau After Boner," *Evening Independent*, July 21, 1949.

APPENDIX A

Top 10 players in lifetime cubic games played at each number

Rank	2		3		4	
1	Billy Sullivan Jr.	13	Mickey Vernon	466	Brandon Phillips	700
2	Mike Heath	12	Harmon Killebrew	439	Joe Gordon	74
3	Rick Wilkins	8	Bill Terry	418	Bill Cissell	52
4	Tim McCarver	5	George McQuinn	366	Johnny Hodapp	26
5	Frankie Pytlak	3	Joe Kuhel	264	Odell Hale	25
6	Brent Mayne	2	Jimmie Foxx	228	Bobby Grich	23
7	Tom Satriano	1	Ripper Collins	137	Johnny Berardino	16
8			Elbie Fletcher	110	Wilmer Flores	14
9			Tony Lupien	110	Scooter Gennett	13
10			Ed Morgan	93	Rogers Hornsby	11

Rank	5		6		7	
1	Brooks Robinson	668	Eric McNair	152	David Murphy	127
2	Pinky Higgins	541	Rico Petrocelli	151	Jake Powell	73
3	David Wright	326	Billy Rogell	81	Gregor Blanco	53
4	Bob Horner	300	Irv Hall	67	Jim Rivera	42
5	Jim Tabor	258	Stephen Drew	61	Billy Ashley	25
6	Pinky Whitney	173	Travis Jackson	43	Kenny Lofton	24
7	Kevin Kouzmanoff	167	Ron Hansen	34	Augie Galan	17
8	Cookie Lavagetto	145	Billy Cox	32	Cody Ross	15
9	Cecil Travis	118	Mark Christman	31	3 tied with 13	
10	Bill Madlock	108	Billy Urbanski	18		

Rank	8		9	
1	Peter Bourjos	49	Bombo Rivera	12
2	Joe Marty	31	Jody Gerut	12
3	Rip Repulski	21	Ernie Young	6
4	Anthony Gose	15	Ryan Raburn	4
5	Max Venable	11	Jason Dubois	4
6	Juan Samuel	11	Skeeter Barnes	3
7	Ian Happ	10	Jim Dwyer	3
8	Gerardo Parra	8	Tomas Perez	3
9	4 tied with 7		Brady Anderson	3
10			2 tied with 2	

Appendix B: Top 10 players in lifetime cubic games played in each decade

Rank	1929–1938		1939–1948		1949–1958	
1	Pinky Higgins	541	George McQuinn	366	Mickey Vernon	466
2	Bill Terry	418	Joe Kuhel	264	Hank Majeski	76
3	Pinky Whitney	173	Jim Tabor	258	Bob Skinner	55
4	Eric McNair	152	Elbie Fletcher	110	Dick Gernert	54
5	Ripper Collins	137	Tony Lupien	110	Eddie Waitkus	48
6	Jimmie Foxx	124	Jimmie Foxx	104	Vern Stephens	45
7	Ed Morgan	93	Irv Hall	67	Dale Long	44
8	Billy Rogell	81	Cookie Lavagetto	64	Jim Rivera	39
9	Cookie Lavagetto	81	Joe Gordon	45	Dee Fondy	36
10	Cecil Travis	77	Cecil Travis	41	Joe Gordon	29

Rank	1959–1968		1969–1978		1979–1988	
1	Brooks Robinson	393	Brooks Robinson	259	Bob Horner	235
2	Harmon Killebrew	269	Harmon Killebrew	170	Bill Madlock	108
3	Rico Petrocelli	150	Bob Horner	65	Johnny Bench	40
4	Pete Runnels	71	Jim Spencer	61	Bobby Grich	23
5	Jim Lefebvre	59	Bob Bailey	20	Randy Ready	21
6	Bubba Phillips	39	George Scott	17	Mike Heath	12
7	Ron Hansen	34	Ed Spiezio	15	Rance Mulliniks	11
8	Ed Charles	19	Ed Charles	15	Dave Meier	10
9	Ken Harrelson	14	Danny Cater	13	Roy Smalley	9
10	Walt Moryn	12	Jim Lefebvre	11	Hector Cruz	9

Rank	1989–1998		1999–2008		2009–2018	
1	Sean Berry	29	David Wright	245	Brandon Phillips	505
2	Billy Ashley	25	Brandon Phillips	195	David Murphy	120
3	B.J. Surhoff	13	Kevin Kouzmanoff	86	Kevin Kouzmanoff	81
4	Tony Fernandez	12	Adrian Beltre	79	David Wright	81
5	Juan Samuel	11	Ed Sprague	62	Juan Uribe	55
6	Max Venable	11	Stephen Drew	50	Gregor Blanco	53
7	F.P. Santangelo	10	Nomar Garciaparra	28	Peter Bourjos	49
8	Ron Gant	9	Kenny Lofton	24	Matthew M. Duffy	27
9	3 tied with 8		Jorge Cantu	21	Eduardo Escobar	25
10			Albert Pujols	15	Ian Desmond	16

Baseball 1858–65

By the Numbers

Bruce S. Allardice

Little serious statistical or analytical research has been done on baseball prior to 1871 (the year that the National Association of Professional Base Ball Players started), in large part because there was no organized record-keeping of games. Several very good general histories of the period have been published, notably John Thorn's *Baseball in the Garden of Eden*, Peter Morris's *But Didn't We Have Fun?*, and Bill Ryczek's *Baseball's First Inning*. Larry McCray's Protoball website has compiled data—albeit not systematically—on over 10,000 early clubs and games in 161 different countries, along with learned essays on the early game.[1] But for the statistic-minded "sabermetrician," these resources provide only anecdotal evidence of how games prior to 1871 were played. This contrasts with the thousands of web pages, articles, and books statistically analyzing professional baseball post-1870. Key questions about early baseball, such as where the game was played or how many runs were scored each game, have never been addressed.

This article attempts to address this gap in baseball historiography, and answer some of these questions.

THE THOLKES DATA

"Data! Data! Data! He cried impatiently. "I cannot make bricks without clay."[2]

Thanks largely to SABR member Bob Tholkes, sabermetricians finally have a large enough and random enough sample of early ballgames to analyze and draw statistically valid conclusions. The Tholkes Excel spreadsheet covers the years 1858 to 1865, the eight years after the 1857 rules changes which are usually considered to have created the modern game of baseball, and is viewable at the Protoball website.[3] It lists all the games played under National Association rules as reported by multiple sources, mainly the four major baseball-covering newspapers of the time: the New York metropolitan-area-based *New York Clipper*, *New York Mercury*, *Porter's Spirit of the Times*, and the *Brooklyn Daily Eagle*.

A typical game report, from the Brooklyn Daily Eagle, *June 26, 1865*

The data comprise reports of 4,673 games.[4] Most reports include date the game was played, the source of the report of the game, the team names, scores, innings played, and whether the teams were junior or senior. Not all game reports list all these items. A few lack detailed scores, some don't mention the innings played, and a handful don't mention the senior or junior status of the clubs.[5] However, even with these gaps, the data are robust enough for valid analysis. The number of games per year averages 584, a number greater than the games played per year in the major leagues from 1876 to 1891.

So what do the data tell us about early, amateur/pre-professional, baseball?

EARLY SCORES

In this era the runs scored per game were dramatically greater than in baseball games today, reminiscent of softball scores—which should not be surprising, since 1858–65 baseball resembled modern softball as much as it resembled modern baseball.

The median game score was 27–17. The highest single club score was 162 runs (the Philadelphia

Athletic vs. the evidently hapless Alert of Danville, who scored 11, October 20, 1865. And only 8 innings were played!). The highest total score was 148–139 (Toronto vs. Hamilton, September 24, 1864). On the other end, 5 clubs scored zero runs (including a 47–0 shutout in Syracuse, New York, in 1865), and 18 scored only 1 run.

In 1987 historian John Thorn expressed the conventional wisdom on scoring in the 1860s when he noted that "the baseball games of the 1860s typically featured 35 or more combined runs per game, with scores of 60–100 runs not unusual."[6] With these new data, it can be said that the scoring for the early 1860s, at least, was significantly higher:

Year	Games	Runs scored per game (RPG)
1858	377	48.96
1859	597	47.62
1860	1024	46.07
1861	428	45.04
1862	257	44.08
1863	271	41.38
1864	448	48.26
1865	1260	55.37
Avg.	–	50.95[7]

RUNS PER INNING (RPI)

The 1857 rules changes mandated a nine-inning standard game, with extra innings if there was a tie after nine. However, clubs seemed slow to adopt this new rule, with games called because of weather or oncoming darkness, or by agreement. The average innings per game slowly climbed upward almost every year after 1858. Considered by runs per inning played (RPI)—a more accurate measure than straight runs per game (RPG), the scoring averages show the same trend as RPG, but with a more uniform 1858–63 decline:

Year	RPI[8]	Change from Prior Year
1858	6.23	–
1859	6.00	-.23
1860	5.73	-.27
1861	5.52	-.21
1862	5.24	-.28
1863	4.98	-.26
1864	5.70	+.72
1865	6.78	+1.08

Several trends can be seen here. The average RPG declines about a run per year (approximately 3%) every year through 1863. This percentage change is not out

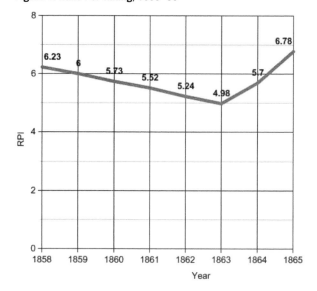

Figure 1. Runs Per Inning, 1858–65

of line with scoring fluctuations we've seen in major league baseball in the past 100 years. This accords with speculation in some histories that as the game became more practiced and more familiar, the skill level of the fielding increased, which caused the scores to go down.

However, this trend towards lower scores dramatically reverses in 1864 and 1865, jumping seven RPG each of these years. The percentage increases in RPG are 16.60% for 1864 and 14.73% for 1865. Looking at the records for major league baseball we see several scoring jumps that meet or exceed those of 1864–65, as follows:

- 15.9% from 1886 to 1887
- 28.78% from 1888 to 1889
- 28.95% from 1892 to 1893
- 17.7% from 1910 to 1911
- 25.45% from 1919 to 1921
- 19.00% from 1968 to 1969[9]

While the increase in raw number of RPG was greater in 1864–65 (due to the higher overall scores), percentage-wise the increase is not unprecedented.

The major-league RPG increases in the years listed above can all be attributed to specific rules changes or changes in equipment. For example, in 1889 the walk rule was changed from 5 balls to 4. The livelier corked ball was introduced for 1911. For 1969, the strike zone was shrunk and the pitching mound was lowered from 15 inches to 10. So is it with 1864 and 1865. The December 9, 1863, convention of the National

Association of Base Ball Players changed the rules to allow the umpire to call "balls" and "walks," and restrictions were placed on how a pitcher could pitch. The December 14, 1864, convention abolished the "bound game" rule whereby fair hit balls caught on the first bounce were "out," and mandated that fair hit balls must be caught on the fly (the modern rule) to become an "out."[10]

Notice that these rules changes would result in increased scoring, whether this increase was intended or not. It was in fact widely expected at the time that the changes would increase scoring. In early 1864 the *New York Clipper*, baseball's then-equivalent of a "newspaper of record," predicted that the 1863 changes in pitching rules "must perforce result in there being less speed in pitching…and the transfer of the interest of a match from the pitcher to the basemen and outfielders. Of course we must expect to see a large increase in scoring, the probability being that the average runs of a match [for each team] will be increased from twenty to thirty in a majority of games played."[11] The difference between the "bound game" and "fly game" rules was recognized in 1862 by Brooklyn's prominent "Star" Club. The Star played an inter-squad game, first nine (regulars) versus second nine (backups) and to even the contest, the first nine fielded via the "fly game" whereas the second nine used the "bound game" rule. Despite this handicap, the first nine won 35–15.[12]

The 1863 and 1864 conventions changed the rules (which changed scoring) but one caveat remains: How quickly and completely were these rule changes actually implemented? Put another way, would the scoring differences be greater if the rules changes had been immediately and uniformly adopted by the clubs? Richard Hershberger's new book, *Strike Four*, goes into some detail in discussing the rules changes and concludes that, for the new ball-strike rules at least, 1864 umpires rarely enforced the rules. "(T)he base on balls was a new and strange idea…. [In addition to the vagueness of the new rules] the challenge was to get umpires to call balls and strikes at all…Players didn't like the new rule. Umpires…didn't like the new rule either."[13] One indirect indicator of an implementation delay is shown below, where scoring for "elite" clubs increased in 1866 as well, suggesting the 1864 and 1865 rules changes took years to fully take hold.[14]

SCORES OVERALL COMPARED TO SCORES OF "FIRST CLASS" TEAMS

The data here can be compared to the data of the scoring of the "first class" teams for 1861, 1864, 1865, 1866 and 1869. The Beadle Baseball Guides recounted the

yearly scoring of what they defined as the "first class" clubs (almost all in the New York City area) in the games they played against "first class" opponents under National Association rules.[15]

Year	First Class Games[16]	First Class RPG	Overall RPG
1861	64	41.60	45.04
1864	179	40.20	48.26
1865	258	48.60	55.37
1866	485	53.13	
1867	–	62.84	
1869	1138	51.63	

The "first class" teams scored somewhat fewer runs than the overall average. That might be explained by the fact that the better teams would feature better defense, or that the first-class games would feature fewer high-scoring mismatches. The 1864 difference is a bit of an outlier and may be accounted for by the fact that many "first class" teams already played by the new rules and had already adjusted their defenses.

SCORES, JUNIOR CLUBS vs. SENIOR

A surprising 43.6% of the reported games were games between two "junior" clubs, with 50.9% exclusively "senior" and 1.7% involving a junior/senior matchup.[17] A look at the scoring differences between junior and senior teams in the two biggest years, 1860 and 1865, reveals little difference in RPG.

Year	RPG Junior Games	RPG Overall[18]	Difference
1860	43.61	46.01	2.40 RPG
1865	53.70	55.37	1.67 RPG

Year	RPG Junior Games	RPG Senior Games	Difference
1860	43.61	47.61	4.0 RPG
1865	53.70	56.90	3.2 RPG

Since the junior games averaged fewer innings than the senior (7.7 innings versus 8.4), the runs per inning (rpi) were roughly equal:

Year	RPI Junior Games	RPI Senior Games
1860	5.66	5.81
1865	6.97	6.73
Avg.	6.31	6.27

RUNS PER GAME, NEW YORK CITY vs. ELSEWHERE

Of the games we have scores for, 65.8 percent (3067) were played in the greater New York City (GNYC) area. This proportion reflects the New York City origins of the game, as well as the locus of the four major source newspapers. In these games, the GNYC clubs scored significantly fewer runs per game (45.58) than did teams outside of GNYC (54.80). This disparity probably reflects the fact that the GNYC clubs were older and more experienced at the game, had better defenses, and were less likely than newer teams to play in mismatched games.

Looking only at "first class" clubs, the same scoring disparity occurs. For example, in 1867, NYC/Brooklyn teams averaged 8.28 fewer runs scored in their games than teams elsewhere.[19]

WHEN WERE THE GAMES PLAYED?

The following charts the games on a yearly basis:

Year	Games
1858	377
1859	597
1860	1024
1861	428
1862	257
1863	271
1864	448
1865	1260

The dip in games caused by the Civil War is apparent in the 1861–64 seasons. The 1865 number isn't greatly impacted by the war, because Lee surrendered in April and (as seen below) usually very few games were played prior to May. In essence, in 1865 the game resumes where it left off in 1860.[20]

Most of the games were played in the late summer-early fall, rather than in the spring:

Month	Games
January	11
February	11
March	3
April	24
May	128
June	466
July	606
August	936
September	1111
October	906
November	443
December	28

While in modern times we may think of baseball as the "game of summer," early baseball can better be characterized as the "game of fall."

Figure 2. Games Played, By Year

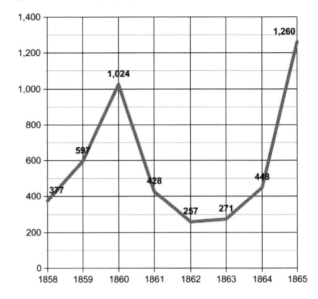

Figure 3. Games Played, By Month

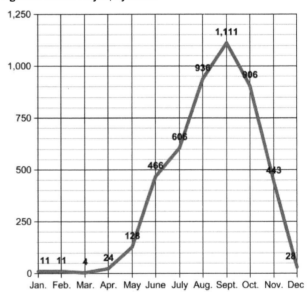

WHERE WERE THE GAMES PLAYED?

Of games where a state or region is indicated, 68.2% were played in GNYC. A further 14.9% were played elsewhere in New York state.[21] By state/region, the breakdown is as follows:

Region/State	Games	Region/State	Games
GNYC	2984	MI	57
NY (non-GNYC)	650	WI	1
NJ (non-GNYC)	32	IA	1
PA	216	MN	4
CT	51	KY	4
RI	6	VA	2
MA	131	MO	42
ME	21	MD	44
DE	4	DC	37
OH	2	LA	18
IL	30	CA	12
IN	3	Canada	18

HOW MANY INNINGS FOR EACH GAME?

The 1857 rules changes established the nine-inning game as standard. This standard was not always followed. One recent history posits that in 1856, the average game lasted only six innings, and that after the 1857 changes, "the nine-inning game was soon firmly established."[22] The data suggest otherwise—that the nine-inning standard, like other rules changes, took some time to become the standard:

Year	2	3	4	5	6	7	8	9	10+ Innings
1858	2	1	5	24	36	49	38	174	1
1859	1	2	7	32	59	64	71	274	5
1860	3	4	9	70	55	82	71	466	9
1861	0	1	0	20	28	27	29	193	0
1862	0	0	0	7	13	14	23	133	5
1863	0	3	1	4	9	19	11	114	2
1864	0	1	1	11	13	12	13	185	2
1865	1	1	5	59	60	79	58	503	9

Games with Innings Played Indicated

Year	Innings Per Game	Percentage of Games Less than 9 innings
1858	7.86	45.4
1859	7.93	45.8
1860	8.03	38.3
1861	8.16	33.2
1862	8.42	29.2
1863	8.31	28.8
1864	8.46	21.4
1865	8.17	33.2
		Overall: 36.2

Just as today, games could be and were shortened because of rain, approaching darkness, agreement between the teams, or time constraints. Since rain during a game generally causes few postponements, then as well as today, it appears the majority of shortened games involved some sort of club agreement and thus some casualness toward the nine-inning standard. More research needs to be done to explain the 1865 uptick in shortened games.

EXTRA-INNING GAMES AND TIE GAMES

The 1857 rules changes allowed for extra-inning games, in case the score was tied after nine innings. This change was in part to eliminate tie games. Just as with the other rules changes, it appears clubs were slow to adopt the new rule:

Year	Games[23]	Extra Inning Games	Tie Games
1858	321	1	6
1859	515	5	5
1860	768	9	22
1861	289	0	6
1862	195	5	4
1863	163	2	6
1864	238	2	9
1865	766	9	12

For this period, only 1% of the games were extra inning games—much less than in today's game. Since 2012, one game in eleven (8.7%) is tied after nine and goes to extra innings. In part this disparity may reflect the higher scoring of the early games, the higher scoring making it less likely that a game would be tied after nine. The early games were in fact more likely to end in a tie than in extra innings, with about 1.5% of the games (mostly, nine inning games) ending in a tie.[24]

JUNIOR GAMES AND SENIOR GAMES, PERCENT COMPARISON

Year	Junior	Junior/Senior	Senior[25]
1858	46.3	5.3	47.9
1859	41.5	4.0	52.6
1860	44.3	5.4	48.5
1861	44.0	4.4	49.2
1862	37.5	2.3	59.8
1863	37.8	6.3	55.2
1864	45.9	2.0	48.5
1865	44.7	1.9	51.8
Total	43.6	3.8	50.9

There was a slight dip in junior baseball during the middle of the Civil War. The war appears to have hurt junior clubs even more than it did senior clubs.

FUTURE RESEARCH

Sabermetric statistical research has covered major league baseball in the years from 1876 to present in great detail. This article will hopefully fill the gap for 1858–65, as much as it can be filled with the available data. The author is compiling similar data for the years 1866–70 to enable similar analysis. ■

Notes

1. John Thorn, *Baseball in the Garden of Eden: The Secret History of the Early Game* (New York, Simon & Schuster, 2012); Peter Morris, *But Didn't We Have Fun? An Informal History of Baseball's Pioneer Era, 1843–1870* (Chicago, Ivan R. Dee, 2008); William J. Ryczek, *Baseball's First Inning: A History of the National Pastime Through the Civil War* (Jefferson, NC, McFarland & Co., 2009). www.protoball.org.
2. Sherlock Holmes, in Arthur Conan Doyle's "The Adventure of the Copper Beeches."
3. www.protoball.org.
4. 4,881 total entries, including games postponed because of rain.
5. For reports where the junior/senior status of the clubs is not given, Mr. Tholkes researched and filled in that information whenever possible. Tholkes has also analyzed the average time of the games, based on an admittedly smaller and non-random sample. See "Time of Game in the Amateur Era: 1860–65," *19th Century Baseball Newsletter*, Fall 2019, 3–4.
6. Our Game blog, Aug. 6, 2014, at https://ourgame.mlblogs.com.
7. By comparison, NA games in 1871 averaged 20.94 RPG, and in 2019 (as of July 15) MLB games have averaged about 9.6 RPG.
8. Not all game reports with innings have scores, and vice-versa. This table compares recorded RPG and recorded average innings per game for each year.
9. Numbers taken from Baseball-Reference.com.
10. For the 1863 convention, see the *Brooklyn Daily Eagle*, December 10, 1863. For the 1864 convention, see the *New York Clipper*, December 14, 1864. For a more general discussion of these rule changes, see Richard Hershberger, *Strike Four: The Evolution of Baseball* (New York, Rowman & Littlefield, 2019), chapters 9, 12 and 13; Ryczek, *Baseball's First Inning*, pp. 178–83. The 1863 changes impacted Rules 5–7.
11. *New York Clipper*, May 7, 1864. This article presents a detailed discussion of the rules changes for 1864.
12. *New York Clipper*, May 24, 1862. *New York Clipper*, Nov. 19, 1864 opines that the "fly game" was best for "first class" clubs, whereas the "bound game" "unquestionably" suited the lesser clubs, and notes that the Excelsior and Star of Brooklyn, two leading first class clubs, played only fly games in 1864.
13. Hershberger, *Strike Four*, 85.
14. Historians have advanced other factors that could have increased scoring, such as the Civil War (where call-ups to the army could create more mismatches) and the ball being made more lively. For the latter reason, see the *New York Clipper*, April 16, 1870.
15. See Beadle's *Dime Base-Ball Player*, 1862, 55–69; 1865, 59–63; 1866, 59–65; 1867, 75–91; 1868, 94–97; 1870, 71–72. The 1868 guide presents runs scored in a different way, and the RPG is an estimate based on the offensive runs scored per game per team for the 94 teams listed, plus the opponents' estimated RPG. The 1869 guide gives no similar figures.
16. Some double counting of games here, which wouldn't impact the RPG. As can be seen, the "first class" games were a significant percentage of the overall games.
17. In the Civil War era "junior" teams generally consisted of young men in their late teens. See Robert Pruter, *The Rise of American High School Sports and the Search for Control: 1880–1930* (Syracuse U. Press, 2013), 9.
18. The overall number includes the junior games.
19. Beadle's *Dime Base-Ball Player*, 1868, 94–97. The number is an estimate (see fn. 15 for methodology).
20. This trend can be seen in another study of baseball, focusing on yearly newspaper mentions of the game. See Bruce Allardice, "The Spread of Baseball, 1859–1870," at http://protoball.org/The_Spread_of_Base_Ball,_1859_-_1870
21. This GNYC emphasis may in part reflect the fact that the newspapers reporting the games were all based in New York.
22. Hershberger, *Strike Four*, 47.
23. Where innings are indicated.
24. For a discussion of the reasons why the nine-inning and extra-inning rules were adopted in 1857, see Hershberger, *Strike Four*, 46–47. From the data, it appears the tie games were NOT "thoroughly abolished" by the new rules (Hershberger, *Strike Four*, 47).
25. Percentages don't add up to 100 because a small percentage of games (less than 2%) have no junior/senior status indicated.

Using Clustering to Find Pitch Subtypes and Effective Pairings

Gregory Dvorocsik, Eno Sarris, and Joseph Camp, PhD

INTRODUCTION

Using Statcast data, it is now possible to compare individual pitches across baseball based on characteristics like movement, velocity, and spin rate that become obvious and meaningful even in a single outing. Various research has used those physical characteristics to define optimal pitches.

However, to be effective even an elite pitch must be mixed with less optimal ones, especially for starting pitchers. Therefore, it is imperative to study the interactions between pitches to fully understand the best shape a particular pitch should have and whether pairing a pitch with others improves or decreases effectiveness. Here, we define pairing as when both pitches are present in a pitcher's arsenal.

This work has potential impact on pitch design, player development, and scouting. For the former, teams could focus efforts on teaching young pitchers new subtypes that have specific shapes according to the characteristics of the best pitches already thrown by that pitcher. For the latter, with very little in-game data, teams could seek to add pitchers that already possess effective pairings or avoid pitchers with ineffective pairings.

BACKGROUND

Pitch design has advanced to the point that tinkering in a lab with high-speed, high-resolution cameras is commonplace to potentially modify the ideal shape of a given pitch. These systems capture the way in which a pitch leaves the fingers, having potential impact on the spin axis, spin rate, velocity, and resulting horizontal and vertical movement. With such fine precision, the traditional classes of pitches might be called into question since sub-classes of pitch types could be forming based on a number of minor alterations to the grip, release point, and other pitching mechanics. We could potentially rely on existing works that have studied the following:

1. classifying pitches in an unsupervised manner pre- and post-Statcast[1]

2. the characteristics of an effective changeup[2]

3. the optimal distribution of pitches[3]

4. a survey of publicly available data and existing methods to evaluate pitch types and performance[4]

However, these works have not evaluated how one pitch type or subtype can affect another when a pitcher throws multiple pitches. We seek to understand whether a particular pitch—with its physical characteristics of spin rate, velocity, and break—can have better or worse outcomes when a second pitch of different physical characteristics is paired with it.

In this paper, we use clustering within each of the most common pitch classifications as determined by Statcast to find subtypes of pitches and evaluate their performance when paired with all other subtypes to determine if performance can increase or decrease by these pairings. Looking at the 9 most common MLB pitch types for left-handed and right-handed pitchers across all pitches thrown in the 2016 and 2017 seasons, we find the total number of subtypes that result to be 30 for both types of pitchers. (Levels of subtypes differed between left-handers and right-handers.) We consider four performance metrics:

- swinging strike percentage (whiff rate)

- exit velocity (how hard the ball was hit)

- percentage of time the launch angle is below 0 percent (ground ball rate)

- percentage of time the launch angle is above 40 percent (pop-up rate)

We created a reference for each of these subtypes by studying the average performance of each of these 30 pitch subtypes for each handedness. We found that even within the same Statcast pitch types, there are sizable differences in effectiveness for these four performance metrics across pitch subtypes.

Then, we compared this reference performance against the performance of that same reference subtype for all occurrences where a pitcher throws that second subtype and created lists ordered according to the change in each performance metric. Hence, we found the highest and lowest performing subtype pair for whiff, pop-up, and ground ball rates and exit velocity, calling these the best and worst subtype pairings for each reference subtype and performance metric. For example, looking at CH1 of LHP in the top left corner of Table 2 and Table 3, the highest positive difference in swinging strike rate for CH1 was when FC3 was paired with it, and the greatest negative difference in swinging strike rate for CH1 was when SI2 was paired with it. After repeating this for all reference subtypes and all possible subtype pairs across all performance metrics, we found that each of these best and worst pairing subtypes are typically distinct across these performance metrics for a given reference subtype. When we consider the average gains across each of these metrics, we see an improvement of 1.6 percent swinging strike percentage, 3.8 percent pop-up rate, 4.2 percent ground ball rate, and a reduction of 1.2 MPH on exit velocity. Conversely, by performing the same process for finding the worst pairing subtypes, we see reductions in the swinging strike rate by 1.9, pop-up rate by 2.9, ground ball rate by 4.8, and increase the exit velocity by 1.2 MPH.

PITCH SUBTYPE CLASSIFICATION USING STATCAST-DRIVEN K-MEANS CLUSTERING

In order to immediately broadcast pitch type across various platforms from in-stadium scoreboards to the MLB AtBat application, Major League Baseball classifies each pitch based on Statcast metrics. While we cannot know the exact algorithms used to perform the classification, based on per pitch data from 2016 and 2017, we know there are 9 predominant pitch types for both right-handed and left-handed pitchers:

- four-seam fastball (FF)

- two-seam fastball (FT)

- cutter (FC)

- splitter (FS)

- sinker (SI)

- curveball (CU)

- knuckle curve (KC)

- slider (SL)

- changeup (CH)

Since these classifications are broad in nature, there are differences in horizontal and vertical movement, velocity, and spin rate, even within the same class of pitch. Movement of pitches is relative to a gyroball, which is a ball spinning in a spiral shape (like a football). A gyroball-shaped pitch is considered the theoretical zero/zero from which other pitches are defined. Unlike a perfect gyroball, almost all pitches exhibit some form of magnus effect—the forces that deflect the ball in a particular direction based on the velocity, spin, and spin axis. To understand the degree to which these four physical characteristics differ within each class, we use clustering within a four-dimensional space as represented by these four physical parameters:

Horizontal Movement: From the catcher's viewpoint and with respect to the movement of a gyroball, a negative value would move toward a right-handed hitter, whereas a positive value would move toward a left-handed hitter.

Vertical Movement: From the catcher's viewpoint and as compared to the movement of a gyroball, a negative value would move downward, whereas a positive value would rise.

Velocity: The miles per hour that a pitch travels as measured out of the pitcher's hand.

Spin Rate: The revolutions per minute along the spin axis of a particular pitch.

We use K-means clustering to form the clusters, meaning we partition n observations into the k clusters where there exist an n of the number of pitches thrown in 2016 and 2017 from a particular handedness from a particular MLB pitch classification. The k is determined via the elbow method where with each of the increasing k values, we evaluate the aggregate Within-Cluster-Sum-of-Squares (WCSS) error between all the data points and the k cluster centroids. In particular, over all k for a given MLB pitch type, when the WCSS value begins to flatten, an elbow is created in

LHP Type/Subtype	Count	SwK (%)	Exit Velo (MPH)	LA>40° (%)	LA<0° (GB %)	Velo (MPH)	Spin (RPM)	Xbrk (in.)	Ybrk (in.)	RHP Type/Subtype	Count	SwK (%)	Exit Velo (MPH)	LA>40° (%)	LA<0° (GB %)	Velo (MPH)	Spin (RPM)	Xbrk (in.)	Ybrk (in.)
CH	45948	15.7	81.3	16.0	37.1	83.1	1811	7.0	4.8	CH	97836	15.0	82.1	15.0	37.8	84.3	1741	-6.3	5.5
CH 1	18837	15.7	82.0	17.1	36.3	84.1	1961	6.3	6.3	CH 1	28814	14.1	83.5	14.1	38.4	86.6	1912	-5.6	5.6
CH 2	13286	15.9	82.2	13.9	39.9	81.2	1529	6.5	5.9	CH 2	27372	16.0	82.8	12.1	42.9	83.4	1480	-5.7	5.3
CH 3	13825	15.5	79.5	16.6	35.5	83.5	1878	8.5	6.0	CH 3	16232	15.3	81.2	24.1	29.1	79.7	1901	-6.0	6.0
CU	28233	12.5	81.5	13.0	38.8	76.7	2440	-3.0	-2.7	CH 4	25418	14.7	80.5	14.9	37.7	85.4	1725	-7.8	5.4
CU 1	6561	12.1	79.2	10.9	42.8	75.7	2551	-4.2	-3.7	CU	87674	12.2	81.8	13.9	36.0	78.1	2498	4.0	-4.7
CU 2	10644	13.2	82.4	16.0	33.1	79.0	2259	-3.1	-3.0	CU 1	35888	10.7	82.5	12.3	38.2	76.1	2589	3.4	-5.0
CU 3	11028	12.0	82.1	11.2	42.4	75.1	2550	-2.4	-3.7	CU 2	31387	13.9	82.2	16.5	32.5	80.6	2336	3.9	-4.3
FC	15322	10.6	82.1	16.7	32.8	87.4	2193	0.6	5.6	CU 3	20399	12.3	80.1	12.8	37.4	77.8	2589	5.1	-4.9
FC 1	5524	11.8	81.8	16.0	33.0	86.1	2278	0.8	6.4	FC	50020	11.4	81.9	19.6	29.6	88.7	2363	-0.1	7.3
FC 2	4876	9.4	82.2	15.9	33.5	86.8	1995	0.4	6.6	FC 1	17663	10.8	81.3	22.7	27.2	91.7	2441	0.0	7.7
FC 3	4922	10.6	82.3	18.3	31.8	89.4	2292	0.7	6.9	FC 2	12402	9.5	82.3	19.5	30.6	87.3	2091	0.0	7.5
FF	130063	7.7	83.1	25.4	21.7	92.2	2234	5.4	8.6	FC 3	19955	13.1	82.1	17.1	31.1	86.9	2462	-0.1	7.0
FF 1	34481	7.6	81.9	24.5	21.9	92.6	2206	6.4	10.2	FF	376138	7.9	83.6	26.1	20.6	93.1	2269	-4.7	10.6
FF 2	41537	5.9	84.5	21.5	26.6	90.4	2110	4.9	10.2	FF 1	103554	8.0	82.1	25.2	20.8	93.9	2266	-5.7	10.5
FF 3	54045	9.1	82.9	29.1	17.6	93.2	2348	5.1	10.6	FF 2	124287	5.8	84.6	24.2	23.3	91.1	2145	-4.3	10.5
FS	2679	18.7	81.8	16.4	38.7	83.4	1562	8.3	3.8	FF 3	148297	9.4	84.0	28.7	18.1	94.4	2376	-4.3	10.8
FS 1	503	20.1	83.9	13.3	41.0	84.6	1474	7.5	4.6	FS	16782	17.2	82.5	13.0	40.6	84.7	1516	-5.3	4.3
FS 2	863	20.3	83.9	11.3	42.1	81.3	1255	7.7	4.4	FS 1	5310	16.2	82.5	14.6	36.9	82.2	1241	-5.1	4.1
FS 3	719	13.9	78.9	30.0	29.4	84.2	2154	8.5	5.4	FS 2	7366	16.2	83.7	11.8	44.0	86.3	1693	-4.7	4.5
FS 4	594	21.2	79.5	11.7	42.2	84.5	1368	9.6	4.5	FS 3	4106	18.0	80.6	13.2	39.6	85.3	1554	-6.8	4.2
FT	55588	6.1	84.1	15.6	35.4	91.5	2134	8.1	5.9	FT	144139	5.7	84.5	15.6	35.1	92.4	2170	-7.9	7.7
FT 1	23008	7.0	85.2	18.4	32.4	92.8	2206	7.3	7.6	FT 1	46996	5.7	82.2	16.0	33.8	92.6	2155	-9.5	7.5
FT 2	15669	5.0	85.0	12.6	41.5	89.4	2030	7.5	7.2	FT 2	47317	6.5	85.7	15.3	31.5	93.9	2298	-7.2	7.9
FT 3	16911	5.8	82.0	14.8	34.1	91.7	2132	9.7	7.3	FT 3	49826	4.9	85.7	12.5	39.9	90.9	2062	-7.0	7.6
KC	8318	12.6	82.7	8.6	41.9	79.3	2229	-2.7	-3.3	KC	22914	13.3	82.5	10.6	43.5	80.7	2520	4.2	-6.0
KC 1	2172	12.1	83.9	8.3	40.8	78.8	2474	-2.2	-3.9	KC 1	7884	9.6	84.4	9.7	44.3	78.2	2424	3.8	-6.2
KC 2	1571	10.4	81.1	5.6	44.4	77.7	2350	-3.6	-4.4	KC 2	6206	17.6	82.7	10.8	45.4	83.4	2732	3.7	-5.9
KC 3	1994	12.2	84.2	4.6	56.9	79.4	2137	-2.3	-4.5	KC 3	6056	13.4	80.1	10.0	43.7	80.9	2615	5.1	-6.2
KC 4	2581	14.7	81.9	13.3	31.3	80.7	2022	-2.9	-3.4	KC 4	2768	14.0	82.3	13.6	37.3	81.0	2113	4.4	-5.5
SI	23387	6.8	83.7	17.1	35.9	90.8	2107	7.9	4.5	SI	59971	5.5	84.8	13.2	38.5	91.6	2124	-7.8	6.1
SI 1	13200	6.8	84.6	21.1	30.0	91.7	2172	7.4	6.3	SI 1	26596	5.9	85.6	14.8	35.9	92.1	2230	-7.3	6.3
SI 2	4846	6.3	84.6	8.9	47.3	87.5	1953	7.3	5.6	SI 2	12880	5.5	82.4	14.1	38.2	91.8	2126	-9.9	6.0
SI 3	5341	7.2	81.1	14.9	40.0	91.4	2083	9.6	5.8	SI 3	20495	5.1	85.6	10.6	42.0	89.5	1984	-7.3	5.9
SL	44923	15.9	81.8	17.0	33.9	83.1	2275	-1.4	1.4	SL	142297	15.8	81.6	18.4	32.4	85.0	2345	2.0	2.3
SL 1	10902	16.2	79.6	18.2	32.3	80.9	2307	-2.1	1.4	SL 1	32906	15.5	82.6	18.6	30.3	82.2	2457	1.4	2.0
SL 2	20593	15.9	82.3	17.0	35.3	85.9	2326	-1.4	2.0	SL 2	71972	15.5	81.2	18.2	33.3	87.1	2338	2.0	2.6
SL 3	10881	15.7	82.6	15.1	33.5	80.4	2385	-0.7	1.3	SL 3	6199	15.3	83.0	17.9	33.4	84.2	1278	1.9	2.4
SL 4	2547	15.7	83.0	18.2	30.5	81.0	1252	-1.5	1.9	SL 4	31220	17.0	80.2	18.8	32.3	83.4	2457	2.6	2.0

Table 1. LHP and RHP type/subtype performance metrics and physical characteristics.

the curve, signaling the reduction of error by increasing the number of clusters has lessened significantly and forming the appropriate number of clusters. To ensure that each physical trait does not dominate, we scale the smallest and largest value of each field to be in the same range of –1 to + 1. Since the elbow method is known to suffer from some ambiguity in terms of the precise location of the bend, we have favored a lower number of clusters to avoid multiple versions of the same subtype.[5] In other words, we use the inflection point where the slope first begins to flatten.

Interestingly, while each number of pitch subtypes is not the same per MLB Statcast pitch type, the total number of pitch subtypes ends up being 30 for both right-handed pitchers (RHP) and left-handed pitchers (LHP). We now consider varying levels of performance across the types and subtypes for each pitch. Since pitches could be successful in different manners, we choose different performance metrics evaluated when each pitch type or subtype is thrown:

1. swinging strike percentage, meaning the percentage of all pitches thrown of that kind that generate swings and misses,

2. average exit velocity, meaning the MPH off the bat when contact is made with that kind of pitch, and

3. extreme launch angles, which we define as the angle off the bat for all batted balls off of that kind of pitch that are either less than 0 degrees (ground ball) or greater than 40 degrees (pop fly).

We first consider the aggregate performance of all pitches thrown in each subtype regardless of what other types of pitches are combined to form a pitch arsenal. Table 1 captures all 9 of the predominant pitch types for left-handed pitchers and right-handed pitchers on the left and right side of the table, respectively. Below each of the 9 types are the subtypes as defined by the aforementioned k-means clustering and elbow method. For the type and subtypes, we have presented the count of the total number of times each pitch has been thrown over the two seasons, the performance metrics, and the four physical dimensions over which we based the clustering.

The performance of some subtypes can be vastly different, even for the same type of pitch. For example, RHP KC1 has a swinging strike percentage of only 9.6 percent as compared to an average of 13.3 and as high as 17.6 for KC2. The key distinction between KC1 and KC2 subtypes is that the lower-performing KC1 is 5.2 MPH slower but has a similar pitch shape in terms of horizontal and vertical break. To give a feel for another performance metric, we turn to the situation where the launch angle is above 40 degrees, producing a routine fly ball. For LHP, a high-spin splitter (FS3) produces a fly ball at a 30 percent rate versus 11.3 percent for a low-spin splitter (FS2). This relationship is flipped for changeups, where there is an advantage to reduced spin for increasing the ground ball rate (launch angle below 0 degrees). This can be seen in the low-spin version of the changeup (CH2 for both) versus a changeup with a higher spin (CH3 for both) with the RHP version increasing the ground ball rate by 13.8 percent.

We can more easily see the physical characteristics of spin in revolutions per minute (RPM) and the horizontal and vertical break in inches in Fig. 1, where we have separated the spin and velocity into one graph and horizontal-vertical break into another graph. We observe that there is more horizontal-break diversity in subtype characteristics than vertical-break diversity. For example, while subtypes rarely span more than 1 or 2 vertical inches, they can have over 6 inches of difference in horizontal movement (e.g., RHP FT). There is far greater distinction in the spin and velocity of subtypes, as observed in Fig. 1. For example, the cluster centers for sliders can vary by more than 1200 RPMs and over 7 MPH for changeups.

When we focus on the shape of the spin-velocity figures by types, we can observe the two places that LHP and RHP had most dissimilar subtype clustering. First, LHP had a high-spin splitter that was not present in the RHP figure. Second, RHP had a changeup that had a relatively higher spin rate for the lower velocity of the pitch. Lastly, while we observe the same number of knuckle curves for both pitcher types, the shape is far more distinct for RHP, where there is a high-spin, high-speed version that is not present with LHP.

EVALUATING THE EFFECTIVENESS OF PITCH SUBTYPE PAIRINGS

Our goal in this section is to quantify the effect of a single pitch subtype when the pitcher pairs that subtype with another subtype. In other words, when a pitcher has both subtypes in his arsenal, we say that the two subtypes have a pairing. To do so, we consider any time these reference subtypes are paired with each of the other subtypes, meaning the pitcher throws both subtypes. We evaluate all combinations of pitch pairings according to the same four performance metrics, as introduced in Section 2. In other words, we compare the aggregate performance of a pitch subtype

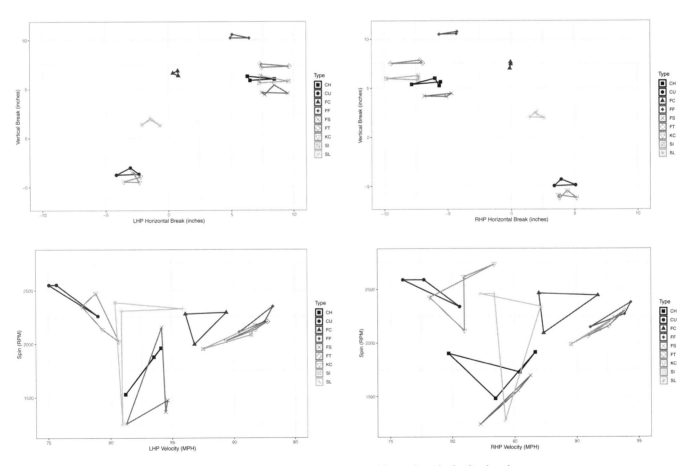

Figure 1: Four physical dimensions for pitch subtype clustering separated into spin-velocity (top) and horizontal-vertical break (bottom) for left-handed (left) and right-handed (right) pitchers.

(shown in Table 1) against the performance of that same pitch when paired with each of the 29 other subtypes to determine the most extreme gains and losses in performance. To do so, we create ordered lists for each of the performance metrics for each reference subtype when paired with all other subtypes, using a cutoff of at least 100 pitches thrown. Almost all of our subtypes have a sample of at least 200 thrown, where most of our pitch type statistics should be considered statistically "stable."[6] We left a few smaller-sample pitch types (four in total) in the study in order to improve the breadth of pitch types included. Then, we identify the best subtype pair (Table 2) and worst subtype pair (Table 3) and show the difference (Δ) in performance from the reference of all occurrences of that subtype being thrown, presented in Table 1.

First, we generally observe the difference in physical characteristics that have extreme gains along each of the performance metrics. Across both RHP and LHP changes in the vertical movement between the reference subtype and paired subtype led to improvements in popup percentage but at the cost of reductions in ground ball percentage. For improvements in exit velocity for both LHP and RHP, a large difference in

horizontal break between the reference and paired subtype is very beneficial. We observe that for increases in swinging strike percentage changes in velocity from the reference subtype and the paired subtype is a primary driver for RHP. For LHP, we found that changes in vertical break between the reference subtype and the paired subtype also played a significant role in swinging strike improvements.

We now discuss some noteworthy observations from Table 2 and Table 3, going from top to bottom. We find that there is an interesting trend for the best changeup pairings based on different performance metrics. We find that the greatest swinging strike rate happens when there is a high level of distinction in at least one physical factor from the reference of a changeup, but distinct by handedness: LHP experience the best swinging strike pairings with subtypes that have the greatest horizontal separation from the changeup, whereas the greatest change in velocity is the key for RHP. Conversely, the biggest changes in exit velocity occur for both handedness when pitches are of similar break to changeups, inducing weak contact. What is striking with the poor pairings for changeups, especially for RHP, the FS that is most

LHP Subtype	ΔSwK (%)		ΔExit Velo (MPH)		ΔLA>40° (Pop-up %)		ΔLA<0° (GB %)		RHP Subtype	ΔSwK (%)		ΔExit Velo (MPH)		ΔLA>40° (Pop-up %)		ΔLA<0° (GB %)	
CH1	FC3	1.3	FC2	−0.3	SI3	2.9	FC1	3.2	CH1	FC1	0.2	SI3	−0.5	SI1	1.8	SI2	2.1
CH2	KC4	1.9	SI3	−1.4	KC2	1.2	FS1	9.2	CH2	FS1	3.0	FS1	−1.6	FS1	2.6	SI2	3.8
CH3	FC2	1.8	FT2	−0.3	FF3	0.8	FC1	1.7	CH3	SI1	2.5	FS2	−2.3	FS1	14.6	KC2	4.6
CU1	FC2	0.7	SI3	−1.2	SI3	5.5	FF3	1.5	CH4	FF3	0.2	SI1	−0.7	CH3	0.8	SI3	1.2
CU2	SI3	1.2	SI3	−0.4	SL1	0.3	SI3	4.7	CU1	SI3	1.4	FS1	−0.7	FS1	2.4	KC2	12.1
CU3	SI3	4.2	SI3	−1.4	SI3	1.5	SL1	2.8	CU2	SI2	3.6	SI3	−1.6	FS1	3.9	KC4	10.7
FC1	KC3	2.8	SI3	−0.3	KC1	5.1	SI3	3.9	CU3	SI3	2.4	FS2	−0.9	FS1	4.4	FS2	4.9
FC2	SI2	1.9	FS1	−1.6	FS1	3.8	FS1	5.2	FC1	SL1	0.8	SL4	−0.5	FS3	7.4	SI2	1.3
FC3	SI3	1.4	SI3	−1.9	SI2	2.8	SL1	3.0	FC2	FT2	0.6	KC2	−1.8	FS3	1.9	FC3	1.3
FF1	FS2	0.8	FC3	−0.4	FS2	6.1	SI1	3.1	FC3	SL3	2.5	SL3	−0.4	KC1	2.1	SL3	1.4
FF2	SI3	1.0	SI3	−1.3	KC1	2.1	FS4	6.6	FF1	KC2	0.6	FS2	−0.4	FC1	1.1	SI2	2.1
FF3	FS2	1.6	KC2	−0.4	FS2	6.0	SI3	1.1	FF2	SI1	0.6	SI1	−0.5	FS1	2.6	SI2	4.1
FS1	FC3	2.5	SL4	−3.1	SL4	10.9	SL3	0.7	FF3	KC4	0.8	SI3	−0.3	FS2	1.6	SI2	3.5
FS2	CU3	0.4	SL3	−1.5	SL3	2.3	FS4	0.5	FS1	CH1	1.5	CH1	−1.6	KC3	4.0	SI2	8.1
FS3	FT1	0.4	CU3	−6.0	FT2	1.6	FS1	0.2	FS2	CH2	1.4	CH3	−0.7	CH4	2.7	SI2	6.8
FS4	CH2	2.8	CU3	−1.6	CU2	3.8	CH2	2.7	FS3	SI2	3.1	SI2	−1.4	CH3	3.4	SI1	7.9
FT1	FS1	0.7	KC1	−1.2	KC1	5.6	SI2	3.5	FT1	SI2	0.3	SI1	−0.2	KC2	2.0	FS2	4.3
FT2	CU2	0.4	KC3	−1.2	KC1	9.2	SI1	4.7	FT2	SI2	1.2	FS1	−1.4	SI2	6.1	KC3	1.6
FT3	SI3	3.2	SI3	−1.2	KC1	4.7	SL4	3.0	FT3	FS3	0.6	CH3	−0.2	KC1	0.7	FC1	1.9
KC1	SL3	2.4	CH3	−0.1	FT3	1.7	FC2	4.8	KC1	FS3	3.3	SI3	−2.4	FC3	3.0	CU2	3.3
KC2	SL2	3.3	FT3	−0.7	SL2	3.2	FC2	3.5	KC2	FC2	3.1	SL4	−1.3	SL4	2.8	FC3	4.0
KC3	SL2	0.5	FS4	−0.8	SL2	1.6	FT1	1.5	KC3	FC3	0.8	SI1	−2.2	SI1	2.2	CU2	5.4
KC4	KC2	1.6	KC2	−1.0	SI3	6.6	KC2	5.1	KC4	KC2	1.3	KC2	−0.9	FS3	4.8	CU2	5.4
SI1	CU2	0.6	KC2	−0.6	FC2	8.8	FT2	7.9	SI1	FS3	2.0	FT3	−1.7	FT3	3.1	KC1	3.5
SI2	FF1	1.5	FT1	−1.5	CU1	5.9	FC3	6.1	SI2	SL4	0.3	FT3	−0.7	FS1	3.9	KC1	4.0
SI3	FF1	0.4	FF3	−1.5	CU1	5.5	FC2	13.0	SI3	FT2	0.8	FF3	−0.6	FS1	3.6	KC4	4.5
SL1	FS2	1.2	FS4	−3.3	FS4	2.8	FS3	4.9	SL1	KC2	2.3	SI2	−1.8	KC4	2.8	KC2	7.3
SL2	SI2	0.9	KC1	−1.5	SI3	6.8	FC2	3.2	SL2	SI1	0.9	SI2	−0.8	FS2	3.3	FF3	0.1
SL3	FC2	0.7	FS4	−1.0	CU3	2.7	FC1	4.3	SL3	KC1	2.9	SI3	−2.2	KC1	3.9	KC3	4.6
SL4	FS1	1.2	CU3	−0.9	FS3	0.9	CU1	4.8	SL4	KC2	4.3	SI2	−0.8	FS1	4.0	KC2	2.8
AVG. GAIN		1.5		−1.3		4.1		4.0	AVG. GAIN		1.7		−1.1		3.5		4.3

Table 2. Best subtype pairings in terms of gain in each of the four performance metrics for the reference subtype for LHP (left) and RHP (right).

similar in break and velocity to the reference changeup subtype (see CH1, FS3, CH3, and FS1 in Table 1) dramatically reduces the swinging strike and ground ball rate outcomes of the changeup.

Sinkers (especially SI3) pair fairly universally well with curveballs, especially across performance metrics for LHP but even RHP. However, a lower-spin splitter (FS1) is the best match for all RHP curveball types for pop-up percentage and the more downward knuckle curve dramatically helps the CU to induce more ground balls. In fact, SI can pair both well and poorly with FS and driven by the velocity separation, since they have very similar movement and can have large spin differences with poor pairings.

For RHP cutters (FC), we see a compelling opposite trend. Namely, cutters play up (Table 2) when they are paired with pitches with more positive horizontal break and play down (Table 3) with pitches with more negative horizontal break. Conversely, RHP splitters play up when they are paired with pitches with more negative horizontal break and play down when paired with pitches with more positive horizontal break. LHP cutters play up with pitches with more negative horizontal break, such as sinkers for swinging strike rate

and exit velocity. When SL2 or SL3 is paired with the cutter, the differing horizontal and vertical break induces more ground balls. When SL1 or SL4 is matched with the curveball (SL1, CU2, SL4, and CU1) both losses occur of swinging strike rate going down and stronger contact being induced. The poor pairings seemingly result from differing vertical break between the pitch subtypes.

Both fastball (FF and FT) subtypes seem to be the least affected by the pairings in terms of swinging strike differences (1.6 Δ). Notice though that high-spin FF pairs better with low-spin KC (and better velocity separation) versus low-spin FF with high spin KC. Also, notice that the highest speed, highest spin class of FT pairs best with SI and worst with the slowest changeups. With lefties, SI2 or SI3 is paired well with FF2 or FF3 with respect to swinging strike rate. Four-seam fastballs pair poorly with splitters with regards to failing to induce ground balls (significant spin difference and vertical break change).

For RHP, knuckle curves can have very positive pairings with FS (similar velocity but very different vertical and horizontal movement) and FC (similar horizontal movement but substantial speed difference and vertical

LHP Subtype	ΔSwK (%)		ΔExit Velo (MPH)		ΔLA>40° (Pop-up %)		ΔLA<0° (GB %)		RHP Subtype	ΔSwK (%)		ΔExit Velo (MPH)		ΔLA>40° (Pop-up %)		ΔLA<0° (GB %)	
CH1	SI2	-2.1	SI1	0.5	FC1	-1.9	SI2	-2.2	CH1	FS3	-3.2	FS2	1.9	FC3	-1.2	FS3	-6.8
CH2	CU3	-0.6	FS1	2.7	SI2	-2.6	CU2	-1.6	CH2	KC3	-0.7	CU2	0.4	SI2	-1.7	FS2	-2.5
CH3	KC4	-1.0	KC4	1.3	KC4	-3.0	KC2	-2.0	CH3	FS1	-2.6	KC3	2.0	KC1	-4.4	FS1	-11.0
CU1	SL3	-0.4	SL3	1.0	FC1	-2.8	SL4	-4.0	CH4	KC4	-2.0	KC1	1.1	KC2	-2.8	CH3	-1.1
CU2	SL3	-0.6	FC1	0.9	SI1	-1.7	FC3	-1.0	CU1	FS1	-2.3	KC2	3.1	KC2	-4.5	FS1	-6.0
CU3	SL1	-2.2	FC1	0.8	FT1	-1.3	SI2	-5.4	CU2	FS1	-4.0	SL4	0.5	KC4	-7.2	FS1	-6.5
FC1	CU3	-1.2	SL3	1.0	SI3	-1.2	KC1	-6.1	CU3	SL4	-1.2	KC4	1.6	KC4	-1.6	SI2	-3.5
FC2	FS1	-2.5	FF3	0.2	FF3	-0.2	SI1	-3.3	FC1	CH3	-1.6	CH3	0.7	CH3	-1.0	FS3	-7.6
FC3	SL3	-2.3	KC3	1.6	SL1	-2.0	CU1	-1.5	FC2	SI3	-1.9	FS3	2.1	SI3	-1.7	FS3	-3.8
FF1	SI2	-0.9	FS1	0.7	SI2	-3.4	FS2	-6.5	FC3	FS3	-3.5	FT2	0.3	SI3	-1.5	KC2	-3.4
FF2	KC4	-0.7	KC1	2.9	FS4	-5.3	FS3	-2.6	FF1	SI2	-0.9	KC1	0.3	SI2	-3.0	FS2	-1.7
FF3	SI3	-2.7	FS4	1.9	SI3	-5.1	FS2	-3.1	FF2	KC3	-0.9	KC2	0.5	SI2	-3.8	FS1	-1.5
FS1	SL1	-2.2	CU3	1.4	CU3	-7.0	SL4	-4.6	FF3	CU2	-0.4	FS1	0.3	SI1	-1.8	CH3	-1.1
FS2	SL1	-1.8	FC2	0.3	CU2	-0.8	SL1	-1.5	FS1	SI2	-2.3	FC1	2.4	SI2	-4.6	KC3	-7.4
FS3	FF2	-0.1	SL4	1.0	CU3	-6.2	FT1	-1.8	FS2	FC2	-2.6	CU3	0.9	SI2	-2.3	CH4	-4.3
FS4	FT3	-2.0	CH1	2.2	CH2	-7.4	FT1	-2.7	FS3	CH3	-3.6	KC1	2.3	KC4	-3.2	CH3	-4.7
FT1	SI1	-1.7	CU3	0.5	SI2	-1.7	KC2	-6.7	FT1	SI3	-0.6	KC1	1.3	SI3	-1.9	KC2	-4.5
FT2	KC2	-1.3	FC3	0.5	SL4	-1.8	KC2	-11.8	FT2	CH3	-0.6	SI2	2.5	CH4	-0.9	SI2	-10.3
FT3	CU3	-1.1	FC2	0.5	SL4	-1.5	KC1	-10.7	FT3	SI3	-0.9	KC3	1.0	FS2	-1.8	KC1	-4.4
KC1	FT3	-1.6	FC2	1.2	FC2	-4.0	FT3	-5.8	KC1	SI2	-2.1	FC3	0.3	CU2	-5.7	CU1	-6.5
KC2	FT3	-1.3	KC4	0.4	KC4	-1.6	FT3	-5.3	KC2	SI2	-6.4	SI2	1.0	CH3	-1.2	CU3	-5.0
KC3	FT2	-0.4	FT1	0.7	FT1	-0.7	SL2	-1.5	KC3	SL1	-3.0	CU1	1.3	CU2	-3.1	SI3	-5.1
KC4	SL4	-4.1	SI2	1.8	FC3	-3.6	SI3	-10.9	KC4	SL3	-3.5	SL3	1.2	CU2	-4.7	SL3	-9.2
SI1	KC1	-2.0	FC1	0.8	FT2	-5.5	FC2	-6.8	SI1	KC1	-1.0	CH3	0.8	KC1	-1.3	FS1	-5.0
SI2	CU3	-1.3	FC2	2.5	FC3	-2.9	CU3	-10.8	SI2	FS3	-1.3	FS1	1.6	KC1	-2.8	FS1	-6.3
SI3	FC1	-1.2	SL4	0.5	FT2	-5.2	CU1	-9.9	SI3	FS1	-1.2	FS2	0.9	KC1	-1.7	FS1	-7.0
SL1	FC2	-2.4	FC2	1.2	FS3	-4.2	CU1	-3.7	SL1	FS1	-3.2	FC2	0.5	KC1	-5.8	CU1	-1.4
SL2	FC3	-4.0	CU3	0.5	FC2	-1.9	KC1	-3.2	SL2	KC1	-2.3	FS1	0.6	KC1	-0.9	SI2	-2.5
SL3	FS4	-3.9	CU3	0.8	FS4	-3.3	CU3	-4.1	SL3	CU3	-1.4	FT2	0.4	FC2	-2.9	CH1	-0.5
SL4	FC1	-2.0	FC1	1.2	CU1	-1.3	FC3	-4.3	SL4	CU3	-1.0	KC1	1.7	FC2	-0.6	FS1	-4.7
AVG. LOSS		-1.7		1.1		-3.0		-4.8	AVG. LOSS		-2.1		1.2		-2.7		-4.8

Table 3. Worst subtype pairings in terms of loss in each of the four performance metrics for the reference subtype for LHP (left) and RHP (right).

action). However, from Table 3, we find that KC pairs poorly with SI (dissimilar speed and dissimilar movement in both directions) and SL (similar speed and most similar movement other than CU) for RHP. Unlike for RHP, the KC and SL2 or KC and SL3 is a positive pairing (very different vertical movement) for swinging strike rate for LHP. For LHP, KC and FT has a negative pairing (very different horizontal and vertical movement and very different velocity) and plays down for swinging strike rate and ground ball rate.

For RHP, slider subtypes have various KC subtypes that pair well for increasing swinging strike rate and increasing ground and fly balls, whereas SI2 and SI3 reduce exit velocity. For LHP, sliders when paired with cutters, especially FC2 or FC3, seemed to reduce swinging strike rate and induce harder contact.

To accentuate the value of this pitch pairing research there are a couple of examples of one pitch in isolation having different performance than when paired with others. One example of a mediocre pitch having profound pairing impact is RHP SI2, which has only a 5.5 percent swinging strike rate and a decent ground ball rate (38.2). However, there are 17 instances where SI2 helps another subtype to have improved performance. For example, SI2 greatly helps slider with reducing hard contact. Conversely, RHP FS1 with low speed and low spin is somewhat of a black hole of pitch pairing, having 16 instances where it worsens the performance of a subtype. RHP, slider subtypes have various KC subtypes that pair well for increasing swinging strike rate and increasing ground and fly balls, whereas SI2 and SI3 reduce exit velocity. For LHP, sliders when paired with cutters, especially FC2 or FC3, seemed to reduce swinging strike rate and induce harder contact.

EXTREMES IN PAIRING FREQUENCY AND PITCHER PERFORMANCE LEVEL

In this section, we exemplify these pairings with five examples: Aaron Nola, Corey Kluber, Jeff Samardzija, Aaron Bummer, and Sean Newcomb.

Aaron Nola throws two types of curve balls (CU1 and CU3). Both of these types of curveballs have the greatest increase in swinging strike percentage when they are paired with the type of sinker that Nola throws, SI3. In other words, the optimal pairing for CU1 and CU3 are both SI3 for RHP, with the latter curve ball having the greatest increase. When we compare the physical characteristics, CU3 is faster with greater horizontal break. Therefore, Nola could potentially work with a pitching coach to increase the horizontal move-

ment on his curve even further to generate even more swinging strikes.

Corey Kluber is a particularly good example of a positive pairing with CU2 and SI2. Despite below-average velocity on the sinker, Kluber has had great success with those two pitches. In particular, since Kluber's sinker is of the SI2 variety, it helped his curve ball play up from a pitch subtype average swinging strike rate of 13.9% to a remarkable 26.2% swinging strike rate.

Jeff Samardzija also throws multiple breaking pitches, but many of them have bad outcomes. For example, CU2 and KC4 do not pair well for balls in play, KC4 and SL3 do not pair well for swinging strikes, and CU1 and FS1 do not pair well for whiffs or grounders. However, there is a silver lining here. In the last three springs, Samardzija has been working on a new breaking pitch, SL3, which has an excellent pairing with KC1 for RHP. He could work on his knuckle curve having more depth, which is the distinguishing feature of the KC1 and could take his SL3 to the next level, adding 2.9% of swinging strikes and 3.9% of pop-up rate.

Aaron Bummer and his short sample of one season with above-average results might well represent how minor league or amateur pitch tracking systems might pay great dividends. A good pitch pairing is the SI3 with the FF1 for LHP, which allows greater swinging strikes. He throws the four-seamer high in the zone following his sinker to get batters to swing under it. The pairing certainly contributed to the White Sox extending him for five years and $16M even with his limited MLB success. With FF1 in his arsenal, his SI3 swinging strike rate was 9.0%, 1.8% more than the average SI3.

Sean Newcomb is another left-handed pitcher with a fairly short track record but has some interesting pairings that could produce high levels of performance in the future. Specifically, Newcomb pairs a CU1 and FF3 (a pairing that is not shown in Table 2, but very positive nonetheless) that generates a very high rate of ground balls. Since he had FF3 in his arsenal, his CU1 had a 56.0% ground ball rate, 13.2% above the average CU1. Despite his iffy command, it looks like Newcomb may return to the rotation this year, and that fly ball suppression may be part of the reason why.

CONCLUSION

In this paper, we used k-means clustering and the elbow method to classify pitch subtypes from previously-labeled MLB Statcast pitch types. In doing so, we understood the degree to which subtypes differ across a type and evaluated the effectiveness of pairing subtypes. Between the best and worst pairing of subtypes, we found that there is an average change of 3.5 percent swinging strike rate, a 2.4 MPH exit velocity, 3.3 percent pop-up rate, and 4.5 percent ground ball rate. Lastly, based on frequency of the best and worst pairings, we showed examples of pitchers and discussed their level of performance. We hope that this work leads to intuition on where to focus efforts with pitcher scouting, pitch design, and development. ■

Notes

1. Max Marchi, "Pitch classification revisited." https://tht.fangraphs.com/pitch-classificationrevisited, July 2010, and, Ethan Moore, "An unsupervised approach for pitch classification," in *Proc. of Sabermetrics, Scouting, and the Science of Baseball (Saberseminar)*, 2019.

2. Harry Pavlidis, "What makes a changeup good?" https://www.baseball-prospectus.com/news/article/ 21675/what-makes-a-good-changeup-an-investigation-part-three, Aug. 2013.

3. Glenn Healey and Shiyuan Zhao, "Finding the optimal pitch distribution," in *Proc. of Sabermetrics, Scouting, and the Science of Baseball (Saberseminar)*, 2019.

4. Carson Sievert and Brian M. Mills, "Using publicly available baseball data to measure and evaluate pitching performance," 39–66, New York, New York, USA: Chapman and Hall/CRC, 2017.

5. Tirthajyoti Sarkar, "Clustering metrics better than the elbow-method," https://towardsdatascience.com/clustering-metrics-better-than-the-elbow-method-6926e1f723a6, Sep. 2019.

6. Jonah Pemstein, "A long-needed update on reliability," https://blogs.fangraphs.com/a-long-neededupdate-on-reliability, Sep. 2016.

cWAR: Modifying Wins Above Replacement with the Cape Cod Baseball League

Fr. Humbert Kilanowski, O.P.

Evaluating a player's talent, ability, and contributions to his team is an important task of analyzing the game of baseball. In recent years, the prevalent metric for player evaluation has been Wins Above Replacement (WAR), which distills the evaluation into a single number that can be compared directly with that of other players. WAR measures a player's contributions in units of games won as compared to the expected contribution of a readily available replacement player. Yet this metric suffers from three shortcomings. First, many competing algorithms for computing WAR exist, and they do not agree on how players are to be ranked, demonstrating that the algorithms are imprecise and may be muddled by confounding variables. Second, the baseline for replacement level is arbitrarily chosen; rather than refer to an actual average of minor-league players who see action in the major leagues for part of the season, the baseline is selected so that the total of WAR across the major leagues is a fixed number. Third, in order not to give an unfair advantage to players who have a greater opportunity to contribute to scoring runs (based on their team, competition, or place in the batting order), WAR is designed to be context-neutral; yet this does not give any greater value to players' performance in high-leverage or clutch situations, which are helpful in determining their value to their teams. Modifying WAR to account for this would make it more difficult to compare directly to other formulas.

To remedy the first two problems with WAR we have written an algorithm, based on the methods of FanGraphs and the openWAR project, using the data from the Cape Cod Baseball League—a high-ranked summer league for collegiate players—in which several confounding variables can be directly controlled and temporary players provide a built-in replacement level, and to address the third, we have experimented with adding a leverage term into the formula to improve the linear fit between a team's aggregate WAR and its actual wins. Our Wins Above Replacement statistic, cWAR, can be used to evaluate and rank college players and aid the work of major league scouts, as well be adapted to find a more effective baseline and more precise metric for the majors.

SUMMARY OF PREVIOUS WORK

The computation of a single-valued metric to measure a baseball player's overall contributions to his team dates back to 1984 with the "Total Player Rating" devised by John Thorn and Pete Palmer in their groundbreaking book, *The Hidden Game of Baseball*.[1] This formula, rooted in the linear weights for each type of play, based on how many runs each play is expected to produce, has undergone many versions and modifications, such as Value Over Replacement Player (VORP) by Baseball Prospectus and Win Shares by Bill James, until the currently used statistic of Wins Above Replacement, which converts the number of runs a player contributes into units of wins, came into use around 2008.[2] This statistic, WAR, is now so common that MLB.com uses it to describe players, and has even appeared on baseball cards alongside traditional metrics such as slugging percentage and earned run average.

Each of the three main sabermetric web sites (Baseball-Reference.com, FanGraphs, and Baseball Prospectus) has its own formula, and these often disagree in how players are to be ranked.[3] While currently the formulas differ only in such details as how baserunning and defensive contributions are to be computed, or how much data should be used to calculate park factors, the algorithms did use different baselines for replacement level. Notably, Baseball-Reference and Fangraphs agreed on a unified replacement level in 2013, so that a hypothetical team full of replacement players would perform at a winning percentage of .294.[4] This figure of .294 means that a league-average MLB team (with a record of 81–81 over a full 162-game season) would be worth 33⅓ wins above replacement level, and consequently, the entirety of MLB would have 1000 WAR. This creates a convenient visual image of WAR as a large pie with one thousand slices to be distributed among all players, but the round figure is derived from an arbitrary estimate of how a replacement-level team would perform, which in the past two seasons has been very close to the actual worst team in the majors.[5]

Because of this, some analysts have sought a more reliable baseline. Some have chosen to work with Wins Above Average (WAA) instead, since league average is better defined than replacement level; yet this does not prove to be as applicable, since a team cannot call up a league-average player from the minors, nor easily trade for a league-average player. Another approach is to redefine replacement level; the authors of the openWAR Project have done so by taking the players on MLB rosters at any given time, identifying the 750 with the most in-game appearances (namely, the 390 batters with the most plate appearances and the 360 pitchers with the most batters faced), and then regarding all other players as replacement players.[6,7] The average rate of run value among these replacement players then becomes the baseline, and this results in a higher total of WAR (1166.3 in 2012 and 1173.5 in 2013) for all of MLB. Yet even this does not accurately reflect replacement level. An All-Star player whose time is limited due to injury (such as Giancarlo Stanton in 2019) would count as a replacement player and skew the replacement level to be too high. Therefore, a replacement level criterion similar to that of the temporary player in the Cape Cod Baseball League may yield a more effective baseline, and this is one of the modifications that we make to the formula.

To improve further on our base model taken from the CCBL with a replacement level based on temporary players, another modification is the inclusion of a leverage term. This would give greater weight to a player's performance in high-leverage situations. Current formulas for WAR only include leverage for relief pitchers; for FanGraphs' formula (fWAR), only the leverage of the moment at which a pitcher enters the game is considered.[8]

Finally, there has been no evidence so far of any similar work done with the data of the CCBL to compute a WAR-like formula. The league's official website, with statistics collected with PointStreak software, includes a page for "Sabermetric Stats." The page only lists some rate statistics such as walks per plate appearance, isolated power, secondary average, and component ERA, with a listing for "runs created" without any explanation of how it is computed.[9] Therefore, our project looks to be the first that calculates WAR for the Cape Cod Baseball League, using its temporary players as the baseline for replacement level.

METHODOLOGY OF OUR RESEARCH

The main data source for our research was a digital file graciously provided by the league's official statistician of the collected boxscores from all of the regular-season games from the 2019 Cape Cod Baseball League season, formatted to be input as a data frame in RStudio. Our computer program to analyze this file was written in the language R, chosen for its ability to handle large data frames (particularly with its additional commands in a package called the "tidyverse") and for its built-in statistical capabilities. Our algorithm for computing WAR for each player in the league involves the following steps.

First, we calculated the run expectancy matrix for the league. We found the empirical expected value of the number of runs that the team at bat would score, given the state (outs and base runners), until the end of the inning. This was done according to a method similar to the one in *Analyzing Baseball Data with R* (Marchi/Albert/Baumer), modified in order to work with our data set (the book's algorithm is designed to work with Retrosheet data).[10] After filtering the play-by-play data file, which includes a line for every pitch, to include only the plays during which either the state changes or a run scores, we counted the number of runs that the team at bat scores from that point until the end of the inning, and computed the average number of runs scored for each state across the whole season, excluding incomplete innings that ended before three outs were recorded. This matrix, however, contained some anomalies; for example, the state of runners on second and third with no outs had a higher run expectancy than bases loaded with no outs, since the samples were small (as few as 53 instances) and were easily skewed by a few high-scoring innings in the former case. To rectify this, we averaged 50 instances of each state from the major-league data from the 2019 season, normalized so that the basic state (bases empty and no outs) remained unchanged, meaning the MLB values were multiplied by (0.5354/0.5439). This gives the following run expectancy matrix. Notice that in the Cape League, the team at bat expects to score fewer runs with two outs than in the majors, and the run expectancies for a runner on first base only and second base only are closer together in the CCBL than in MLB. The run-scoring environment on the Cape is lower, since batters are hitting with wooden bats in competition, often for the first time.

Outs	Runners	CCBL (raw)	MLB	CCBL (buffered)
0	Bases empty	0.5354	0.5439	0.5354
0	1st only	0.9656	0.9345	0.9635
0	2nd only	1.0790	1.1465	1.0856
0	3rd only	1.4151	1.3685	1.3821
0	1st and 2nd	1.5799	1.5371	1.5700
0	1st and 3rd	1.9765	1.7591	1.8858
0	2nd and 3rd	2.4286	1.9711	2.2363
0	Bases loaded	2.2813	2.3617	2.2962
1	Bases empty	0.2797	0.2983	0.2800
1	1st only	0.5696	0.5641	0.5691
1	2nd only	0.6924	0.7134	0.6933
1	3rd only	1.0053	0.9528	0.9912
1	1st and 2nd	1.0513	0.9792	1.0437
1	1st and 3rd	1.2827	1.2186	1.2655
1	2nd and 3rd	1.4694	1.3679	1.4444
1	Bases loaded	1.6460	1.6337	1.6392
2	Bases empty	0.0877	0.1147	0.0884
2	1st only	0.2134	0.2422	0.2144
2	2nd only	0.2780	0.3391	0.2817
2	3rd only	0.3823	0.3907	0.3826
2	1st and 2nd	0.4448	0.4666	0.4460
2	1st and 3rd	0.4645	0.5182	0.4714
2	2nd and 3rd	0.6128	0.6151	0.6115
2	Bases loaded	0.6667	0.7426	0.6778

Table 1. Run expectancy matrix for each state (outs and base-runners) for the Cape Cod Baseball League in 2019. The rightmost column (CCBL data buffered by 50 instances of the MLB data) is what we use for our run value calculations.

The next step was to use the run expectancy of each state to calculate the average run value of each type of play, such as a single, walk, or out. This was done by creating a factor variable that gives a label to each play, and then using the "summarize" command in R to compute the average value of each play in units of runs. Following the algorithm from FanGraphs, we then converted these values to the linear weights to calculate weighted on-base average (wOBA) for each batter and wOBA allowed for each pitcher.[11] Notably, the weights for singles, walks, and hit-by-pitch were higher in the CCBL than in almost any era of MLB.[12] This suggests that batters reach base at a premium in the Cape League; the weight for a triple was nearly as high as that of a home run. The conversion factor to make wOBA on the same scale as on-base average (so that the league average for both statistics is the same) was comparable to that of MLB, namely 1.205 in the Cape League as opposed to 1.157 in the majors.[13]

Event	Run value	Value relative to out	Weight for wOBA
Out	-0.298	0.000	0.000
Walk	0.341	0.639	0.769
Hit by pitch	0.360	0.658	0.792
Single	0.492	0.790	0.951
Double	0.762	1.060	1.277
Triple	1.403	1.701	2.048
Home Run	1.445	1.743	2.099

Table 2. Linear weights for events in the Cape Cod Baseball League for the 2019 season. The leftmost column is calculated from the average change in run expectancy for each event, and the rightmost column contains the values used for calculating wOBA. Errors count as outs for the purposes of wOBA but have a run value slightly less than that of a single.

A simple linear transformation applied to wOBA gives the rate statistic that measures a batter's weighted runs created (wRC) when multiplied by his plate appearances. (For the purposes of wOBA and WAR, intentional walks and sacrifice bunts do not count as plate appearances, since they do not consist of a confrontation between the pitcher and batter.)[14] The rate statistic of wRC/PA is used to compare the baseline for batters.

For pitchers, however, the algorithm is more complicated. Again, we follow the routine of FanGraphs and calculate each pitcher's fielding-independent pitching (FIP) statistic, scaled to the league average of runs allowed.[15] This was normalized by the number of games in which each pitcher appeared to produce the rate statistic of Wins Per Game Above Average (WPGAA).[16] For the two cases in which a pitcher appeared only once in a game and never retired a batter, we used a scaled version of the pitchers' wOBA against in order to avoid division by zero.

These two rate statistics, wRC/PA and WPGAA, are compared for each player to replacement level, which itself is determined with a criterion based on the temporary players in the Cape League. CCBL coaches set their rosters in the fall, several months before the next season, but roster vacancies are created for several reasons. Some of the players they choose suffer injury during the college season or play for a team that advances to the College World Series. Some also play for national teams for part of the summer, and others leave the Cape League before the season finishes—typically after the Cape League All-Star Game—to avoid the risk of injury. Coaches must add temporary players to fill out their rosters, chosen from among local colleges or lower-ranking summer collegiate leagues.

We have chosen to identify temporary players by both of the following criteria:

(a) the player only appears in games before June 30 (before players return from the College World Series) or after July 21 (the day of the CCBL All-Star Game), or appears in games over the course of fewer than seven days

(b) the player sees fewer than 40 plate appearances (for batters) or faces fewer than 40 batters (for pitchers).[17]

Any player who satisfies criteria in both (a) and (b) is identified as a temporary player, and the average wRC/PA and WPGAA among the temporary players is set as the baseline for replacement level. Notice that our routine departs from FanGraphs in that no separate baselines are used for starting pitchers and relief pitchers, since in the CCBL there is less of a distinction between the two than in MLB, especially early in the season. Also, pitchers do not bat in the CCBL, but any non-pitcher who pitches (typically at the end of the season) is counted as a temporary player among the pitchers. For each batter or pitcher, then, the difference between that player's pertinent rate statistic and the baseline is multiplied by plate appearances or innings pitched, respectively, and then converted from runs to wins based on the average number of runs per plate appearance in the league. This yields the value of Wins Above Replacement for each CCBL player, which we can call cWAR.

This measure only accounts for batting and pitching, which are not all of the actions that contribute positively or negatively to a player's team's runs scored or allowed. In particular, baserunning and fielding are also areas in which a player can perform above or below replacement level. FanGraphs uses methods—Ultimate Baserunning (UBR) and Ultimate Zone Rating (UZR)—which require video analysis to determine when a baserunner should be credited for taking an extra base or when a fielder should be credited for making a play requiring above-average skill. Such information is not available to us from the Cape League database. What we have done is to find the average run value for non-batted ball events such as stolen bases (0.122) and caught stealing (−0.478), and added these contributions to each position player's wRC

totals, which in turn affect his WAR. Similarly, runs due to wild pitches (0.268) were incorporated into pitchers' WAR totals. Notably, a stolen base in the CCBL has a lower value than that in MLB.[18]

Another modification that we made to the weights and run values was the park factors, following a method described in Marchi, Albert, and Baumer.[19] We computed each team's park factor as the ratio of the number of runs scored at home to those scored on the road, multiplied by 100. In our original model, we considered the park factors for the 2019 season only, and regressed them toward the mean by a factor of (44/162) to make the single 44-game CCBL season comparable to an MLB season.[20] The average park factor was then computed for each position player and pitcher, and the player's WAR was divided or multiplied, respectively, by the park factor, since a higher park factor favors hitters. A later modification includes a park factor computed from the past ten seasons combined to provide a more accurate value.

A final contribution to our values of WAR is a leverage factor. While we have not yet performed a complete analysis on how leverage and clutch performance affect WAR, some members of our research team have done a preliminary analysis, using the leverage values for each state and score differential as given by the "Inside The Book" website.[21] The most comprehensive treatment of leverage that we have explored involves expressing each player's contribution to runs scored as a discrete Riemann-Stieltjes integral.[22] Each play's run value (the difference in run expectancy before and after the play) is multiplied by the leverage at the start of the play, and these are summed together, so that the effective run value is the leverage integrated against the run expectancy matrix, rather than a simple RE24 which only totals the changes in run expectancy.

Team	Home Park	Park Factor (one year regressed)	Park Factor (ten year)
Bourne Braves	Doran Park	102.3	90.1
Brewster Whitecaps	Stony Brook	111.5	115.2
Chatham Anglers	Veterans Field	104.9	98.9
Cotuit Kettleers	Lowell Park	94.4	100.4
Falmouth Commodores	Arnie Allen Diamond	108.6	104.8
Harwich Mariners	Whitehouse Field	95.3	85.2
Hyannis Harbor Hawks	McKeon Park	91.6	102.9
Orleans Firebirds	Eldredge Park	97.8	94.0
Wareham Gatemen	Spillane Field	104.2	100.3
Yarmouth-Dennis Red Sox	Red Wilson Field	101.0	112.2

Table 3. Park factors for the ten ballparks in the Cape Cod Baseball League, with both the original (one-year) and modified (ten-year) values.

With these considerations in place, we find that replacement level is 0.08387 runs created per plate appearance for batters, and 0.02846 wins per nine-inning game for pitchers. Comparing each player's pertinent rate statistic to these baselines and multiplying by plate appearances or innings pitched, respectively, yields the desired cWAR statistic.

TESTING OF OUR RESEARCH

We have tested our algorithm in two ways: first, by comparing our leaders in WAR for both position players and pitchers to the list of players who were given various awards at the end of the season; and second, by totaling the WAR for each team, and running a least-squares regression to the teams' aggregate WAR and their actual winning percentage during the season.

Player	RE24	wOBA	wRC	WAR
Nick Gonzales, COT	22.2	.499	48.5	3.17
Zach DeLoach, FAL	9.9	.453	33.7	1.97
Austin Wells, Y-D	10.5	.422	36.1	1.92
Hayden Cantrelle, FAL	9.5	.409	30.9	1.67
Kaden Polcovich, CHA	14.2	.417	30.9	1.67
Shay Whitcomb, ORL	2.7	.436	25.9	1.56
Zavier Warren, BOU	7.2	.398	29.4	1.53
Wyatt Young, Y-D	13.0	.412	27.5	1.37
Niko Kavadas, HAR	7.4	.386	25.1	1.29
Jared DeSantolo, HYA	11.3	.407	24.9	1.29

Table 4. Top 10 position players by WAR in the CCBL in 2019, with their total change in run expectancy (RE24), weighted on-base average, runs created, and WAR.

One position player, second baseman Nick Gonzales of New Mexico State University and the Cotuit Kettleers, has a significantly higher WAR, wOBA, and wRC than anyone else.[23] This is confirmed in that he easily won the league MVP award as he led his team to the league championship, and he is the highest ranked prospect according to MLB.com among all players who played a full season in the Cape League.[24] Typically, a higher wOBA leads to a higher WAR, but some players benefit from contributing more runs due to stolen bases (Hayden Cantrelle) or from being a power hitter in a more pitcher-friendly park (Niko Kavadas).

The list of position players with the highest WAR corresponded better with the end-of-season awards than the list of pitchers did.[25] The pitchers also tended to have lower WAR values than the position players. This is likely because the pitchers tend to see less playing time than other position players; many pitchers are placed on innings limits by their college coaches for the summer, and teams carry many pitchers on their rosters, so that only four pitchers ended up pitching enough innings to qualify for the league's ERA title.[26] As a result, only one pitcher (Ian Bedell, who won the Outstanding Pitcher award) finished with a WAR higher than 1.

Pitcher	RE24	wOBA	FIP	WAR
Ian Bedell, WAR	-15.0	.186	1.58	1.06
Sean Sullivan, COT	-9.4	.242	1.98	0.91
Ryan Cusick, BOU	-7.6.	255	2.44	0.85
Jacob Palisch, HAR	-14.5	.214	2.24	0.81
Carmen Mlodzinski, FAL	-9.3	.201	2.33	0.75
Logan Allen, HAR	-5.9	.163	0.93	0.63
Will Heflin, HAR	-10.9	.223	1.98	0.63
Brandon Pfaadt, WAR	-9.5	.235	2.90	0.58
Kolby Kubichek, CHA	-6.5	.212	2.78	0.57
Joseph Nahas, COT	-7.3	.177	1.80	0.56

Table 5. Top 10 pitchers by WAR in the CCBL in 2019, with their total change in run expectancy (RE24), wOBA allowed, fielding-independent pitching metric, and WAR. The best pitchers have negative RE24 values since their performance causes a net decrease of runs.

In addition to testing our results with a qualitative list of awards, we have also run a more quantitative test. Since each player's contributions to his team are measured in units of wins, one could, in theory, add the WAR values for all players on a team and obtain a value comparable to the actual number of games that the team has won. Although WAR is often imprecise, this calculation can be used as a means of testing our WAR algorithm as compared to the methods used in MLB. We have run a least-squares linear regression between each team's aggregate WAR and its winning percentage, counting each tie as half of a win and half of a loss.[27]

RESULTS OF OUR RESEARCH

The plot shown in Table 6 demonstrates the linear fit between each team's total WAR (x) and winning average (y), and the least-squares regression line is $\hat{y} = 0.2841 + 0.0311 x$, with a correlation coefficient of $r = 0.8560$. This is lower than the correlation coefficients for the WAR models used in the MLB for last season; FanGraphs' algorithm gave $r = 0.9438$, and Baseball-Reference's gave 0.9560 when applied to the MLB data from 2019. However, the CCBL data have a lower correlation due to the shorter season and smaller sample, and the linear fit is still statistically significant at the $\alpha = 0.001$ level ($t = 4.683$ with 8 degrees of freedom).

103

Some teams (such as the Falmouth Commodores) won more games than their WAR would indicate, while others (such as the Cotuit Kettleers) won fewer, but no residual is as large as 0.071 in winning average. The team with the worst record in the league, the Hyannis Harbor Hawks, is an influential observation that drags the trend line down towards it slightly. While we have only done some preliminary work on considering leverage, an early result is that replacing RE24 with the sum of leverage multiplied by the run value for each play does decrease the residuals and make for a more accurate fit between team WAR and winning percentage.

A further analysis of the regression line shows that its slope, 0.03109, is 36.8% higher than one would expect from a linear relationship in which an increase of team WAR by one would also increase a team's win total by one. This would occur with a slope of 1/44, or 0.02273, for a 44-game season. Yet while the slope of our regression line looks alarmingly high, corresponding to 1.368 wins per WAR, its difference from 1/44 is not statistically significant at even the $\alpha = 0.1$ level, as a one-sided t-test for $H_a > 1/44$ gives a P-value of 0.1216. Therefore, the higher slope can be attributed to the random effects of working with a small sample, and the intercept of 0.2841 is close to the baseline winning average in MLB: 0.2942.

If the influential observation (Hyannis) were to be removed, the regression line becomes y = 0.3833 + 0.01895x, with a higher intercept and lower slope, corresponding to only 0.834 win per WAR, also not a statistically significant difference from 1. Notably, the correlation coefficient of the fit drops to 0.5913,

suggesting that the last-place team improves the fit. Naturally, the fit can be improved further by taking more data. After completing this pilot study of the 2019 CCBL season, our next step will be a retrospective study of the past ten seasons (2010–19).

Another observation comes from our comparison of our cWAR values with the end-of-season awards.[28] While all of our top ten position players made the All-League Team, only five of the twelve pitchers from the All-League Team made our top ten. Notably, our second and third-ranked pitchers in WAR—Sean Sullivan and Ryan Cusick—did not make the team, and our list also includes some pitchers who did not pitch the full season (Logan Allen and Joseph Nahas) but still pitched well enough, with a low enough FIP, to make our top ten without qualifying for awards. Also, the winner of the league's award for the best closer, Zachary Brzykcy, finished with a WAR of only 0.07. This is because as a closer, his innings were limited, and while he only allowed two runs all season, both scored on solo home runs, which greatly increased his FIP and diminished his WAR. This explains some of the discrepancies between our pitching WAR values and the league's awards, but it should also be noted that for the whole league, pitchers' WAR adds up to 12.5 while other position players' WAR sums to 56.9.[29] This suggests that WAR for pitchers ought to be scaled, or the baseline modified, to make the contributions from batting and pitching closer in magnitude.

CONCLUSION

The Cape Cod Baseball League is an environment in which confounding variables such as age and ability level can be directly controlled and which contains a built-in replacement level, resulting in a useful formula for Wins Above Replacement. Two important consequences for analysts and scouts in the major leagues result from this research. First, since professional scouts have become intent on recruiting players from college (rather than high school) since the sabermetric revolution as described in *Moneyball*, the importance of accurately ranking and evaluating college players has increased, and our project provides a way to do this.[30] Second, our criteria for replacement level can be applied to the majors. By identifying conditions based on playing time and days spent on the roster, we can meaningfully determine who should be included among replacement-level players, and yield a more accurate baseline. In these ways, our analysis can contribute toward refining the methods that professional baseball analysts use in evaluating players. ∎

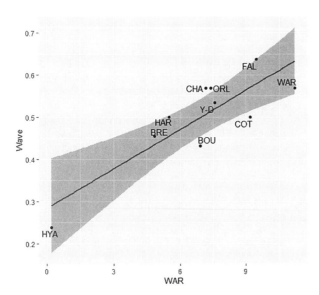

Table 6. Plot of winning average (y) vs. total Wins Above Replacement (x) for the ten teams in the Cape Cod Baseball League in the 2019 season.

Acknowledgments

I would like to thank Chris Thoms, the official statistician for the Cape Cod Baseball League, for providing us with the play-by-play data from the 2019 season; Jim Albert, for his encouragement and advice with the project; and all of my research students, especially Peter Graziano and Helen Nguyen for their work on the discrete Riemann-Stieltjes integral model for incorporating leverage, and Casey Sullivan and Thomas Zinzarella for calculating and explaining the ten-year park factors for the league.

Works Cited

Baseball-Reference.com, "WAR Comparison Chart." https://www.baseball-reference.com/about/war_explained_comparison.shtml, accessed January 2, 2020.

Baumer, Benjamin S., Shane T. Jensen, and Gregory J. Matthews, "openWAR: An Open Source System for Evaluating Overall Player Performance in Major League Baseball." arXiv:1312.7158v3[stat.AP], 2015.

Cape Cod Baseball League, "2019 CCBL All-League Team Announced." http://www.capecodbaseball.org/news/league-news/index.html?article_id=2659, accessed January 6, 2020.

FanGraphs, "What is WAR?" library.fangraphs.com/misc/war, accessed January 6, 2020.

Lewis, Michael. *Moneyball*. New York: Norton, 2004.

Major League Baseball, "2020 Prospect Watch." http://m.mlb.com/prospects/2020?list=draft, accessed January 5, 2020.

Marchi, Max, Jim Albert, and Benjamin S. Baumer. *Analyzing Baseball Data with R*, 2nd ed. Boca Raton, FL: CRC, 2018.

PointStreak, "CCBL 2019 – Stats." pointstreak.com/baseball.stats.html?leagueid=166&seasonid=31871, accessed January 6, 2020.

Tango, Tom M., Mitchel G. Lichtman, and Andrew E. Dolphin, *The Book*, "Crucial Situations," http://www.insidethebook.com/li.shtml, accessed January 6, 2020.

Thorn, John, and Pete Palmer. *The Hidden Game of Baseball: A Revolutionary Approach to Baseball and Its Statistics*. Chicago: University of Chicago, 1985.

Notes

1. John Thorn and Pete Palmer, *The Hidden Game of Baseball: A Revolutionary Approach to Baseball and Its Statistics* (Chicago: University of Chicago, 1985). The first edition was published in 1984.
2. Baseball Reference, "WAR Comparison Chart." https://www.baseball-reference.com/about/war_explained_comparison.shtml, accessed January 2, 2020.
3. For example, to determine the players with the highest WAR in the 2017 MLB season, Baseball-Reference gives Corey Kluber (8.2) as the overall leader and Max Scherzer in the top five; while FanGraphs places Kluber fifth (7.2) and deems Chris Sale as the best pitcher, with Aaron Judge being the overall leader.
4. Dave Cameron, "Unifying Replacement Level," FanGraphs Blog, March 28, 2013, https://blogs.fangraphs.com/unifying-replacement-level, accessed May 4, 2020.
5. In 2019, for example, the Detroit Tigers finished with a record of 47–114 (.292), and in 2018, the Baltimore Orioles finished 47–115 (.290); each had the worst record in MLB that year, slightly below replacement level.
6. This number is 750 before the 2020 season, when rosters expand to 26 players per team for a total of 780.
7. Benjamin S. Baumer, Shane T. Jensen, and Gregory J. Matthews, "openWAR: An Open Source System for Evaluating Overall Player Performance in Major League Baseball" (arXiv:1312.7158v3[stat.AP], 2015).
8. FanGraphs, "What is WAR?", library.fangraphs.com/misc/war, accessed January 6, 2020.
9. PointStreak, "CCBL 2019 – Stats," pointstreak.com/baseball.stats.html?leagueid=166&seasonid=31871, accessed January 6, 2020.
10. Max Marchi, Jim Albert, and Benjamin S. Baumer, *Analyzing Baseball Data with R*, 2nd edition (Boca Raton, FL: CRC, 2018), 113–16.
11. We chose the algorithm used by FanGraphs since it is the most transparent one in use by a major outlet.
12. FanGraphs. The only MLB eras with higher weights were World War II and the Deadball era.
13. FanGraphs. The factor was 1.226 for MLB in 2018 and tends to increase as the average runs per game decreases.
14. FanGraphs. The calculation is wRC = (((wOBA − league wOBA) / wOBA scale) + (league R/PA)) * PA.
15. The formula for FIP is 13 * home run rate + 3 * walk rate − 2 * strikeout rate, where hit batters count as walks and popups caught by an infielder count as strikeouts. A coefficient of 3.80 must be added, to bring the league average FIP (0.41) in line with the league average ERA (4.21).
16. FanGraphs. WPGAA is given by the pitcher's runs allowed per nine innings (based on FIP), divided by the measure of the pitcher's own run environment, known as Dynamic Runs Per Win.
17. The figure 40 is chosen as the typical number of batters a team sends to the plate in a game.
18. This means that a team should only attempt a stolen base when the runner has an 80% chance of succeeding, higher than the 75% in the majors.
19. Marchi, Albert, and Baumer, 263–66.
20. This is actually not a very accurate regression factor, since it does not take into account the actual correlation between the CCBL and MLB park factors. Our later modification, with the 10-year park factors, replaced it.
21. Tom M. Tango, Mitchel G. Lichtman, and Andrew E. Dolphin, *The Book*, "Crucial Situations," http://www.insidethebook.com/li.shtml, accessed January 6, 2020. *The Book* itself does not have the table of leverage values, but the companion Web site does.
22. This is an integral from measure theory in which one function f is integrated against the change in another function g. If we let f represent the leverage factor and g the run expectancy, and apply the discrete version of the integral, we have a way to incorporate leverage into the WAR formula.
23. His WAR of 3.17 translates to 10.6 WAR on a major-league scale. On this scale, the WAR for all position players totals 570 for a 162-game season. Gonzales is therefore comparable to Mookie Betts' MLB-leading WAR in 2018.
24. Major League Baseball, "2020 Prospect Watch." http://m.mlb.com/prospects/2020?list=draft, accessed January 5, 2020. Gonzales is ranked fourth; Spencer Torkelson, who is ranked second, played a week on the Cape, where he also played the previous summer, but spent most of last summer playing for the US national team.
25. Cape Cod Baseball League, "2019 CCBL All-League Team Announced," http://www.capecodbaseball.org/news/league-news/index.html?article_id=2659, accessed January 6, 2020.
26. PointStreak. The minimum is 0.8 innings pitched per team game, or 35⅓ innings for the season.
27. In the Cape League, a game is called off and counted as a tie if it remains tied after the tenth inning. Games may also end as ties due to weather, or darkness at one of the three fields (Cotuit, Brewster, or Yarmouth-Dennis) that does not have lights.
28. Cape Cod Baseball League, "2019 CCBL All-League Team Announced."
29. This is a ratio of 4.552 for batters to pitchers, as opposed to 1.326 for FanGraphs and Baseball-Reference's formulas for MLB.
30. Michael Lewis, *Moneyball* (New York: Norton, 2004), 16: "In any case, you only had to study the history of the draft to see that high school pitchers were twice less likely than college pitchers, and four times less likely than college position players, to make it to the big leagues. Taking a high school pitcher in the first round—and spending 1.2 million bucks to sign him—was exactly the sort of thing that happened when you let scouts have their way. It defied the odds; it defied reason. Reason, even science, was what Billy Beane was intent on bringing to baseball."

Multi-Attribute Decision-Making Ranks Baseball's All-Time Greatest Hitters

William P. Fox

INTRODUCTION AND HISTORY

I have taught or co-taught sabermetrics in the mathematics department at the United States Military Academy several times. We covered all the metrics but what always interested me most was the direction student projects took to solve or analyze various issues in baseball. In one of these courses, for example, the group project came up with a new metric for percentage of extra base hits. In reading Bill James and examining all the metrics available to enthusiastic baseball fans, it struck me that every fan has an opinion as to the best or greatest hitter ever in baseball, each using the metric that best suited their choices.

Through basic research, I found many such conclusions:

a) Ted Williams was the greatest hitter ever.[1]
b) The top five hitters voted online were Ruth, Cobb, Hornsby, Gehrig, Williams.[2]
c) The Britannica chose Ruth, Mays, Bonds, Williams, Aaron.[3]
d) Baseball's All Time Greatest Hitters shows how statistics can level the playing field and concludes Tony Gwynn is the best.

Just Google "Greatest Hitters in Baseball All-time" and see the many results. Google found 851,000 results when I tried. Many have similar but slightly different conclusions but one thing that all seemed to have in common was their subjective nature. The basic results of (a)–(d) support that.

If raw home runs were the most important metric, the top five all time would be Barry Bonds (762), Hank Aaron (755), Babe Ruth (714), Alex Rodriguez (696), and Willie Mays (660). If hits, then Pete Rose (4256), Ty Cobb (4189), Hank Aaron (3771), Stan Musial (3630) and Tris Speaker (3514) would be the top five. Only Hank Aaron is in the top 5 in both lists. One article argues that Tony Gwynn was the all-time greatest hitter. In the table below, we present the best in the categories of home runs, extra base hits, RBI OBP, SLG and OP just for players who have been inducted into the National Baseball Hall of Fame in Cooperstown. It is easy to see why there are disputes.

Table 1. Leaders for players in the Hall of Fame

Home Runs	Extra Base Hits	RBI	OBA	SLG	OPS
Aaron	Aaron	Aaron	Williams	Ruth	Ruth
Ruth	Musial	Ruth	Ruth	Williams	Williams
Mays	Ruth	Anson	McGraw	Gehrig	Gehrig
Griffey	Mays	Gehrig	Hamilton	Foxx	Foxx
Thome	Griffey	Musial	Gehrig	Greenberg	Greenberg

Table 2. Leaders for all players

Home Runs	Extra Base Hits	RBI	OBA	SLG	OPS
Bonds	Aaron	Aaron	Williams	Ruth	Ruth
Aaron	Bonds	Ruth	Ruth	Williams	Williams
Ruth	Musial	Rodriguez	McGraw	Gehrig	Gehrig
Rodriguez	Ruth	Anson	Hamilton	Foxx	Bonds
Mays	Pujols	Pujols	Gehrig	Bonds	Foxx

We could perform this same exercise using newer metrics instead of counting stats, but ultimately the same debate arises. Therefore, in lieu of a single metric, I propose using a multi-attribute decision-making algorithm that allows for the use of many metrics. There is no limit to the number of metrics that might be used in such an analysis. We point out that the metrics chosen for our analysis might not be the metrics chosen by many readers.

In using multi-attribute decision-making (MADM) algorithms, the attributes (in this case the chosen baseball metrics) must have assigned weights where the sum of all weights used must equal one. The MADM algorithms themselves call for weighted metrics. Additionally, there are several weighting algorithms that can be used. Some are subjective and at least one is objective. Subjective weights are, or can be, not much different from just choosing one metric, ordering, and stating the result. However, objective weighting weights allow the data elements themselves to be used in the calculation of the weights. This appears as a more objective method as it allows the user data (as many data metrics as the user desires) to be used to calculate the weights and in a ranking decision-making algorithm. The selection of the players in the analysis, and the choice of metric used, affect the calculation of the weights and in turn the ranking of the players. We choose TOPSIS, the technique of order preference by similarity to the ideal solution, to be our MAMD algorithm because TOPSIS is the only algorithm that allows these attributes (criteria and in our case metrics) to either be selected to be maximized or minimized. For example, home runs could be maximized but perhaps strikeouts, as a metric, should be minimized.

Quantitative analysis is one method that can be used where at least the reader can see the inputs and outputs used for the analysis. The mathematics used and their results are not without fault. However, the assumptions behind the metrics and which players to use or exclude can be questioned and argued just as subjective decisions might be argued among fans. In this article, we suggest a quantitative method—the technique of order performance by similarity to ideal solution (TOPSIS)—and discuss why we think it is has merit to be used in analysis.

MULTI-ATTRIBUTE DECISION MAKING (MADM)

The two main types of multi-attribute decision methods are (1) simple additive weights (SAW) and (2) the Technique of Order Preference by Similarity to Ideal Solution (TOPSIS). These methods require a normalization process of the data and multiplication by weights found by either subjective methods or entropy. TOPSIS has a clear advantage if any of the attributes (metrics) being used should be minimized instead of maximized. As previously mentioned, home runs should be maximized but strikeouts should be minimized. If all attributes being utilized should be maximized both are adequate for analysis. But if we were using stolen bases (SB) and caught stealing (CS), then we would maximize SB and minimize CS.

THE TECHNIQUE OF ORDER PREFERENCE BY SIMILARITY TO IDEAL SOLUTION (TOPSIS)

TOPSIS was the result of research and work done by Ching-Lai Hwang and Kwangsun Yoon in 1981.[4] TOPSIS has been used in a wide spectrum of comparisons of alternatives including: item selection from among alternatives, ranking leaders or entities, remote sensing in regions, data mining, and supply chain operations. TOPSIS is chosen over other methods because it orders the feasible alternatives according to their closeness to an ideal solution.[5] Its strength over other decision making methods is that with TOPSIS, we can indicate which metric (attributes) should be maximized and which should be minimized. In all other methods, everything is maximized.

TOPSIS is used in many applications across business, industry, and government. Jeffrey Napier provided some analysis of the use of TOPSIS for the Department of Defense in industrial base planning and item selection.[6] For years, the military used TOPSIS to rank order the systems' request from all the branches within the service for the annual budget review process. MADM and TOPSIS are being taught as part of decision analysis.

So why are we using TOPSIS as our MADM method and entropy as our weighting scheme? We are using TOPSIS because in our selected dataset all variables are not "larger is better." As mentioned, for strikeouts (SO), we'd prefer a smaller value. Entropy weights allows the data themselves to be used mathematically to calculate the weights and is not biased by subjectivity as are the other weighting schemes methods such as pairwise comparison method. Again, if we were using stolen bases (SB) in our analysis then we would like SB to be maximized and caught stealing (CS) minimized.

TOPSIS METHODOLOGY

The TOPSIS process is carried out through the following steps.

Step 1. Create an evaluation matrix consisting of m alternatives (players) and n criteria (metrics), with the intersection of each alternative and criterion given as x_{ij}, giving us a matrix $(X_{ij})_{mxn}$.

$$D = \begin{array}{c} \\ A_1 \\ A_2 \\ A_3 \\ . \\ . \\ . \\ A_m \end{array} \begin{array}{cccccc} x_1 & x_2 & x_3 & \cdot \cdot & \cdot & x_n \\ \left[\begin{array}{cccccc} x_{11} & x_{12} & x_{13} & \cdot & \cdot & x_{1n} \\ x_{21} & x_{22} & x_{23} & \cdot & \cdot & x_{2n} \\ x_{31} & x_{32} & x_{33} & \cdot & \cdot & x_{3n} \\ . & . & . & . & & . \\ . & . & . & . & & . \\ . & . & . & . & & . \\ x_{m1} & x_{m2} & x_{m3} & \cdot & \cdot & x_{mn} \end{array} \right] \end{array}$$

Step 2. The matrix shown as D above is then normalized to form the matrix $R = (R_{ij})_{mxn}$, using the normalization method to obtain the entries,

$$r_{ij} = \frac{x_{ij}}{\sqrt{\sum x_{ij}^2}}$$

for $i = 1,2...,m; j = 1,2,...n$

Step 3. Calculate the weighted normalized decision matrix. First, we need the weights. Weights can come from either the decision maker or by computation using entropy.

Step 3a. Use either the decision maker's weights for the attributes $x_1, x_2,...x_n$, pairwise comparisons method, or the entropy weighting scheme, as we use here.

$$\sum_{j=1}^{n} w_j = 1$$

The sum of the weights over all attributes must equal one regardless of the weighting method used.

Step 3b. Multiply the weights to each of the column entries in the matrix from *Step 2* to obtain the matrix, T.

$$T = (t_{ij})_{m \times n} = (w_j r_{ij})_{m \times n}, \quad i = 1,2, ..., m$$

Step 4. Determine the worst alternative (A_w) and the best alternative (A_b): Examine each attribute's column and select the largest and smallest values appropriately. If the values imply larger is better (profit) then the best alternatives are the largest values and if the values imply smaller is better (such as cost) then the best alternative is the smallest value.

We suggest that if possible make all entry values in terms of positive impacts.

Step 5. Calculate the L2-distance between the target alternative i and the worst condition A_w

$$d_{iw} = \sqrt{\sum_{j=1}^{n} (t_{ij} - t_{wj})^2}, i=1,2,...m$$

and the distance between the alternative i and the best condition A_b

$$d_{ib} = \sqrt{\sum_{j=1}^{n} (t_{ij} - t_{bj})^2}, i=1,2,...m$$

where d_{iw} and d_{ib} are L2-norm distances from the target alternative i to the worst and best conditions, respectively.

Step 6. Calculate the similarity to the worst condition:

$$s_{iw} = \frac{d_{iw}}{(d_{iw} + d_{ib})}, \quad 0 \leq s_{iw} \leq 1, i = 1,2, ..., m$$

$s_{iw} = 1$ if and only if the alternative solution has the worst condition; and
$s_{iw} = 0$ if and only if the alternative solution has the best condition.

$$A_w = \left\{ \left\langle \max(t_{ij} \Big| i = 1,2, ..., m \mid j \in J_- \right\rangle, \left\langle \min(t_{ij} \Big| i = 1,2, ..., m) \mid j \in J_+ \right\rangle \right\} \equiv \left\{ t_{wj} \Big| j = 1,2, ..., n \right\},$$

$$A_{wb} = \left\{ \left\langle \min(t_{ij} \Big| i = 1,2, ..., m \mid j \in J_- \right\rangle, \left\langle \max(t_{ij} \Big| i = 1,2, ..., m) \mid j \in J_+ \right\rangle \right\} \equiv \left\{ t_{bj} \Big| j = 1,2, ..., n \right\},$$

where,

$J_+ = \left\{ j = 1,2, ...n \Big| j \right\}$ associated with the criteria having a positive impact, and

$J_- = \left\{ j = 1,2, ...n \Big| j \right\}$ associated with the criteria having a negative impact.

Step 7. Rank the alternatives according to their value from S_{iw} $(i = 1,2,...,m)$.

SIMPLE ADDITIVE WEIGHTS (SAW)

SAW is a very straightforward and easily constructed process within MADM methods, also referred to as the weighted sum method.[7] SAW is the simplest, and still one of the widest used of the MADM methods. Its simplistic approach makes it easy to use. Depending on the type of the relational data used, we might either want the larger average or the smaller average.

Here, each criterion (attribute) is given a weight, and the sum of all weights must be equal to one. If equally weighted criteria then we merely need to sum the alternative values. Each alternative is assessed with regard to every criterion (attribute). The overall or composite performance score of an alternative is given simply by Equation 1 with m criteria.

$$P_i = (\sum_{j=1}^{m} w_j m_{ij})/m \qquad (1)$$

It was previously though that all the units in the criteria must be identical units of measure such as dollars, pounds, seconds, etc. A normalization process can make the values unitless. So, we recommend normalizing the data as shown in equation 2:

$$P_i = (\sum_{j=1}^{m} w_j m_{ijNormalized})/m \qquad (2)$$

where ($m_{ijNormalized}$) represents the normalized value of m_{ij}, and P_i is the overall or composite score of the alternative A_i. The alternative with the highest value of P_i is considered the best alternative.

The strengths of SAW are (1) the ease of use and (2) the normalized data allow for comparison across many differing criteria. But with SAW, either larger is always better or smaller is always better. There is not the flexibility in this method to state which criterion should be larger or smaller to achieve better performance. This makes gathering useful data of the same relational value scheme (larger or smaller) essential.

ENTROPY WEIGHTING SCHEME

Shannon and Weaver originally proposed the entropy concept.[8] This concept had been highlighted by Zeleny for deciding the weights of attributes.[9] Entropy is the measure of uncertainty in the information using probability methods. It indicates that a broad distribution represents more uncertainty than does a sharply-peaked distribution. To determine the weights by the entropy method, the normalized decision matrix we call R_{ij} is considered. The equation used is

$$e_j = -k \sum_{i=1}^{n} R_{ij}\ln(R_{ij})$$

Where $k = 1/ln(n)$ is a constant that guarantees that $0 \le e_j \le 1$. The value of n refers to the number of alternatives. The degree of divergence (d_j) of the average information contained by each attribute is calculated as:

$$d_j = 1 - e_j.$$

The more divergent the performance rating R_{ij}, for all i and j, then the higher the corresponding d_j the more important the attribute B_j is considered to be.

The weights are found by the equation

$$w_j = \frac{(1 - e_j)}{\sum (1 - e_j)}.$$

Let's assume that the criteria were listed in order of importance by a decision maker. Entropy ignores that fact and uses the actual data to compute the weights. Although home runs might be the most important criterion to the decision maker, it might not be the largest weighted criterion using entropy. Using this method, we must be willing to accept these types of results in weights.

SENSITIVITY ANALYSIS

In the previous work done by Fox and Fox et al. using the pairwise comparison method of obtaining weight, sensitivity analysis was done to determine the effect of changing weights on the ranking of terrorists.[10] The decision weights are subject to sensitivity analysis to determine how the affect the final ranking. Sensitivity analysis is essential to good analysis. Additionally, Alinezhad suggests sensitivity analysis for TOPSIS for changing an attribute weight.[11] The equation they developed for adjusting weights based upon a single weight change that we used is:

$$w_j' = \frac{(1 - w_p')}{(1 - w_p)} w_j$$

where w_j' is the future weight of criterion j, w_p the current selected weight to be changed, w_p' the new value of the selected weight, w_j is the current weight of criterion j. This method of doing sensitivity analysis is valid for any chosen weighting scheme.

Another method of sensitivity analysis might be to change the metric used or the baseball players used in the analysis. We accomplished this by first including strikeouts and then excluding strikeouts in our analysis. We also can alter the players used if we are using the entropy weighting methods. Changing players, as well as changing metrics analyzed, changes the weights that are calculated and in turn might change the rank ordering of the players.

2. APPLICATION TO BASEBALL'S GREATEST HITTERS

We applied these mathematical techniques to baseball's greatest hitters. We started by taking hitters in the National Baseball Hall of Fame (excluding pitchers and managers). We ran our analysis. Then we added some star retired players and current players: Pete Rose, Barry Bonds, Mark McGwire, Alex Rodriguez, Albert Pujols, Mike Trout, Miguel Cabrera, Sammy Sosa, and Ichiro Suzuki, sourcing their statistics from Baseball-Reference.com.[12,13]

DATA

Based upon reviewers' comments, we ran several separate analyses with the Hall of Fame players including the additional mentioned players. We used standard metrics as the criteria for the initial analysis and then more advanced metrics for the second run of our analysis.[14]

STANDARD METRICS

G – Games Played
PA – Plate Appearances
AB – At Bats
R – Runs Scored
H – Hits
2B – Doubles Hit
3B – Triples Hit
HR – Home Runs Hit
RBI – Runs Batted In
BB – Bases on Balls
SO – Strikeouts
BA – Hits/At Bats

ADVANCED METRICS

OBA = (H+BB+HBP)/(At Bats+BB+HBP+SF)
SLG – Total Bases/At Bats or (1B+2*2B+3*3B+4*HR)/AB
OPS – On-Base + Slugging Averages

In our first analysis, we used the first 11 metrics above. In our second analysis we decided to use percentage of extra base hits (2B + 3B + HR/hits), runs, BB, OBA and SLG. Since OPS is the sum of OBA and

SLG, we excluded it from either analysis.

Since entropy is a function of the data, we separated our collected data into sets both with only the data partitioned as stated and for our two separate groups of players. First, we performed our analysis for the Hall of Fame players and then we repeat it for these same players but with the additional players added. We used the entropy method to weigh these criteria for the analysis. We did so because we did not want bias to interfere with our weighting scheme as the other methods for obtaining weights are very subjective. Using the entropy weighting scheme as described previously, we found our weights to use in the analysis. Examining the HoF set, we used the entropy method of weighting for the 11 criteria. We found these weights for the hall of fame players:

METRICS AND WEIGHTS

Metric	Weight
G	0.04128
PA	0.05064
AB	0.04965
R	0.06426
H	0.05876
2B	0.07295
3B	0.11743
HR	0.23904
RBI	0.07459
BB	0.09882
SO	0.12679
BA	0.00579

We found the weights for the second set of metrics for the hall of fame players as:

%X	RBI	BB	BA	OBA	SLG
0.149467087	0.295852	0.465290109	0.016695	0.01822	0.054477

We present the weights when all our additional players are included with the hall of fame players in the analysis.

LARGER METRIC SET

Metric	Weight
G	0.04847
AB	0.04886
R	0.05541
H	0.05014
2B	0.05764
3B	0.06165
HR	0.41781
RBI	0.05905
BB	0.08292
SO	0.08865
BA	0.02941

SMALLER METRIC SET

%X	RBI	BB	BA	OBP	SLG
0.155603773	0.292877	0.463543085	0.015732	0.017507	0.054736

3. MADM MODEL RESULTS

Using our TOPSIS procedures and using "larger is better" for all variables except SO where *smaller* is better, we found the top HoF hitters of all time. TOPSIS ranked them in order as: Babe Ruth, Hank Aaron, Willie Mays, Stan Musial, and Lou Gehrig using our larger group of metrics.

Player	TOPSIS Value	Rank
Babe Ruth	0.731603653	1
Hank Aaron	0.712828581	2
Willie Mays	0.688321995	3
Stan Musial	0.664775607	4
Lou Gehrig	0.653080437	5
Ted Williams	0.639868853	6
Jimmie Foxx	0.623135348	7
Mel Ott	0.619731627	8
Frank Robinson	0.616727014	9
Ken Griffey Jr.	0.602640058	10
Ernie Banks	0.573236285	11
Mickey Mantle	0.572825146	12
Harmon Killebrew	0.566824198	13
Eddie Mathews	0.565000206	14
Frank Thomas	0.561931931	15
Mike Schmidt	0.559451492	16
Carl Yastrzemski	0.556948693	17
Eddie Murray	0.555682669	18
Willie McCovey	0.552158735	19
Dave Winfield	0.536912893	20

The next twenty are:

Billy Williams	0.535553305	21
Joe DiMaggio	0.534463121	22
Al Kaline	0.526047568	23
Reggie Jackson	0.523830476	24
Cal Ripken	0.520103131	25
Andre Dawson	0.508935302	26
Jeff Bagwell	0.506944011	27
Rogers Hornsby	0.506190846	28
Johnny Mize	0.503463982	29
George Brett	0.499767024	30
Duke Snider	0.497691125	31
Yogi Berra	0.495176578	32
Willie Stargell	0.493824724	33
Al Simmons	0.490040488	34
Mike Piazza	0.483583075	35
Goose Goslin	0.474848669	36
Ralph Kiner	0.473649418	37

Ty Cobb	0.46631062	38
Jim Rice	0.460974189	39
Johnny Bench	0.459232829	40

When we ran the analysis with the second criteria using the MADM method, SAW, because all the metrics used were to be maximized We found that our top players were:

1. Babe Ruth
2. Ted Williams
3. Lou Gehrig
4. Jimmie Foxx
5. Hank Greenberg
6. Mickey Mantle
7. Stan Musial
8. Joe DiMaggio
9. Frank Thomas

Note that number one in both approaches among the HoF players is Babe Ruth.

4. "WHAT IF" ANALYSIS: OTHER NON-HALL OF FAME PLAYERS INCLUDED.

Next, we included additional players based upon their performance, and not regarding other issues. We included Pete Rose, Barry Bonds, Mark McGwire, Alex Rodriguez, Albert Pujols, Miguel Cabrera, Mike Trout, Sammy Sosa and Ichiro Suzuki. First, we re-compute the entropy weights and then our ranking.

We present the top 20 ranked players using TOPSIS using all the chosen metrics.

The addition of the new players yielded a slightly different set of results but we see that Ruth and Aaron are ranked one and two:

Hank Aaron	0.70117	2
Barry Bonds	0.69878	3
Willie Mays	0.67513	4
Stan Musial	0.6537	5
Lou Gehrig	0.64057	6
Ted Williams	0.63168	7
Jimmie Foxx	0.61065	8
Mel Ott	0.61013	9
Frank Robinson	0.60508	10
Ken Griffey	0.59135	11
Alex Rodriguez	0.58904	12
Mickey Mantle	0.56287	13
Ernie Banks	0.5604	14
Harmon Killebrew	0.55695	15
Eddie Mathews	0.55434	16
Frank Thomas	0.55274	17
Carl Yastrzemski	0.54894	18
Mike Schmidt	0.54886	19
Mark McGwire	0.54863	20

We also ran analysis with a smaller number of metrics as mentioned earlier. The Top 25 of all time all *including* our stars that are not currently in the Hall of Fame are:

Barry Bonds	1
Babe Ruth	2
Hank Aaron	3
Alex Rodriguez	4
Willie Mays	5
Albert Pujols	6
Ken Griffey Jr.	7
Frank Robinson	8
Sammy Sosa	9
Reggie Jackson	10
Jimmie Foxx	11
Ted Williams	12
Harmon Killebrew	13
Mike Schmidt	14
Mickey Mantle	15
Stan Musial	16
Mel Ott	17
Mark McGwire	18
Lou Gehrig	19
Frank Thomas	20
Eddie Murray	21
Eddie Mathews	22
Willie McCovey	23
Carl Yastrzemski	24
Ernie Banks	25

We see that using the smaller list of metrics Barry Bonds computes as first followed by Babe Ruth. The addition of the new players has made a difference in the ranking of baseball's greatest hitters.

CONCLUSIONS

Using entropy as our method to obtain weights, which is an unbiased weighting method, we found Babe Ruth as the greatest hitter in many of our analyses, while Barry Bonds ranked number one using the smaller metric set. Arguments can be made for any of these players being the greatest hitter of all time. By using more than one sabermetric measure, applying weights to the metrics, and applying a MADM method, we can strengthen the argument for the greatest hitter of all time. Depending on the players and metrics in the analysis, we see that ranking might change. This is why the argument continues regarding *who is the greatest hitter of all time?* ∎

Acknowledgments
I acknowledge and thank Father Gabe Costa, Department of Mathematical Sciences, United States Military Academy for introducing me to sabermetrics and the initial reading and suggestions on this research.

Notes

1. www.espn.com/classic/obit/williams_ted_kurkjian.html) July 5, 2002, accessed September 2017.
2. www.ranker.com/crowdranked-list/best-hitters-in-baseball-history, accessed January 2019.
3. www.britannica.com/list/10-greatest-baseball-players-of-all-time accessed January 2019.
4. Shell, Max, 2005.
5. Ching-Lai Hwang and Kwangsun Yoon, 1981. *Multiple attribute decision making: Methods and applications.* New York: Springer-Verlag.
6. Jacek Malczewski. 1996. "GIS-Based Approach to Multiple Criteria Group Decision-Making." *International Journal of Geographical Information Science - GIS,* 10(8), 955–71.
7. Jeffrey Napier. 1992. Industrial base program item selection indicators analytical enhancements. *Department of Defense Pamphlet,* DLA-93-P20047.
8. Fishburn, P.C. (1967). Additive utilities with incomplete product set: Applications to priorities and assignments. *Operations Research Society of America (ORSA),* 15, 537–42
9. Claude Shannon and Warren Weaver. 1949. *The Mathematical Theory of Communication,* University of Illinois Press. ISBN 0-252-72548-4.
10. Milan Zeleny. 1982. *Multiple Criteria Decision Making.* New York: McGraw Hill.
11. William Fox, Bradley Greaver, Leo Raabe, and Rob Burks. 2017. "CARVER 2.0: Integrating Multi-attribute Decision Making with AHP in Center of Gravity Vulnerability Analysis," *Journal of Defense Modeling and Simulation,* Published on-line first, http://journals.sagepub.com/doi/abs/10.1177/1548512917717054.
12. Alireza Alinezhad and Abbas Amini, 2011. "Sensitivity Analysis of TOPSIS technique: The results of change in the weight of one attribute on the final ranking of alternatives." *Journal of Optimization in Industrial Engineering,* 7(2011), 23–28.
13. Hall of Fame Players Baseball Statistics, https://www.baseball-reference.com/awards/hof_batting.shtml, were accessed September 14, 2017).
14. Players Baseball Statistics, accessed October 1, 2019.
Trout https://www.baseball-reference.com/players/t/troutmi01.shtml
Rose (https://www.baseball-reference.com/players/r/rosepe01.shtml)
Bonds (https://www.baseball-reference.com/players/b/bondsba01.shtml)
McGwire (https://www.baseball-reference.com/players/m/mcgwima01.shtml)
Rodriguez (https://www.baseball-reference.com/players/r/rodrial01.shtml)
Jackson (https://www.baseball-reference.com/players/j/jacksjo01.shtml)
Pujlos (https://www.baseball-reference.com/players/j/pujolis01.shtml)
Trout (https://www.baseball-reference.com/players/j/trout01.shtml)
Caberra (https://www.baseball-reference.com/players/j/caberra01.shtml)
Suzuki (https://www.baseball-reference.com/players/j/susukio01.shtml)
Sosa: (https://www.baseball-reference.com/players/j/sosasa01.shtml)
15. https://www.baseball-reference.com/awards/hof_batting.shtml)

THE SABR DIGITAL LIBRARY

The Society for American Baseball Research, the top baseball research organization in the world, disseminates some of the best in baseball history, analysis, and biography through our publishing programs. The SABR Digital Library contains a mix of books old and new, and focuses on a tandem program of paperback and ebook publication, making these materials widely available for both on digital devices and as traditional printed books.

GREATEST GAMES BOOKS

TIGERS BY THE TALE:
GREAT GAMES AT MICHIGAN AND TRUMBULL
For over 100 years, Michigan and Trumbull was the scene of some of the most exciting baseball ever. This book portrays 50 classic games at the corner, spanning the earliest days of Bennett Park until Tiger Stadium's final closing act. From Ty Cobb to Mickey Cochrane, Hank Greenberg to Al Kaline, and Willie Horton to Alan Trammell.
Edited by Scott Ferkovich
$12.95 paperback (ISBN 978-1-943816-21-7)
$6.99 ebook (ISBN 978-1-943816-20-0)
8.5"x11", 160 pages, 22 photos

FROM THE BRAVES TO THE BREWERS: GREAT GAMES
AND HISTORY AT MILWAUKEE'S COUNTY STADIUM
The National Pastime provides in-depth articles focused on the geographic region where the national SABR convention is taking place annually. The SABR 45 convention took place in Chicago, and here are 45 articles on baseball in and around the bat-and-ball crazed Windy City: 25 that appeared in the souvenir book of the convention plus another 20 articles available in ebook only.
Edited by Gregory H. Wolf
$19.95 paperback (ISBN 978-1-943816-23-1)
$9.99 ebook (ISBN 978-1-943816-22-4)
8.5"X11", 290 pages, 58 photos

BRAVES FIELD:
MEMORABLE MOMENTS AT BOSTON'S LOST DIAMOND
From its opening on August 18, 1915, to the sudden departure of the Boston Braves to Milwaukee before the 1953 baseball season, Braves Field was home to Boston's National League baseball club and also hosted many other events: from NFL football to championship boxing. The most memorable moments to occur in Braves Field history are portrayed here.
Edited by Bill Nowlin and Bob Brady
$19.95 paperback (ISBN 978-1-933599-93-9)
$9.99 ebook (ISBN 978-1-933599-92-2)
8.5"X11", 282 pages, 182 photos

AU JEU/PLAY BALL: THE 50 GREATEST GAMES IN THE
HISTORY OF THE MONTREAL EXPOS
The 50 greatest games in Montreal Expos history. The games described here recount the exploits of the many great players who wore Expos uniforms over the years—Bill Stoneman, Gary Carter, Andre Dawson, Steve Rogers, Pedro Martinez, from the earliest days of the franchise, to the glory years of 1979-1981, the what-might-have-been years of the early 1990s, and the sad, final days.and others.
Edited by Norm King
$12.95 paperback (ISBN 978-1-943816-15-6)
$5.99 ebook (ISBN978-1-943816-14-9)
8.5"x11", 162 pages, 50 photos

ORIGINAL SABR RESEARCH

CALLING THE GAME:
BASEBALL BROADCASTING FROM 1920 TO THE PRESENT
An exhaustive, meticulously researched history of bringing the national pastime out of the ballparks and into living rooms via the airwaves. Every play-by-play announcer, color commentator, and ex-ballplayer, every broadcast deal, radio station, and TV network. Plus a foreword by "Voice of the Chicago Cubs" Pat Hughes, and an afterword by Jacques Doucet, the "Voice of the Montreal Expos" 1972-2004.
by Stuart Shea
$24.95 paperback (ISBN 978-1-933599-40-3)
$9.99 ebook (ISBN 978-1-933599-41-0)
7"X10", 712 pages, 40 photos

BIOPROJECT BOOKS

WHO'S ON FIRST:
REPLACEMENT PLAYERS IN WORLD WAR II
During World War II, 533 players made the major league debuts. More than 60% of the players in the 1941 Opening Day lineups departed for the service and were replaced by first-times and oldsters. Hod Lisenbee was 46. POW Bert Shepard had an artificial leg, and Pete Gray had only one arm. The 1944 St. Louis Browns had 13 players classified 4-F. These are their stories.
Edited by Marc Z Aaron and Bill Nowlin
$19.95 paperback (ISBN 978-1-933599-91-5)
$9.99 ebook (ISBN 978-1-933599-90-8)
8.5"X11", 422 pages, 67 photos

VAN LINGLE MUNGO:
THE MAN, THE SONG, THE PLAYERS
40 baseball players with intriguing names have been named in renditions of Dave Frishberg's classic 1969 song, Van Lingle Mungo. This book presents biographies of all 40 players and additional information about one of the greatest baseball novelty songs of all time.
Edited by Bill Nowlin
$19.95 paperback (ISBN 978-1-933599-76-2)
$9.99 ebook (ISBN 978-1-933599-77-9)
8.5"X11", 278 pages, 46 photos

NUCLEAR POWERED BASEBALL
Nuclear Powered Baseball tells the stories of each player—past and present—featured in the classic Simpsons episode "Homer at the Bat." Wade Boggs, Ken Griffey Jr., Ozzie Smith, Nap Lajoie, Don Mattingly, and many more. We've also included a few very entertaining takes on the now-famous episode from prominent baseball writers Jonah Keri, Joe Posnanski, Erik Malinowski, and Bradley Woodrum
Edited by Emily Hawks and Bill Nowlin
$19.95 paperback (ISBN 978-1-943816-11-8)
$9.99 ebook (ISBN 978-1-943816-10-1)
8.5"X11", 250 pages

SABR Members can purchase each book at a significant discount (often 50% off) and receive the ebook edtions free as a member benefit. Each book is available in a trade paperback edition as well as ebooks suitable for reading on a home computer or Nook, Kindle, or iPad/tablet.
To learn more about becoming a member of SABR, visit the website: sabr.org/join

SABR BIOPROJECT BOOKS

In 2002, the Society for American Baseball Research launched an effort to write and publish biographies of every player, manager, and individual who has made a contribution to baseball. Over the past decade, the BioProject Committee has produced over 2,200 biographical articles. Many have been part of efforts to create theme- or team-oriented books, spearheaded by chapters or other committees of SABR.

THE YEAR OF THE BLUE SNOW:
THE 1964 PHILADELPHIA PHILLIES
Catcher Gus Triandos dubbed the Philadelphia Phillies' 1964 season "the year of the blue snow," a rare thing that happens once in a great while. This book sheds light on lingering questions about the 1964 season—but any book about a team is really about the players. This work offers life stories of all the players and others (managers, coaches, owners, and broadcasters) associated with this star-crossed team, as well as essays of analysis and history.
Edited by Mel Marmer and Bill Nowlin
$19.95 paperback (ISBN 978-1-933599-51-9)
$9.99 ebook (ISBN 978-1-933599-52-6)
8.5"X11", 356 PAGES, over 70 photos

DETROIT TIGERS 1984:
WHAT A START! WHAT A FINISH!
The 1984 Detroit tigers roared out of the gate, winning their first nine games of the season and compiling an eye-popping 35-5 record after the campaign's first 40 games—still the best start ever for any team in major league history. This book brings together biographical profiles of every Tiger from that magical season, plus those of field management, top executives, the broadcasters—even venerable Tiger Stadium and the city itself.
Edited by Mark Pattison and David Raglin
$19.95 paperback (ISBN 978-1-933599-44-1)
$9.99 ebook (ISBN 978-1-933599-45-8)
8.5"x11", 250 pages (Over 230,000 words!)

SWEET '60: THE 1960 PITTSBURGH PIRATES
A portrait of the 1960 team which pulled off one of the biggest upsets of the last 60 years. When Bill Mazeroski's home run left the park to win in Game Seven of the World Series, beating the New York Yankees, David had toppled Goliath. It was a blow that awakened a generation, one that millions of people saw on television, one of TV's first iconic World Series moments.
Edited by Clifton Blue Parker and Bill Nowlin
$19.95 paperback (ISBN 978-1-933599-48-9)
$9.99 ebook (ISBN 978-1-933599-49-6)
8.5"X11", 340 pages, 75 photos

RED SOX BASEBALL IN THE DAYS OF IKE AND ELVIS: THE RED SOX OF THE 1950s
Although the Red Sox spent most of the 1950s far out of contention, the team was filled with fascinating players who captured the heart of their fans. In *Red Sox Baseball*, members of SABR present 46 biographies on players such as Ted Williams and Pumpsie Green as well as season-by-season recaps.
Edited by Mark Armour and Bill Nowlin
$19.95 paperback (ISBN 978-1-933599-24-3)
$9.99 ebook (ISBN 978-1-933599-34-2)
8.5"X11", 372 PAGES, over 100 photos

THE MIRACLE BRAVES OF 1914
BOSTON'S ORIGINAL WORST-TO-FIRST CHAMPIONS
Long before the Red Sox "Impossible Dream" season, Boston's now nearly forgotten "other" team, the 1914 Boston Braves, performed a baseball "miracle" that resounds to this very day. The "Miracle Braves" were Boston's first "worst-to-first" winners of the World Series. Refusing to throw in the towel at the midseason mark, George Stallings engineered a remarkable second-half climb in the standings all the way to first place.
Edited by Bill Nowlin
$19.95 paperback (ISBN 978-1-933599-69-4)
$9.99 ebook (ISBN 978-1-933599-70-0)
8.5"X11", 392 PAGES, over 100 photos

THAR'S JOY IN BRAVELAND!
THE 1957 MILWAUKEE BRAVES
Few teams in baseball history have captured the hearts of their fans like the Milwaukee Braves of the 1950s. During the Braves' 13-year tenure in Milwaukee (1953-1965), they had a winning record every season, won two consecutive NL pennants (1957 and 1958), lost two more in the final week of the season (1956 and 1959), and set big-league attendance records along the way.
Edited by Gregory H. Wolf
$19.95 paperback (ISBN 978-1-933599-71-7)
$9.99 ebook (ISBN 978-1-933599-72-4)
8.5"x11", 330 pages, over 60 photos

NEW CENTURY, NEW TEAM:
THE 1901 BOSTON AMERICANS
The team now known as the Boston Red Sox played its first season in 1901. Boston had a well-established National League team, but the American League went head-to-head with the N.L. in Chicago, Philadelphia, and Boston. Chicago won the American League pennant and Boston finished second, only four games behind.
Edited by Bill Nowlin
$19.95 paperback (ISBN 978-1-933599-58-8)
$9.99 ebook (ISBN 978-1-933599-59-5)
8.5"X11", 268 pages, over 125 photos

CAN HE PLAY?
A LOOK AT BASEBALL SCOUTS AND THEIR PROFESSION
They dig through tons of coal to find a single diamond. Here in the world of scouts, we meet the "King of Weeds," a Ph.D. we call "Baseball's Renaissance Man," a husband-and-wife team, pioneering Latin scouts, and a Japanese-American interned during World War II who became a successful scout—and many, many more.
Edited by Jim Sandoval and Bill Nowlin
$19.95 paperback (ISBN 978-1-933599-23-6)
$9.99 ebook (ISBN 978-1-933599-25-0)
8.5"X11", 200 PAGES, over 100 photos

SABR Members can purchase each book at a significant discount (often 50% off) and receive the ebook editions free as a member benefit. Each book is available in a trade paperback edition as well as ebooks suitable for reading on a home computer or Nook, Kindle, or iPad/tablet.
To learn more about becoming a member of SABR, visit the website: sabr.org/join

The Henry Chadwick Award was established by SABR to honor baseball's great researchers—historians, statisticians, analysts, and archivists—for their invaluable contributions to making baseball the game that links America's present with its past.

Apart from honoring individuals for the length and breadth of their contribution to the study and enjoyment of baseball, the Chadwick Award will educate the baseball community about sometimes little known but vastly important contributions from the game's past and thus encourage the next generation of researchers.

The contributions of nominees must have had public impact. This may be demonstrated by publication of research in any of a variety of formats: books, magazine articles, websites, etc. The compilation of a significant database or archive that has facilitated the published research of others will also be considered in the realm of public impact.

Tom Tango

by Dave Studenmund

Tom Tango (1968–) was born in the suburbs of Montreal, where he found that baseball spoke to him even more than the Canadian national sport of hockey. He particularly enjoyed watching Red Sox games on TV and was entranced by Fenway Park. He eventually became an Expos fan as well, but it was a love of the game itself that stayed with him.

In school, Tom's favorite subject was math, so he was naturally drawn to sports statistics. His mathematical imagination was first captured by the Plus/Minus stats in the *Hockey News*. He subsequently stumbled upon Pete Palmer's Linear Weights in the *Baseball Digest* and started reading sabermetric classics such as the *Hidden Game of Baseball* and Bill James's *Baseball Abstracts*.

Tom majored in computer science in college and, upon graduation, found jobs as a programmer, analyst, and database developer. Tom never lost his enthusiasm for baseball statistics, however. In the late 1990s he became a regular participant on the Baseball Boards (aka Fanhome), where he met many other passionate baseball statistics fans, including Mitchel Lichtman. Thus began Tom's formidable presence online, where he mastered the skills of presenting insightful analyses, explaining difficult topics, encouraging discussion, and building consensus.

Tom co-authored (along with Lichtman and Andy Dolphin) *The Book: Playing the Percentages in Baseball*. This 2007 book, which introduced wOBA and included detailed analytic chapters on platoons, sacrifice bunts, and many other strategic topics, remains one of the most influential baseball analytic books of all time. Its sales are still strong nearly 15 years later.

On the Internet, Tango investigated, discussed, and published new frontiers in baseball statistics such as Fielding Independent Pitching (FIP, building on the work of Voros McCracken), Wins Above Replacement (WAR), Marcel the Monkey forecasting system, WOWY (With and With Out You) analysis, and dollars per WAR free agent contracts—among many other topics.

During this time, Tango was also hired as a consultant by several baseball teams, including a four-year stint with the Chicago Cubs. In 2016, he was hired by MLBAM on a full-time basis to develop systems and statistics driven by new on-field radar and camera technology. In his short time there, he has introduced new stats—including Barrels, Batted Ball Exit Velocity, and Outs Above Average—that have quickly become part of the national baseball conversation.

Tom has been one of the most influential voices in baseball analysis and sabermetrics for more than 20 years. His impact can be seen on the field, in the broadcast booth and in many teams' analytic departments. Tom has not just created new statistics; he has introduced new ways of understanding the game. By interacting with readers on the Internet in a fully open, transparent manner, he has deepened the baseball community's understanding of baseball statistics, analytics and strategy. ■

Michael Haupert

by Dan Levitt

Mike Haupert (1961–) dramatically expanded our understanding of the business of baseball through his research of player contract cards at the National Baseball Hall of Fame and Museum in Cooperstown. Haupert, a professor of economics at the University of Wisconsin-La Crosse, extracted and made available the information for roughly 100,000 player seasons, providing the first comprehensive accurate salary and contract information for a large swath of baseball history. With his additional groundbreaking research on the New York Yankees, Negro Leagues, and AAGPBL financial records, Haupert has perhaps become the foremost authority on the long history of baseball's evolving economics.

Haupert grew up in Dubuque, Iowa, where he quickly became a Cubs fan. Dubuque was one of the first cities wired for cable, and Haupert would catch the Cubs on TV when he came home from school. He stayed in Dubuque for his undergraduate degree at Loras College before heading to Washington University in St. Louis for his advanced degrees. As a graduate student Haupert first applied baseball to one of his assignments, using city size and games won to predict attendance. While he was in college, the first Rotisserie baseball book came out, and Haupert and friends set up a league that lasted for 26 years.

Once he became a professor at La Crosse, Haupert had the opportunity to design a new course. He was concerned that the limited availability of data at the time precluded a course solely on the economics of sport, so he introduced a class on the economics of the entertainment industry, which included sports. Today, that course has morphed into two separate courses, one on the economics of sports, the other covering the performing arts.

In 2000 Haupert traveled to Cooperstown to see what financial information might be available, particularly relative to salaries. He was serendipitously introduced to the Yankees' financial ledgers, which required a significant amount of deciphering to formulate meaningful interpretations. From this research

Haupert published a couple of groundbreaking studies: "Pay Ball: Estimating the Profitability of the New York Yankees, 1915–1937" (with Ken Winter), and a three-part series, "Purchasing Pennants: the New York Yankees Then and Now."

During his semiannual trips to Cooperstown, Haupert was further introduced to the vast and broadly untapped collection of player contract cards. Over a number of years and many trips to the Hall, Haupert collected the data off of these cards, creating a database of around 100,000 player seasons. (Many of these players never played in the big leagues—the salaries were contingent on the player making it to the majors. Cards likewise exist for non-playing personnel, including scouts and managers. Moreover, these cards help add to our knowledge of the history of the structure of baseball. Scouts, for example, were sometimes compensated based on how far a player advanced through a team's farm system.) The data on the cards included all the information filled into the blanks on a player's contract, including his salary and provisions outside the standard language such as bonus clauses. The cards also list player transactions and occasionally purchase prices. Haupert has made the salary information publicly available through Baseball-Reference.com.

In 2018 Haupert synthesized much of his financial research from the 1920s when he coauthored *The Age of Ruth and Landis: The Economics of Baseball during the Roaring Twenties* (with David Surdam). The book added important new economic insights outside Organized Baseball, such as Negro League financial information.

Business of baseball research has come a long way since 1991 when insufficient course material existed for Haupert to put together a class on the economics of sport. That instructors today have a wealth of information to use in such a class owes much to Haupert's efforts to track down and catalog player salary information. We can only hope that Haupert will continue to use his research knowhow and interpretive skills to enlarge our business of baseball knowledge. ∎

Tom Shea

by Dick Thompson

Thomas Shea (1904–95) was one of the 16 founding members of SABR, making the drive to Cooperstown from his home in Hingham, Massachusetts, for the organization's first meeting in August 1971. Shea's baseball work was devoted to collecting biographical details on players, umpires, and other personnel.

The oldest of the SABR founders, Tom spent his early school years in and around Boston and Providence, Rhode Island. Tom never paid much attention to player stats but was fascinated by biographical and demographic data on players, as well as umpires, magnates, and other baseball persons. After graduating from Boston College in 1926, he traveled the Northeast and Midwest selling textbooks to schools for Macmillan Publishers, and later Nelson Publishing and Encyclopedia Britannica.

Wherever he went he carried index cards and small scraps of paper in his pocket. While waiting for appointments with school administrators, he would kill time taking notes from the local newspapers of whatever small town he was in. During the evenings he would use his Macmillan expense account—these were Depression years—to buy drinks in an area establishment and steer the conversation toward local baseball.

In 1939 Tom married Elizabeth Griffith. It was she who transformed Tom's scrawled notes into legible copy. At the end of World War II, Tom and Betty settled in Hingham, where he engaged in real estate work.

Tom had begun a correspondence with Ernie Lanigan in the mid-1920s, and through Lanigan, Tom met S.C. Thompson some time in the 1930s. Shea left behind an extensive trove of correspondence with both men, along with J.G. Taylor Spink, publisher of *The Sporting News*. In 1941, Shea responded at length to Spink's plaintive requests for help in marketing the *Baseball Register*. Shea's advice worked, but his only payment was a lifetime subscription—which was abruptly cut off when Spink died.

It is obvious from the materials in his files that Shea supplied a high percentage of the biographical facts for Turkin and Thompson's *Official Encyclopedia of Baseball*, first published in 1951. Tom trustingly thought he was a co-author, and the fact that he got only a brief credit in the preface turned him off baseball research for almost a decade.

In the early 1960s Lee Allen resumed his own correspondence with Shea, and his letters make it clear that Shea had been out of the field for a number of years. For the rest of the decade, however, he continued to supply Allen with numerous facts that informed Allen's columns in *The Sporting News* as well as the first edition of Macmillan's *The Baseball Encyclopedia*.

Allen's 1969 death was a shocking blow to the research community, but Shea remained involved enough that he answered Bob Davids's call to come to Cooperstown in August 1971.

In the very first *Baseball Research Journal* (1972), Joe Simenic wrote, in an article about biographical sleuthing, "Those of us who attended the organizational meeting of SABR in Cooperstown last August will long remember that walking-talking baseball encyclopedia, Tom Shea of Hingham, Mass. He had many of us spellbound as he recounted in his fine New England twang innumerable anecdotes and personal data of the early day players."

Shea and Bill Haber, along with Allen and S.C. Thompson, were baseball's greatest biographical researchers. One thing, though, is certain. Whenever Haber, Allen, or Thompson had a tough nut to crack, the man they turned to was Tom Shea. ∎

NOTE: This article is heavily excerpted from Dick Thompson's much longer piece on Shea from SABR's Biography Project. Additional biographical material was added from the "SABR Salute" Shea received from Bob Davids in 1990.

Contributors

BRUCE S. ALLARDICE is a Professor of History at South Suburban College, near Chicago. Professor Allardice has authored numerous articles on the Black Sox, along with biographies of the Black Sox gamblers for the SABR Bio Project. His article "The Spread of Baseball in the South Prior to 1870" received SABR's McFarland Award at the 2013 SABR Convention.

TERRY BOHN is an original member of the Halsey Hall SABR chapter. He has previously been published in the *Baseball Research Journal*, has written numerous biographies for the SABR BioProject, and has completed three books on baseball history in North Dakota. His other interests include the Negro League Baseball Grave Marker Project. He works as a hospital administrator in Bismarck, North Dakota.

JOE CAMP is an Associate Professor in Electrical and Computer Engineering (ECE) at Southern Methodist University (SMU). While his research efforts focus on wireless systems and drone communications, his hobby is baseball analytics and he has collaborated with the Rangers for multiple years to give a SABR 101 talk to fans before games.

WARREN CORBETT of Pawleys Island, South Carolina, is the author of *The Wizard of Waxahachie: Paul Richards and the End of Baseball as We Knew It* and a contributor to SABR's BioProject.

STEPHEN DAME is a teacher of Humanities in Toronto. He is a member of the Hanlan's Point chapter of SABR and has presented research papers at three of the four Canadian Baseball History Conferences which take place each November in London, Ontario, Canada.

WILLIAM P. FOX is an Emeritus professor at the Naval Postgraduate School in Monterey, CA. He is currently an adjunct professor of mathematics at the College of William and Mary in Williamsburg, VA, where he teaches applied mathematics courses. He has authored over twenty books, over twenty additional chapters in other books and over a hundred journal articles.

DAVID GORDON is a native Chicagoan who grew up in the '50s within earshot of Wrigley Field. After graduating from the MD-PhD program at the University of Chicago, he moved to Bethesda, MD, and spent 43 years in public health and biomedical research at the National Institutes of Health. In retirement, he has come full circle to write a book on the history of major league baseball and its greatest players. Dr. Gordon is married (Susan) and has two adult children (Sam and Emily).

STEVE GIETSCHIER taught history to undergraduates for eleven years, including courses on American sport and baseball. From 1986 until 2008, he worked for *The Sporting News*, responsible, with the help of many others, for developing an unorganized collection of historical materials into The Sporting News Research Center. He is the editor of *Replays, Rivalries, and Rumbles: The Most Iconic Moments in American Sports* (University of Illinois Press, 2017) and is a former member of the SABR Board of Directors.

DOUGLAS JORDAN is a professor at Sonoma State University in Northern California, where he teaches corporate finance and investments. He's been contributing articles to *BRJ* since joining SABR in 2014. He runs marathons when he's not watching or writing about baseball. You can contact him at jordand@sonoma.edu.

FR. HUMBERT KILANOWSKI, O.P. became involved in sabermetrics while working as the statistician for the baseball team at his high school. He earned a PhD in mathematics from The Ohio State University in 2010 and was ordained a Catholic priest in 2018. Since then, he has taught as an Assistant Professor of Mathematics at Providence College, and is a member of the Lajoie-Start Southern New England Chapter of SABR.

RANDY KLIPSTEIN has been a SABR member for thirty-five years. A Yankee fan, he lives happily in Dobbs Ferry, New York, with his wife Lisa, a Red Sox fan. Randy hopes to see an alphabetical batting order. Contact Randy at rbk65@optonline.net.

BRIAN MARSHALL is an Electrical Engineering Technologist living in Barrie, Ontario, Canada, and a long time researcher in various fields including entomology, power electronic engineering, NFL, Canadian Football and MLB. Brian has written many articles, winning awards for two of them, and two books in his 65 years. Brian has been a SABR member for seven years. Growing up, Brian played many sports, including football, rugby, hockey, and baseball, along with participating in power lifting and arm wrestling events, and aspired to be a professional football player. But when that didn't materialize he focused on Rugby Union and played off and on for 17 seasons in the "front row."

JOHN T. PREGLER is a lifelong baseball fan from the land of the Field of Dreams with an interest in early baseball history. This is Pregler's first *BRJ* article.

DAVID SIEGEL has been a member of SABR since 2006. After 40 years as a Professor of Political Science and administrator at Brock University in St. Catharines, Ontario, Canada, he has now turned his attention to doing research on baseball. Contact: dsiegel@brocku.ca.

JEB STEWART is a lawyer in Birmingham, Alabama, who enjoys taking his sons (Nolan and Ryan) and his wife Stephanie to the Rickwood Classic each year. He has been a SABR member since 2012 and is co-President of the Rickwood Field SABR Chapter. He is an Executive Committee Member on the Board of the Friends of Rickwood Field and is a regular contributor to the *Rickwood Times*. He has written several biographies for SABR's Baseball Biography Project. He wrote part of his article on the 1967 Dixie Series in the press box at Rickwood Field. He presented the topic at the 16th annual Southern Association Baseball Conference in Birmingham, Alabama, on March 2, 2019.

CHRISTIAN TRUDEAU is a Professor of Economics at the University of Windsor. For the last 20 years, he has also researched Quebec baseball history, and published in *The Hardball Times, The Baseball Research Journal* and in *Dominionball: Baseball Above the 49th*.

Society for American Baseball Research

◀SABR▶

Cronkite School at ASU
555 N. Central Ave. #416, Phoenix, AZ 85004
602.496.1460 (phone)
SABR.org

Become a SABR member today!

If you're interested in baseball — writing about it, reading about it, talking about it — there's a place for you in the Society for American Baseball Research.

SABR memberships are available on annual, multi-year, or monthly subscription basis. Annual and monthly subscription memberships auto-renew for your convenience. Young Professional memberships are for ages 30 and under. Senior memberships are for ages 65 and older. Student memberships are available to currently enrolled middle/high school or full-time college/university students. Monthly subscription members receive SABR publications electronically and are eligible for SABR event discounts after 12 months.

Here's a list of some of the key benefits you'll receive as a SABR member:

- Receive two editions (spring and fall) of the *Baseball Research Journal*, our flagship publication
- Receive expanded e-book edition of *The National Pastime*, our annual convention journal
- 8-10 new e-books published by the SABR Digital Library, all FREE to members
- "This Week in SABR" e-newsletter, sent to members every Friday
- Join dozens of research committees, from Statistical Analysis to Women in Baseball.
- Join one of 70+ regional chapters in the U.S., Canada, Latin America, and abroad
- Participate in online discussion groups
- Ask and answer baseball research questions on the SABR-L e-mail listserv
- Complete archives of *The Sporting News* dating back to 1886 and other research resources
- Promote your research in "This Week in SABR"
- Diamond Dollars Case Competition
- Yoseloff Scholarships

- Discounts on SABR national conferences, including the SABR National Convention, the SABR Analytics Conference, Jerry Malloy Negro League Conference, Frederick Ivor-Campbell 19th Century Conference, and the Arizona Fall League Experience
- Publish your research in peer-reviewed SABR journals
- Collaborate with SABR researchers and experts
- Contribute to Baseball Biography Project or the SABR Games Project
- List your new book in the SABR Bookshelf
- Lead a SABR research committee or chapter
- Networking opportunities at SABR Analytics Conference
- Meet baseball authors and historians at SABR events and chapter meetings
- 50% discounts on paperback versions of SABR e-books
- Discounts with other partners in the baseball community
- SABR research awards

We hope you'll join the most passionate international community of baseball fans at SABR! Check us out online at SABR.org/join.

- - - ✂ -

SABR MEMBERSHIP FORM

	Standard	Senior	Young Pro.	Student
Annual:	❏ $65	❏ $45	❏ $45	❏ $25
3 Year:	❏ $175	❏ $129	❏ $129	
5 Year:	❏ $249			
Monthly:	❏ $6.95	❏ $4.95	❏ $4.95	

(International members wishing to be mailed the Baseball Research Journal should add $10/yr for Canada/Mexico or $19/yr for overseas locations.)

Participate in Our Donor Program!

Support the preservation of baseball research. Designate your gift toward:
❏ General Fund   ❏ Endowment Fund   ❏ Research Resources   ❏ _____
❏ I want to maximize the impact of my gift; do not send any donor premiums
❏ I would like this gift to remain anonymous.

Note: Any donation not designated will be placed in the General Fund.
SABR is a 501 (c) (3) not-for-profit organization & donations are tax-deductible to the extent allowed by law.

Name _____

E-mail* _____

Address _____

City _____ **ST** _____ **ZIP** _____

Phone _____ **Birthday** _____

* Your e-mail address on file ensures you will receive the most recent SABR news.

Dues $_____

Donation $_____

Amount Enclosed $_____

Do you work for a matching grant corporation? Call (602) 496-1460 for details.

If you wish to pay by credit card, please contact the SABR office at (602) 496-1460 or sign up securely online at SABR.org/join. We accept Visa, Mastercard & Discover.

Do you wish to receive the *Baseball Research Journal* electronically? ❏ Yes   ❏ No
Our e-books are available in PDF, Kindle, or EPUB (iBooks, iPad, Nook) formats.

Mail to: SABR, Cronkite School at ASU, 555 N. Central Ave. #416, Phoenix, AZ 85004

Friends of SABR

You can become a Friend of SABR by giving as little as $10 per month or by making a one-time gift of $1,000 or more. When you do so, you will be inducted into a community of passionate baseball fans dedicated to supporting SABR's work.

Friends of SABR receive the following benefits:
- ✓ Annual Friends of SABR Commemorative Lapel Pin
- ✓ Recognition in This Week in SABR, SABR.org, and the SABR Annual Report
- ✓ Access to the SABR Annual Convention VIP donor event
- ✓ Invitations to exclusive Friends of SABR events

SABR On-Deck Circle - $10/month, $30/month, $50/month

Get in the SABR On-Deck Circle, and help SABR become the essential community for the world of baseball. Your support will build capacity around all things SABR, including publications, website content, podcast development, and community growth.

A monthly gift is deducted from your bank account or charged to a credit card until you tell us to stop. No more email, mail, or phone reminders.

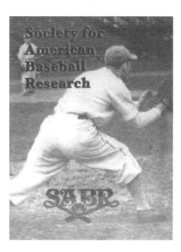

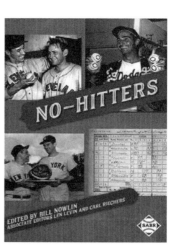

Join the SABR On-Deck Circle

Payment Info: _____Visa _____Mastercard

Name on Card: _____

Card #: _____

Exp. Date: _____ Security Code: _____

Signature: _____

- ○ $10/month
- ○ $30/month
- ○ $50/month
- ○ Other amount _____

Go to sabr.org/donate to make your gift online